NATURE AND GRACE IN ART

CHAPEL HILL
THE UNIVERSITY OF NORTH CAROLINA PRESS

NATURE
AND
GRACE
IN ART

By JOHN W. DIXON, Jr.

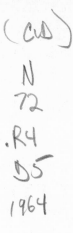
Manufactured in the United States of America

TO VIVIAN

PREFACE

Art scholarship since its beginning has necessarily been occupied with certain tasks. It had first of all to establish the very body of evidence it had to work with for it was faced with a vast conglomeration of objects without identification or with faulty identification, objects that required the most elementary kind of sorting before they could be used in further research. Then, too, it was necessary to establish the essential critical tools, to learn how to analyze the works in their own terms.

This work had to be done and, by and large, it was well done. In fact, much of it remains to be done and it will continue to be a concern of responsible historians and critics for a long time to come. Yet the concern with this necessary task has required less attention to other tasks equally necessary: no comparable attention has been given, by critics and historians at least, to the place of art in the human enterprise. Partly this has been taken for granted, for every man assumes that what is important to him is important generally but this does not help those who have their own preoccupation with other areas of experience.

Thus the general intellectual work becomes impoverished because too many scholars work with the arts only on the periphery of their concern. The understanding of the arts is also impoverished, for the sense of purpose in art is weakened to the extent that a sense of its ultimate relevance is not defined. The content and character of that relevance is the concern of this book.

To define relevance is to define motive and purpose, the human context out of which any work grows and the ends to which it is directed. This cannot be done except on the foundation of the historical and critical work which has been built up in several generations of art studies but neither is it made explicit by those studies. On the other hand, scholarship has rightly learned to be mistrustful of explanations of any work of the mind which are brought to it from the outside. Philosophies of history are in themselves interesting historical phenomena but inevitably they distort or omit the actuality of history and they provide no help at all to the work of the historian. The enthusiasms of any partisan interpretation of history, whether Marxist, Freudian, or Christian, may uncover information that had not been sufficiently noticed before or put things in an order that reveals unexpected aspects of their meaning. Yet again, and inevitably, they omit, distort, and fail the historian's purpose. Thus the historian continues to cling to his ancient ideal of absolute objectivity at the same time he discovers that there is no such thing as objectivity. Even in the limited sense of particular research it is doubtful if a historian ever frees himself from his preconceptions. Certainly no work of any size or substance is free from the historian's basic attitude toward the world and man.

This dichotomy between objectivity and subjectivity is not to be bridged by any such simple process as acknowledging and making overt one's presuppositions. This would lead inevitably into the same partisan errors that have so obscured the study of history in the past. What is needed is the development of a new and workable relation between the evidence of history and the creative mind of the historian.

Thus this book, if it succeeds in its purpose, cannot be described as a "Christian interpretation of art history," or a "Christian criticism of the arts," even though its obsessive concern is with the definition of the relation between Christianity and the arts. There is a dogma which is assumed as the starting point of the work but there is nothing about this particular dogma which has any special relevance to Christianity. This dogma holds that what a man believes, both as his overtly held propositional faith and those fundamental attitudes that go deeper than propositions, determines the substance and details of what he does. Further, this dogma holds that it applies equally to the historian and to history, to the artist, and to the historian and critic of art. Thus, if a man works on the basis of certain fundamental assumptions, Christian or otherwise, they determine the essential shape and character of his work. Similarly when a man studies the events and works of the past he does so on the basis of comparable assumptions. This determines what he responds to most sensitively, how he interprets the evidence. It also determines how he uses what he sees of the past in the clarifying of his own understanding of the world.

This begins to lay out the concerns of this book and, incidentally, indicates the type of critique which can be aimed at it. If an artist has worked on the basis of Christian assumptions then a clear definition of those assumptions should clarify the understanding of his work. The Christian critic might here serve a useful purpose in defining the appropriate categories but the critic who does not share those assumptions can still accept the validity of the work, judging it only on the basis of its adequacy to the evidence. In a different direction the Christian critic, working on the basis of his assumptions will use those assumptions to measure and define the work of non-Christian artists. The non-Christian critic has no interest in the enterprise as such but again he can use it strictly on the basis of its adequacy to the evidence. The question is, do such categories say anything that illuminates, in their own terms, the work of the artists being studied? The third part of the enterprise is of interest to the Christian only for it directs the communication the other way: the Christian artist has a great deal to say to the Christian who is trying to understand the world in terms of his faith, and the non-Christian artist has a great deal to say in his own terms that the Christian and the Christian church ignore at their peril and only in poverty of their spirit.

Art scholarship has labored effectively in the account of the place of Christian subject matter in art. Inevitably art scholarship has been less interested in the matter of Christian assumptions. Good critics who pursue a work back to its essentials do define the Christian attitudes of particular artists but to my knowledge, no attempt has been made to bring the formulation of these attitudes into any kind of systematic ordering that can make them usable as tools while at the same time guarding against subordinating the work of art to the tool. This is the purpose of this book, to formulate the categories of the appropriately Christian attitude toward art; to test these categories by applying them to the experience of the actual works of art; and to use the analysis art makes of reality to illuminate the formulation of the Christian attitude. This is no more (or no less) a Christian critique of the arts than it is art's critique of Christianity.

There are two rather obvious stages of the argument required to prove or demonstrate its character. There must be a theoretical justification of the process in aesthetic theory and the principles of criticism. There must be a demonstration and testing of these principles in critical practice. The theory is important to justify the procedure and determine the direction of the practice. The critical demonstration is vital, for the theory is useless if it cannot serve to illumine the actual work of art or to make it accessible to the Christian imagination which is trying to discover the meaning of its activity.

The text of this book divides itself according to these purposes. Part One considers the aesthetic and critical theory. Part Two examines the evidence and attempts to apply the critical principles. The two parts are not mutually exclusive and their division is, in part, arbitrary. It is not altogether possible to discuss either apart from the other and the attempt has not been made. The ordering of the two parts is particularly arbitrary and probably is to be accounted for largely by an atavistic philosophical notion that practice ought to grow out of theory. Those who prefer to begin with the concrete material are invited to turn to Part Two first, remembering that the condensation of some of the discussion is justified, if at all, only by the foundation laid in Part One.

The course of the argument might be described as circular rather than linear with Part One centripetal and Part Two centrifugal. Part One works from the theologically general, the place of creating or making in the life of the Christian as determined by theological principles, to the more particular problems of critical activity and definitions. On the way it examines the general nature of communication as I conceive it to be involved in the Christian life in order to place the distinctive activity of the artist in its proper context. A more extended displacement of the main line of the argument is necessary to establish certain critical principles and terms for the benefit of those who may wish to read the book without a background of familiarity with the technical procedures involved. This section is necessary also to indicate the choice made of terms in professional dispute.

Part Two is not intended to be a history of Christian art or art in the light of Christianity, a task too large for the purposes of this publication. It is intended, rather, that it examine certain typical examples of relevant works. One period, the Renaissance, is chosen for examination in some detail; several others would have served the purpose as well. I chose the Renaissance, partly to compensate for the critical and historical cliché that makes the Renaissance a secular enterprise altogether and partly because the Renaissance, as the confluence of many forces, dramatizes the problem to an unusual degree.

From the Renaissance, the study moves to a briefer examination of the work of Christian artists of other periods and, finally, to a consideration of the problems of mannerism and of modern art. These are problems of a different nature, as their motives lie outside the immediate influence of the church, but they are styles of a particular relevance to the thought of the church.

Further than this the study cannot safely go in terms of a demonstration based on the evidence. Those ideas still a matter of speculation rather than proof are placed in an epilogue. They are important, even vital, in establishing the relevance of the study beyond the immediate concerns, but honesty suggests they should be placed where they can be seen as matters of conviction or intuition rather than matters to be submitted for objective professional judgment.

It is only when a man has actually written a book himself that he realizes fully that the conventional paragraphs of acknowledgments at the end of prefaces are not in the least formalities but small enough expressions of gratitude for assistance of the most important kind. Therefore, I would like to offer my thanks to the Research Committee of Emory University for its help in the first stages of this work, to the Research and Publications Committee of Florida Presbyterian College, and to the Ford Foundation for a grant under its program for assisting American university presses in the publication of works in the humanities and the social sciences; to my mother, Mrs. J. W. Dixon, who carried a major responsibility for the reading of both manuscript and proof; to Professor Joseph Sloane for a detailed and useful reading of the manuscript; and to Professor Arnold Nash for his understanding reading of the manuscript and much assistance of a practical kind. I acknowledge with appreciation the permission granted me by the Methodist Student Movement for the use of several long passages from the study book I did for them: *Form and Reality : Art as Communication*. Chapters Two-Four of that work make up the bulk of Chapter Six in this one.

I am grateful to Houghton Mifflin Company for permission to quote from Archibald MacLeish, *J. B.*, and to the University of Chicago Press for permission to use several long passages from my article "Is Tragedy Essential to Knowing?" which appeared in *The Journal of Religion*, October, 1963.

I would like to make special acknowledgment to Professor Theodore Greene of Scripps College. Some years ago the two of us planned to do a book of the kind together. Our work got no further than preliminary exploratory conversation before Professor Greene transferred from Yale to Scripps and, under difficulties of distance, the joint project languished. I owe much to those conversations, the results of which are to be noted particularly in the formulations in Chapter Four.

I owe special gratitude to my family who provided and protected the many hours that are essential for any serious work.

Finally, I feel the gratitude felt by all its graduates to the University of Chicago's Committee on Social Thought. All this work was done after I had left the immediate influence of that extraordinary body but little of it would have been possible without the training I received there. The work was done after I left – so I take responsibility for the errors in it. But more is owed than I could ever fully acknowledge or repay to its distinctive combination of a passionate respect for the integrity of evidence and an equally passionate respect for the wholeness of knowledge and its humane purpose.

TABLE OF CONTENTS

TABLE OF CONTENTS

FIGURES (Between pages 112 and 113)

NATURE AND GRACE IN ART

PROLOGUE

THE SEARCH FOR

SACRAMENTAL FORM

> If God is God he is not good.
> If God is good he is not God.
> Take the even, take the odd.
> I would not sleep here if I could,
> Except for the little green leaves in the wood
> And the wind on the water.
>
> Archibald MacLeish, *J.B.*

With beautiful concision, the poet has here stated one of the fundamental theological problems of the human experience, if not the most fundamental problem of theology in its ethical dimension. The conflict in the sensitive human conscience between the presumed goodness and omnipotence of God and the undoubted existence of evil and suffering is a major aspect of human tragedy.

Yet the drama of the poet's statement of the ethical and theological problem ought not to obscure the equally effective statement of the fundamental aesthetic problem. "If God is God he is not good" may be the fundamental theological problem. Yet the answer the poet offers is the little green leaves and the wind on the water. At this point in his drama this is not, to the poet, a problem but the answer to the problem he has already raised. Yet as an answer it is by no means obvious. What do little green leaves and the wind on the water have to do with the power and goodness of God? It is not a self-evident answer. The philosophical and critical mind has almost universally rejected it as an answer. Yet the poet does not include it as an ornament to his problem or a gesture of despair. To a certain type of sensibility it is an answer, the only sufficient answer to the problem to which the theologians and the philosophers can give no answer to sustain the human spirit. This answer, as response to the problem of human tragedy, points directly to the fundamental aesthetic problem.

The answer is not always found only in this specific form. In its specificity it is naturalism. But it is not nature worship. It is only the sentimental mind, not the ethical mind, which can find undefined nature an answer to the fundamental problems of human experience. And even the artist or poet who is content to remain within the confines of pure naturalism can do so only by avoiding the basic ethical questions. Nature itself and in itself alone does not satisfy the serious intellect. McLeish is a serious intellect.

It is not nature alone which answers the question. It is the concreteness of nature. It is the very specific quality of nature. It is not the natural object itself. It is the natural object seen by the artist, isolated and seen by the peculiar temperament of the artist. It would be a hard proposition to check but it is doubtful if the inarticulate mind would ever find the little green leaves an answer to his suffering. The artist can do so, not because the little green leaves in any way refer to the immediate problem, but because the little green leaves are palpable, physical. They have a form, yet can be the intersection in the material world of the artist's sense of order and purpose. Otherwise the cosmos only inflicts on him suffering or unanswerable questions. This search for meaning in the physical form of things is the peculiar prerogative and the defining responsibility of the artist.

It is out of this principle that the understanding, not only of the modern J. B., but also of the ancient Job might grow. There the answer was asserted even more positively than in the modern retelling of the ancient story

4

and to the correspondingly greater dissatisfaction of the modern critic. The critical mind is often philosophical rather than artistic and many critics have accused the writer of Job of failing to answer his own problem. Job hurls his question and his defiance against the almighty God for many pages. God answers the challenge with a catalogue of his power over nature – which Job has already acknowledged – and Job promptly collapses, saying, "I abhor myself and repent in dust and ashes." The liberal modern mind finds this situation and response appalling in its inadequacy. Yet it is very difficult to reject it as bad drama without facing the fact that the poet did not consider it his obligation to give an answer satisfactory to the modern liberal mind. Nor was he satisfied with the answer implicit in the modern ethical mind. Job knew of Leviathan and the little green leaves. He knew more. He knew that God created and controlled both Leviathan and the little green leaves. Yet this knowledge did not answer his anguish. It was only as God spoke to him through the concreteness of the world that he repented, not of what he had done, but what he had been. It was neither the knowledge of little green leaves, nor that God had made the little green leaves, nor even that God told him he had made the little green leaves. It was the majesty and glory and holiness of God as seen in the order and concreteness of nature which spoke directly to Job in his agony and his humility. It was concreteness become sacramental, transforming Job's person. The sacramental did not answer Job's question. It made of him a different man who could then live with his question.

The question is still not fully answered, at least in terms appropriate to this study. The form of concreteness can be the order in which man finds completion that is his shelter against his tragedy. The form of concreteness can be sacramental in linking man to the glory of the eternal God. Yet the concreteness is still primarily the concreteness of nature. Not altogether, because there are two important qualifications. Neither Job nor J. B. has historical existence. Their experience is part of a work of art and it is still a live question whether their experience is an experience of nature or an element of a work of art. Furthermore, the experience as described is an aesthetic, not a natural, experience. It is an experience of a person whose sensibilities are informed by his awareness of the significance of forms. Yet even with these qualifications there is at the heart of the experience the sense of the natural and its sacramental significance. It is later that the man wants to make a form which can have sacramental significance.

Thou art indeed just, Lord, if I contend
With thee; but, sir, so what I plead is just.
Why do sinner's ways prosper? and why must
Disappointment all I endeavour end?
   Wert thou my enemy, O thou my friend,
How wouldst thou worse, I wonder, than thou dost
Defeat, thwart me? Oh, the sots and thralls of lust
Do in spare hours more thrive than I that spend,
Sir, life upon thy cause. See, banks and brakes
Now, leaved how thick! laced they are again
With fretty chervil, look, and fresh wind shakes
Them; birds build – but not I build; no but strain,
Time's eunuch, and not breed one work that wakes.
Mine, O thou lord of life, send my roots rain.

                            GERARD MANLEY HOPKINS

Hopkins here begins with a direct quotation from Jeremiah which is another expression of the perennial moral problem, the reverse of the problem posed by Job and J. B. There the problem was the suffering of the righteous, here it is the problem of the prosperity and productivity of the wicked.

The contrast between Hopkins and his source in Jeremiah is, however, instructive for our purpose. The point of attack is the same. Even the very significant reference to fruitfulness is the same: "Thou plantest them, and they take root; they grow and bring forth fruit" (Jeremiah 12:2). Yet the prayer of Jeremiah as a consequence of this is very different. "Pull them out like sheep for the slaughter, and set them apart for the day of slaughter" (Jeremiah 12:3). Hopkins, on the other hand, prays, not for vengeance, but for productivity. It should be added, even hastily added, that this contrast is not fair to Jeremiah. His desire for vengeance is one point in his spiritual development and is both reproved and transformed by the Lord. Yet, while both Hopkins and Jeremiah are poets and prophets, Jeremiah is primarily a prophet and Hopkins is primarily a poet. Jeremiah goes on to the vision of the new covenant, Hopkins to the writing of poems. The cause of Jeremiah can be fulfilled only within the sacramental covenant, the cause of Hopkins within the sacramental form.

Hopkins is a poet and his development is different from the author of Job. He begins with the knowledge of God's creativity and the fruitfulness of concrete nature. This position, which in its way satisfies both the poet of J. B. and of Job, is no more than the starting point for Hopkins. It is his own fruitfulness that is central to him, the growth of form out of his own creativity. It is this kind of form which is essential to his sense of the sacramental. While nourishing his creativity on the creativity of God it is only his own creativity which can finally order him within the creativity of God.

It is this kind of form that is the object of this essay, the form that not only grows out of man's participation in the divine creativity but fulfills the nature of humanity by adding to creation the meaningful form which was not there before. In this lies man's great temptation, that he should think his own creativity should be the equivalent or replacement of God's.

In this lies also man's glory, that he should make an object in which something of the quality and sense of the divine can rest, to be communicated to him and to those who see it.

PART ONE

FORMS OF THE CHRISTIAN IMAGINATION

I

THE FUNCTION OF

FORMS

IN THE CHRISTIAN LIFE

The Christian church has never throughout its history fully resolved the place of forms in its corporate life. It would perhaps be more accurate to say "images" rather than forms since the question has nearly always been posed in terms of the function or the admissibility of images, rather than of forms. The use, at this point, of the term "forms" rather than the usual one "images" serves both to keep this statement within the limits of the intent of this discussion and also to emphasize that forms and images are not the same thing.

Both extremes of the church's attitudes can be found, not surprisingly, in the same branch of the church and is summed up in the two terms "icon" and "iconoclasm." On the one hand there has never been a higher function given to the image or to the form than that given to the icon of the Eastern Orthodox church. In nearly every sense of the word it is considered sacramental, a channel of communication between God and man, a means of grace and a focus of devotion. On the other hand there has never been a more virulent opposition to images than that of the iconoclasts.

On the one hand, the personality of the sacred person or scene passes to the relics and the representations and "the honor paid to the images passes to its original, and he that adores an image adores in it the person depicted thereby..." (definition of the Second Council of Nicaea, 787 A.D.). On the other hand, the making of images was considered a profound violation of the nature of the holy, a profanation of the sacredness of God. This grew out of the ancient and ever present fear of idolatry but also out of a profound theological and metaphysical mistrust of matter and the flesh.

The Western church has never felt impelled to go to the same extreme in either direction, although the tension did exist. At one extreme, there is, perhaps, St. Bernard of Clairvaux scathingly condemning the immoderate size and expense of the churches of other orders. At the other extreme there is Fra Angelico weeping in agony before one of his painted crucifixions. Yet these very examples are revealing of the different character of the two communions. There is not in Bernard the deep metaphysical anguish of the true iconoclast, torn by the linking of the purity of the eternal with the corruption of matter. He is concerned rather with the dissipation of funds, the vanity, the distraction of the mind, the impropriety. Fra Angelico is perhaps closer to the icon makers (and it is said he is the only Western artist to be recognized by the Eastern church as a true maker of icons) yet there is not the same singleness of intention to make a holy object but often an innocent delight in the world and in paint and a willingness to participate in the development of the new artistic language.

The matter-of-fact practicality of the Western church can be indicated even more directly by a quotation from a letter of Pope Gregory: "It is one thing to worship a picture and another to learn from the language of a picture what that is which ought to be worshipped. What those who can read learn by means of writing, that do the uneducated learn by looking at a picture.... That therefore, ought not to have been destroyed which had been placed in the churches, not for worship, but solely for instructing the minds of the ignorant."

Thus the range of opinion is indicated: the devotion to images verging on idolatry and not always avoiding it; the enmity to images that would destroy them and their makers; and the common sense position in between that would use them without exaggeration.

Yet no one of these positions provides an answer to the concerns of this study. It might, in fact, be asked which of the three attitudes makes a socially effective answer more possible. The problem lies precisely in the fact that each of the three attitudes is formulated in terms of images and not in terms of forms. The devotion to icons is devotion to the saint represented and to the image of the saint which contains his sacred authority. This has interesting consequences for the forms, because appropriate forms eventually became codified. Only certain forms, a certain style, were fit to be the vessel of the holy. Thus the image is primary over the form and the form could not develop anything like a full human existence. The iconoclasts were perhaps more rigorously consistent to the aesthetic problem since they were concerned quite directly about the involvement of the sacred with matter. Under the condition of their final attitude their consistency is not much help, since their only answer was to destroy the images.

The practical attitude of the Western church was a more realistic approach to the problem, since it made possible the great variety of styles when Western art was under the influence of the church. In terms of the problem of this study this attitude is of little or no help for it really evades the problem of the meaning of forms by reducing art to pedagogy. This made possible the development of the range of styles in the church, but that range unhappily includes decadent, degenerate, mindless forms as well as forms which have been the glory of Western man. Pedagogically there is little difference between good and bad art. So it is only in the life of the church, not in its systematic formulations or official attitudes, that an answer to the problem may be found.

Thus, even though the Western church managed to avoid the extremes of the Eastern and made possible the making of the forms that are the evidence for this study, it shut itself off from a serious and consistent answer to the problem of man's incorrigible passion for making new forms. It is altogether unlikely that artists would have endured either the torments or the delights of creativity simply to provide elementary instruction to the faithful. Having found instruction as the grounds for the admission of art to the service of the church, the church could not then formulate, except very incidentally, the deeper purpose and function and intention and responsibility of art as the making of forms. Before the main problem can be explored, therefore, it is essential to make at least a short preliminary statement as an hypothesis to account for the urge to make, which has so strongly characterized man's activities.

In one sense, perhaps the artist's own sense, the search for such an explanation is superfluous since art is an activity with its own purpose and meaning. It does not necessarily exist subordinate to something else but it is its own reason for existence. Yet this is no final satisfaction of the problem, for no human activity is without some reason for existence, even if the verbal statement of that reason falsifies it or is inadequate to it.

Man creates because it is essential to him to find out what it means to be human, to be a man.

Man is born into a chaos of forms and experience. To live he must orient himself within those forms and experiences. At the most elementary level, this means that he learns how to move, to dress, to feed himself, to earn a living. But it also means that he feels a compulsion to find a meaning to what he does. He is not content to exist. He must also understand, he must also find a posture toward experience.

"Meaning," unfortunately, has come to be understood as exclusively verbal. This has been a consequence of man's verbal activity finding the explanation for all things within itself. It has not been the intent of man's general activity, which persists in finding the making of forms a meaningful activity even when that meaning cannot be translated into words. Nor do the makers in any sense consider their activity as a substitute for words or an imitation of words. It is rather the only possible way to the grasp of certain types of meaning. It is in the making of forms (including the verbal form as distinct from discursive statement) that man most uniquely finds order and the posture toward existence which he can assume only if he can grasp with the totality of his being the order of the universe he inhabits.

The making of forms is not the only way to search for order and meaning. It is not the only possible response to the compulsion for meaning and understanding. Men respond by the making of systems, for example, and this is the nature of philosophy. Men respond by meaningful work, or by the analysis of the structure of things, or in the search for power or for status. Or they run away from the compulsion and bury themselves in conformity to the herd. Except the last, which is eminently replaceable, and for power and status which are usually distortions of the primary compulsion, none of these is replaceable by another, none is primary, none can ignore another without peril to its own completeness. There is a particular cogency to the verbal and conceptual system which gives it the appearance of primacy. It can be argued, manipulated, as the others cannot, and this increases its popularity. But the system can cover only part of experience. To many experiences, words and systems are inadequate.

The answer to the question raised by this statement can be indicated by returning to the little green leaves of the prologue. The responsibility and the prerogative of the system maker is the general. The responsibility and prerogative of the maker of forms is the concrete. However the system might state the significance and the relevance of the concrete, it can only talk about them. It is the artist who alone can present the concrete.

The concrete and specific is a part of the experience of all men. Yet, with the exception of occasional flashes of inarticulate intuition, the experience remains casual, inchoate, without significant, and meaningful relation. It is one of the high responsibilities and privileges of the artist to present the concrete as itself, in isolation and enhancement so it is accessible to others in a way which is rarely possible for them, with their less sensitive, more preoccupied view of things. This responsible presentation is not only of things in the world outside the work of art but the structure and material, the order of the work of art itself. Thus the artist grasps and presents the little green leaves and the painting or poem in which the little green leaves might be a part.

Yet the power and responsibility of forms go further. The forms embody not just the things themselves but their meaningful relation, the sense of the order of things which is inherent in their relation. The artist reflects on the meaning of things (the word "reflects" is used deliberately of an activity which, in the artist, is essentially visual) and this meaning is then presented in the order of his work. Furthermore, he explores, by the structure of the work of art, the meanings he feels to be a part of his life and his faith. Thus he reflects and creates and his work is not only a presentation of the concreteness of things but the embodiment of the order which proceeds from his reflection and creation.

Thus forms are the embodiment, the incarnation, of man's sense of the meaning of things in their concreteness, their distinctive personality and individual significance. Forms establish the essential contact with the order, vitality, and fruitfulness of the earth and embody man's insight into the meaning of that order.

There are certain fairly obvious dangers involved in this kind of statement and awareness of the dangers should lead to an articulation of a principal problem involved in the Christian understanding of art. The term sacramental was used earlier. The term incarnation was used immediately above. These are theological terms with a specific reference. To extend the reference of these terms, even analogically, is to tread on dangerous ground. To extend the reference deliberately and literally could be theologically catastrophic, idolatrous, and blasphemous.

It is in the cleft of this semantic difficulty that the nature of the central problem can be seen. The artist makes a thing: both popular and professional usage join in calling this creation and the artist a creator. He brings into existence a thing which had not existed before. It is perhaps well that the artist is generally too busy making his objects to spend much time contemplating the majesty and meaning of the act which he performs, else his ego might suffer badly. Almost alone among men he shares an attribute of divinity which is central to the idea of divinity: creativity.

Artists have not always avoided the temptation involved in this identification of terminology. "The artist as creator" is an analogy with a long history, but it is primarily since the beginning of romanticism that the artist himself has begun to emphasize his own creativity as central to the spiritual history of man, and it has remained for the contemporary artist to assert for his own work an independence of anything outside his own ego while claiming for it a reference for the life of his day which can be described in Christian terms only as sacramental. It has, then, remained for the contemporary artist to assert his own divinity.

There is no point in burning such a person as a blasphemer. Often the works so described are delightfully decorative and many have a more profound formal significance. It is simply true that there is no articulated understanding of the nature of the artist's creative act and it is not surprising that the philosophically naïve minds of some artists should carry certain of the implications of their activity to extremes.

It is unquestionably a fact that the artist makes something which has not existed before. It is equally unquestionable that the thing he makes, if it is a genuine work of art, is not merely a thing but has an order within itself. It may or may not, at the artist's own choice, have a reference to the world outside the work of art. If it does, then there is a significant interaction between the order of the work of art and the order of the world as seen in the work of art. If it does not have such an external reference, its own internal order carries the full weight of significance and meaning. In either case, the structural system by which the parts of a work are related to each other, by which the work is built up, is the peculiar locus of meaning and relevance.

16

It is an order with its own governing principles. And obviously this order proceeds from the hand and the mind of the artist.

The question which remains is the origin of this sense of order in the artist. If he is fully a creator, then the principle of order in his work originates within himself. If God alone is creator, then the order which informs man's creativity proceeds not from himself and his own inner consciousness but from his awareness of the order which exists objectively outside himself. His work, then, would become not the creation of a new order but an embodiment of his relation to the existing order of things.

It is not the purpose of this study to examine this problem in abstract theory, which would be in a real sense to deny the nature of the creative activity it purports to examine. It proposes rather to examine works of art themselves and to find in them the evidence for an understanding of creativity which can be faithful to the nature of the artistic activity without imperiling the omnipotence of God. It is difficult to see how the Christian can accept the idea of a completely free creativity on the part of man. Yet a contrary interpretation can only be assumed as an hypothesis until the evidence has actually been examined. It is essential, for example, to account for the immense variety of personal styles if it is assumed that true art issues only from a relation to the order of creation. It is necessary to protect the individuality of the artist and not reduce him to a mirror of the things which are already in existence.

It is necessary to protect the humanity of man without making him into God.

II

ART AS

STRUCTURE

AND ART AS

SYMBOL

Man, then, creates because it is a part of his function as a man to create. This defines the purpose of his making philosophically. It does not define the immediate practical purpose of that making nor allow for the differences in type that characterize the whole range of art. Theologically or philosophically he might be called a creator. As a maker, a maker of forms, however, he has an immediate purpose and a function within his society. There is a human reason for what he does. Since it is human, this reason ought to be identifiable. If it can be identified in anything like its human complexity, then it can be seen in its principal types even if no classification can hope to be comprehensive.

If the popular mind were to find an articulate statement of its understanding of the function of art, it would undoubtedly locate that function somewhere in the area of imitation. Most contemporary criticism has outgrown the stage of considering imitation or representation as irrelevant, yet professional critics still give imitation nothing like the same importance, nor would they consider it a primary function of the artist's work. Rather modern criticism considers it derivative from other, more central, functions.

The popular mind does not err so badly in understanding art as expression. The popular understanding of art as expression is a heritage from romanticism and is found now only in distortions of the romantic idea. Yet it is not at all wrong to understand that the art work does contain the personal attitude of the artist toward the world and communicates his feelings and his emotions about the world and the things which happen in it and exist in it.

The function of art as constructive is less clear to the popular mind and often the professional mind. There may be a few extremely expressionistic artists to whom art is primarily expressive of their emotional states. All the evidence, however, points to structure as the primary concern of most artists. Art is not, to the artist, a feeling or emotion to be expressed but an object to be made. Even for those artists who may be concerned primarily with expression, structure is the indispensable ingredient for the communication of the expression. For the majority of artists and the majority of art the primary concern must of necessity be the actual character of the material itself and the ordering of the material into a structured form.

No point is more fundamental to the following analysis than this one. The peculiar province of the artist is neither ideas nor philosophical systems. It is only in part emotion. It is primarily the forming of a physical material into an intelligible structure. If he chooses to make the physical material into a resemblance of something other than itself, that is his prerogative and sometimes his power. For a major part of the world's art the artist has, in fact, chosen to pursue or use such resemblance. Yet it is not required of him by any law of his art that it resemble something else and the work is not to be measured by the degree of such resemblance. Rather it is the structure by which the resemblance is achieved and the function of the resemblance in the total structure that determines the character and meaning of the work.

If the popular mind has had difficulties of this kind in accounting for the work of art, the professional mind has had no fewer difficulties. Curiously, these difficulties are intimately related to those of the untrained public. The popular attitude toward art may be most intimately bound up with the ideas of imitation and of beauty, errors which more sophisticated minds rarely any longer commit. Yet the popular and the sophisticated mind are at one in understanding art as expression even if the interpretations as held by the two groups vary widely in sensitivity.

The root of the difficulty in the professional mind is ontological. Insofar as contemporary intellectual attitudes are still controlled by idealism, there are not the philosophical resources for contending with the profoundly human significance of a material object except as it is accessible to the empirical techniques of the sciences and philosophical attitudes appropriate to scientific empiricism. Thus, in much contemporary philosophy, the only way in which art can be saved as a part of the intellectual enterprise is to find in it the power of expressing something fundamental about existence as now distinguished from being. In this complex situation the art professionals have not been of major assistance since few of them are philosophically trained or particularly interested in the larger philosophical problems. They have no difficulty accepting the art work in its fundamental human relevance and, naturally, no difficulty handling it according to its essential structure and nature. But without this common philosophical foundation there is no language in common with other thinkers and, therefore, little participation of the essential activity of art and art criticism in the general intellectual enterprise. Intellectuals generally are increasingly conscious of the pleasures of arts, but the concern is peripheral. The arts do not challenge their positions or contribute to the formulation of them.

Where significant contemporary thinkers have been seriously concerned with the arts, therefore, it is almost always in terms of their existential import, not their metaphysical structure and significance. Since the primary concern of existentialist thinking is with man's tragedy, the arts, then, are seen as representing or expressing the meaningful, passionate life, the brokenness of experience, the tragedy of man's existence, or as the symbolic link with the basic common attitudes.

If it be true, as I believe it to be, that the reasons for this discontinuity in the intellectual life are identifiable, then it should be useful to begin by examining a few characteristic attempts to formulate a viable philosophic position with respect to the arts. Before doing so I should be careful to state the reasons for my account. I am not attempting any sort of exhaustive classification of contemporary aesthetic attitudes. This is a work that has been done by others and I would have nothing to add to what they have already done. The bibliography contains references to those who seem to me to have the greatest interest for this problem.

Furthermore, such a listing would have small relevance to this argument.

Some attempts to "explain" art would have to be included simply for the sake of completeness for many are pointless attempts to subsume the reality of one discipline under the categories relevant to another. The ones which are at a professionally higher level belong, by and large, to the field of aesthetics and this is an essay in criticism and interpretation, not in aesthetics. How far such aesthetic structures should be held accountable for critical practice is a question best left to the philosophers. Certainly aesthetics is a legitimate philosophical discipline but the practical fact is that both artists and critics find such systems and such classifications irrelevant to their concerns.

My purpose here, then, is to attempt a transition between the discussion as it has developed and my own contribution to the discussion in the hope that both the things I would like to say which are new, and those which are derived can be kept clearly in mind. This suggests a selection of sources rather than a comprehensive catalogue and I shall focus on the two or three writers who appear to me to be most relevant to this concern. Another disclaimer should perhaps go without saying: this is not a complete examination of the thought even of those few people I shall consider. It is a device for showing why I do not think current terminology sufficient to this purpose and hence my examination of their work will be brief and one-sided. It may even distort what they are primarily trying to do but this does not indicate any disrespect for their work. I do not choose to consider those whose work I do not respect but those whom I do respect and whose work I have used with profit but whose analysis seems to me to be insufficient for a purpose worth pursuing. Theirs is primarily a philosophical or theological task, mine a critical one. I shall engage their work primarily at the point of its critical manifestation but I shall not attempt to judge the extent of the implications of my analysis of their criticism on their philosophical work.

The earlier mention of popular interpretations of the meaning and function of the work of art was not arbitrary. It seems clear to me that the more developed doctrines of philosophers and theologians reflect primarily a more subtle formulation of conventional attitudes. To repeat: the popular mind conceives the function of art either as imitative or expressive. Both these definitions are linked to the idea of beauty. That is, the popular mind justifies art either in terms of the represented object, the creating subject, or the receiving subject. It is either a substitute for the "real" object or an objectification of the artist's emotions and in either case its primary function is "beauty," crudely felt as an object that gives pleasure to the beholder. In no case is the object valued or justified for itself but only as an instrument to another purpose. Since the purpose is not itself considered primary to human achievement (in this culture defined so much in terms of power or money), then the arts are not even approximately considered part of the central activity of men. They are decorative and so belong to women.

The plight of the intellectuals is comparable. As intelligent and sensitive people they are drawn to the arts and many (but not all) are unwilling to account for this attraction simply in terms of the enhancement of their leisure. They feel art to be meaningful and important; as responsible intellectuals they are compelled to define this meaningfulness, yet they do not have in their ontology the possibility of accounting for a thing that is independently meaningful nor in their epistemology the tools for receiving or expounding this meaningfulness. Therefore they must account for the art work in relation to something else which is accounted for by their ontology and made accessible by their epistemology.

There are many of these accounts which have no particular relevance to this argument, such as art as play, art as magic, the psychoanalytic interpretation, and the economic interpretation. These explanations often have useful things to say and sometimes they are silly but they are doing something else. They might come from a person who is directly concerned about art but they do not have to and often give the impression of having been developed by scientific techniques without emotional involvement. I am concerned rather with those accounts of art which are impelled by a powerful sense of their fundamental human meaningfulness. It seems to me that, when the desire to account for art is accompanied by a passionate conviction of the meaningfulness of art, the account then develops in two related but slightly different directions: art as symbol or art as expression.

I hope it will be clear from all I say that I judge these explanations to be achievements and not errors. They do not represent a false road but a false end. Any contemporary discussion of art would be seriously impoverished were these accounts rejected. It must be stated now and accounted for later that the insights involved in the area of both symbolism and expression are not peripheral contributions but are fundamental to the understanding of art. Yet both contain a flaw that is fatal to the whole enterprise if they are conceived as the final explanation rather than stages on the way.

Both conceive the art work as ancillary to or instrumental to something else. In the theory of art as symbol the art work becomes the objectification of that beyond itself which is meaningful. In the theory of expression, the art work becomes the objectification of the artist's experience of that beyond himself which is meaningful. The argument might make further concessions: the art work might be recognized as affording an irreplaceable insight into this knowledge or experience, for which there is no other substitute. This enhances the importance of the art work far beyond the popular sense of gratification but it still does not, with complete success, establish communication between the artist and the philosopher or incorporate art fully into the total intellectual enterprise, for in each case art is a means to something else. Since whatever definition of the "something else" or art's account of it is incorrigibly verbal and conceptual the art work becomes embedded in a web of words and subordinate to conceptual formulations. The artist and art are made far more important than they have been for many generations but they are still not masters in their own house.

The theories of symbol and expression overlap and their proponents so often use the same terminology that they appear to be saying the same thing. It is not quite the same and so can be considered separately. The separate treatment has the further advantage that the particular writers whose work I shall consider, Susanne Langer and Paul Tillich, have developed these themes in ways which make their treatments particularly cogent. Mrs. Langer's work is deeply involved in the whole recent research into the symbolic function of myth, ritual, sacrament, and all non-discursive manifestations of man's rationality. Professor Tillich has become perhaps the most noted exponent of the theological relevance of the arts. Both of these emphases are intimately involved in this argument, which makes the consideration of their work not simply reasonably representative but directly relevant.

My express intention is to treat these systems in terms of their critical concreteness. This intention was formulated after I had done my general reading and made the selection of the authors whose work I felt most useful to consider. When I then turned to the search for specific materials for examination I was startled to discover that they are virtually non-existent in Mrs. Langer's work (this is not at all a problem with Professor Tillich, whose work is full of precise critical formulations). This might suggest the choice of another writer whose theory is more extensively illustrated in practice but I determined that I should remain with the original choice. There is enough concrete material of a kind to make examination possible. Furthermore, Mrs. Langer's formulation of the symbol, including the whole area of myth, which has proven so important to the contemporary mind, is useful, orderly, and altogether attractive. Too much talk about myth and symbol in contemporary criticism has the function of magical incantation rather than rational thought and this Mrs. Langer avoids with admirable precision and rigor.

Perhaps her failure to make extensive use of the arts simply reflects personal knowledge and predilections; after all, I am writing about the visual arts and not about music or the dance. Yet she proposes, as I do not, to submit a comprehensive theory of art and then substantiates the theory primarily with evidence from that art, literature, which, because it uses words, appears to be most accessible to words. Only about thirty pages in a four-hundred page book (Langer, *Feeling and Form*) deal directly with the visual arts. This might be dismissed as a fault of execution of no direct concern to an argument that is not a book review, but it may also be symptomatic. We should, then, look at such critical statements to see if the condition of those symptoms can be identified.

The first such statement is not direct criticism at all, but it certainly is a critical statement or a statement-in-criticism, "The expressive form, or art symbol, is, as I said before, the work of art itself, as it meets the eye (let us, for simplicity's sake, stay in the realm of pictorial art). It is the visible form, the apparition created out of paint deployed on a ground. The paint and the ground themselves disappear. One does not see a picture as a piece of spotted canvas, any more than one sees a screen with shadows on it in a movie" (Langer, *Problems of Art*, p. 127).

It is singularly unfortunate for her argument that it should appear at a time when a considerable body of perfectly serious art is seen precisely as a piece of spotted canvas. However relevant contemporary painting might be, the argument does not depend on it for it is doubtful if many really significant artists or observers have ever been that indifferent to the actual tangible character of the object in front of them and ever since Titian first applied paint with his thumb the quality and character of that surface for itself have been a principal preoccupation of the artist. Her statement is only partially true even for the most representational of styles for in the work of important artists the struggle to maintain the integrity of the surface despite the depth of space is incessant. Certainly artists vary a great deal in their awareness of this problem and their concern for it. With some it may occupy a subordinate place and it then takes a lot of "virtual space" to compensate for absence of the coherence of surface. Lesser artists may be indifferent to the problem, which is one of the reasons they are lesser artists, as inchoateness in the "spotted canvas" is glaringly apparent to the trained observer. With some artists, such as Poussin and Cézanne, it is a consuming passion.

This is a small point and, as not much is made of it in Mrs. Langer's argument, too much should not be made of it here. But it is a symptom and it does serve to emphasize that it is not the art work as object, the art work as structure that concerns her; it is the art work as symbol. Where her work is more directly relevant to the act of criticism than many others is in the point of contact between the art work and symbol. It is not the represented symbol that concerns her but the symbolic reference of an indubitably formal, structural quality of the work, "virtual space" (Langer, *Feeling and Form*, *passim*, but particularly Chapter 5). This is defined as an artist would define it; i.e., it is not only the three-dimensional represented space but also the two-dimensional surface as a field for action. Furthermore, it is an exceedingly important point and I suspect more than one teacher or lecturer has found it possible to clarify different stylistic attitudes easily by the differences in the attitude toward space. This is partly because it is usually a rather dramatic difference, a demonstrable difference and perhaps, too, precisely because of its symbolic quality. As a symbol of general experience it is accessible to the untrained layman as other qualities of the work might not be and so can serve effectively for this pedagogical purpose.

It is nonetheless true that Mrs. Langer makes this the definition of art, whereas to the artist there are a great many other "virtual" things in a painting which do not seem quite so secondary. This is not the only place where Mrs. Langer says something that seems very good and well-said but then appears to concentrate on that factor too exclusively. This is neither capriciousness nor inadequacy on her part but philosophical consistency: the art work is a symbol and therefore must be defined in terms of its most symbolic quality. It is necessary therefore to move from this brief consideration of her actual critical remarks to the more theoretical statement and see what it is she means by the word "symbol."

Mrs. Langer makes the basic and essential distinction between sign (or in her later terminology, signal) and symbol. Sign "indicates the existence – past, present, or future – of a thing, event, or condition." A sign is proxy for its object, it announces the object.

Symbols, on the other hand, "are vehicles for the conception of objects." Where a sign announces the object, the symbol leads to a conception of the object. It is therefore an instrument of thought (not in the sense of discursive, verbal thought, but of the act of thought involved in the very handling of the symbol). (Quotations and paraphrases from Langer, *Philosophy in a New Key*, pp. 49-51.)

Mrs. Langer is not content to leave this as an assertion but goes on to develop (particularly in her *Feeling and Form*) the critical structure which explores this as a fact of the artistic experience rather than a philosophical assertion without an object. In this she differs from others who have simply asserted the relation without specifying it. Paul Tillich, for example, is fond of asserting that the symbol participates in the reality it symbolizes, yet never makes clear what this participation entails.

Mrs. Langer's philosophical equipment is more precise at this point. The definition in itself maintains a nice balance between objectivity and subjectivity, an important distinction at this point, for a misplaced objectivity leads to an erroneous doctrine of naturalism in art, whereas a misplaced subjectivity leads to an erroneous doctrine of expressionism (or alternatively, decoration). There is an objective reality to which the symbol refers, for the symbol is always the conception of *something*. Yet the symbol is not servilely dependent on that reality for it is the *conception* of something, an event in the mind of the maker of the symbol. Thus the symbol is neither pure sign nor pure expression but is the product of the interaction of the person with the reality and is, in more precise expression, the means for the person's laying hold of reality.

Thus the artistic symbol (in her philosophy symbol has a wider reference than the arts) is the embodiment in a material form of the artist's response to reality.

Where it would appear that Mrs. Langer's definition, finely drawn and effective instrument that it is, falls short of full usefulness is its focus on one aspect only of the experience of reality, "the pattern of affective and sentient being" (Langer, *Key*, p. 209), the forms of feeling. That she should focus so narrowly is not altogether reprehensible for she is seeking thereby to avoid excesses in several directions. The symbol as an instrument of conception focuses on the forms, not the externals of feelings. It is concerned with the morphology, not the description of feelings. Thus art can avoid those things it is not equipped to do and criticism is clarified to approach the art work in terms appropriate to it. Thus the disturbing problem in music, that the same music can serve a variety of purposes or be understood in contradictory emotional terms, is adequately handled (Langer, *Key*, p. 193). If their morphology is the same then contradictory emotions might be understood in the same work, for music is not able to undertake the psychologically precise description of emotions but is conscious only of their underlying form and movement.

This is a profound insight and it is fundamental to the development of this discussion. For it is in these fundamental forms that the act of criticism must take place. Yet simultaneously the weakness of the position becomes evident, for if she has clarified the relation of art to feeling and made it possible to talk intelligently of feelings in art, she has prematurely cut off criticism from going beyond feeling for she limits art to this symbolizing of the essential forms of feeling. This does not seem necessary in her own terms for there would appear to be nothing inherent in the theory which prevents a wider application of the idea of symbol were it not for the need for consistency within her own attitude. The art work as symbol is not simply the embodiment of the feelings of the artist which reflects the forms of feeling inherent in reality. It permits a much more extensive investigation into the nature of things. The art work is the embodiment of the relation between the artist and what he understands reality to be. It is therefore circumscribed in its reference by all that the artist is and knows and believes. This must be described as a circumscribing for no human product can ever lay hold on the total meaning of things or ever be more than partial and finite. Yet it is simultaneously more than a limitation when compared with Mrs. Langer's restriction of the symbol to the morphology of feeling. The artist by virtue of his humanity and the greater sensitivity of his experience participates in reality through its full range and responds to it, according to his own nature, through the whole range of human experiences insofar as they can realize themselves in the material form of the work of art. Feeling is not only one major element in this response; under Mrs. Langer's definition of it, it is probably a vital ingredient of any work of art of significance and vitality. But it does not make up the whole, nor exclude the possibility of other equally significant approaches to the work of art. It is necessary to give an account of these various approaches which are suggested by the word symbol if the discussion of art as a language is to have real meaning, for it is only by so doing that it is possible to make clear the kind of thing art communicates.

The same problem is found acutely expressed in a quotation, ripped unmercifully out of context, from another leading writer on the subject, Phillip Wheelwright, who says bluntly, "A symbol, in the broadest sense of the word, is *that which means*; and the ways in which a symbol can mean are potentially as many as the ways in which one thing can stand for and lead the mind to something else" (Wheelwright, *The Burning Fountain*, p. 19). On the next page he says of symbols, "What they have in common is the property of *being more in intention than they are in existence*. A symbol points beyond itself, means more than it is." Mr. Wheelwright's notions on this issue are both more complex and more relevant than these isolated quotations might indicate but the very baldness of them may serve the purpose here. For the essential act of the artist is with the work and not with that to which the work might or might not, at his choice, point.

A painter friend of mine was once visited in his studio by a famous writer on the psychology of children's art. When asked what he was working on, the painter explained that he was experimenting with encaustic. "No, my boy," said the condescending psychologist, "you are experimenting with yourself." In telling me the story, the painter said rather plaintively, "I still think I was experimenting with encaustic."

Such an anecdote is not conclusive. The art work not only can but inevitably must have more in it than the artist can intend or even be aware of, for creativity remains a mystery beyond the full understanding of anybody. But it nevertheless says something essential. Art is first of all an order manifesting the order, the rhythm, and suspension of this particular man's world. The reference here must be fair to the philosophers who have written on the subject. Other quotations could be chosen to indicate they often sense this fact of existence with subtlety and depth. Yet there is still a problem between the philosophical and the artistic-critical awareness of the work of art. It is the sense of the art work as the carrier of a reference beyond itself and the art work as an order or a world in its own right. Under the first, the philosophical definition, the art work as symbol is by definition (often not by operation), dispensable. Not by operation, because the modern aestheticians (who may be the first philosophers to have a genuine grasp of art) are perfectly aware that that which is symbolized cannot be reached any other way, that the art work is irreplaceable and irreducible to something else as a means of expression. Yet in the definition the art work is humanly and philosophically relevant because of that to which it refers. To the artist, the art work in its own characteristic being is primary and the symbolic reference is thus *primarily* irrelevant.

Primarily irrelevant. Can it be more? Must it be more? It is probably true to say that it not only can be more with this extended symbolic reference but that it necessarily is. First, through the subject, when the subject is present, great art deals with those fundamental aspects of human experience which are the archetypes or the universals of man's life: life, death, the king, the old man, the sea, the forest, sex, struggle. Then in those works with or without subject, even more basic and general elements are present: dark and light, color, movement, tension and release, the square, the circle, the horizontal, the vertical, penetration and openness, ascent and descent, depth. These are the fundamentals of the human experience and they are the fundamental elements in the language of art.

In a curious but directly relevant fashion, the question of quality imposes itself at this point. For it is partly true to say that these basic and archetypal elements appear equally in bad art as well as good art. Any statement of that kind promptly removes the idea from the center of reference for any element that is common to the poor as well as the good must be automatically suspect.

Yet even this has a complicated reference. When criticism emancipated itself from the problem of quality, it found vast ranges of human experience accessible to it which had been closed before. Either a philosophical or a critical justification of judgments of quality is extraordinarily difficult to achieve. Judgments of quality have almost universally been made according to criteria established from the experience of certain types of art. Those which do not conform to these criteria are automatically judged bad and are ignored. When critics (usually artists preceded the critics here) learned to ignore such criteria and concentrate on the problems of structure and essential language a vast range of man's visual forms became available in living relation. This included works which are directly in the range of the arts, such as the art works of primitive cultures, or cultures foreign to that of the artist and critic, yet it also included every variety of form. Remarkably interesting and humanly significant work is done with all varieties of form remote from the concern of art as such: comic strips, advertisements, bodily ornament. This in turn reflected itself on the judgment of quality, for works of very high quality, formerly inaccessible since their essential language was not known, now became seen in the fullness of their quality.

Yet this, too, can lead to a form of scholarly sentimentality. The language of African sculpture was learned and with it an awareness of the astonishingly high quality of much of that sculpture. A surprising and humanly important conclusion appeared with the awareness that a very high proportion of African, and other primitive art, uncorrupted by the mendacity of civilization, has a directness and integrity which are elements of quality and value. It is also true that no work of African sculpture is the equal of the sculpture of Michelangelo, or Chartres, or the Parthenon. Civilization falls lower and the majority of forms produced in civilized societies in their later periods are a shame compared to the regularly high quality of the primitive. Yet civilization rises higher by the dimension of its self-conscious rationality. It is made up of the same archetypal and fundamental human experiences. But a great work of art is not content simply to manifest or express these elements. It *uses* them in the creation of a new order.

Thus the symbolic reference, whether or not it appears associated with an explicit subject matter, occupies the same place in the language of art that subject matter occupies. It is part of the artist's material. Such reference is an indispensable, an unavoidable ingredient of any formed work and therefore any form, even the most meretricious, is grist to the historian's mill. Any form can serve the purpose of defining the language character-istic of a people or a period. But it is not the language as such that is finally important but what is said with the language. It is not the basic and arche-typal elements that define art but the use made of them when the artist incorporates them into his work. They are a part of the order created by the artist in his art work. They are responsible for a great deal of the emotional weight and depth of the work, its relevance in the general life of a people. Yet, for high art, they remain ingredients, part of the material, having final meaning and value in terms of the order into which they have been incorporated. The art work is primarily an order of its own and the grasp of that order is the essential act, to grasp it in its special character. The art work is its own world to be entered if it is to be meaningful. It is important for what it is, not for what it refers to. It incorporates reference and it is meaningful in terms of that reference. It is essentially meaningful in terms of itself.

Thus the symbol is of fundamental importance in the study of art and it is doubtful if art would be nearly so important in the human enterprise were the symbolic dimension of its being absent from it. To this extent Mrs. Langer, Mr. Wheelwright, and many others have performed a signal service, critically and humanly, by developing this line of thought. The error comes only in making what is part into the whole. The symbol is very important when it appears in the art work; the art work functioning as symbol is very important. The symbol, defined either in Mrs. Langer's formal sense or in the sense of the great symbolic motifs, is the means whereby a vast range of human experience and character, religious, sexual, mythical, ritualistic, is incorporated into the structure that an art work basically is. The art work functioning as symbol can then participate intelligibly in so many of these same experiences. The symbolic material and the symbolic role of art, then, are the means of communication between the art work and its setting in the experiencing world without restricting it to those only who are sensitive to the structural language that is of its essence. This does not alter the fact that the symbol is part of the material and the role of art. It is not its definition.

This has a kind of direct relevance to the work and concerns of the church. The church has no sense of a meaningful role for the artist in its work and the artist is himself not very clear what he should do even when he wants to. Good artists reject the role of illustrator ancillary to pedagogy that is asked of them, as well as the soft, effete devotionalism so common to ecclesiastical art. Some, however, do genuinely want to work in the church but they are not clear how. Much of what they do, therefore, is an adaptation of the more creative styles, principally expressionism and constructivism. Partly, this comes from the fact that the major artists rarely work for the church any more, only the followers. But this is not a sufficient answer. They may be followers but many are honest, yet the results of their work are usually denatured expressionism and denatured constructivism. Much of the trouble arises from a misunderstanding of the role of the symbol. Styles are artificially wedded to symbolic representation that is not appropriate to them and the result is artificial and therefore sterile.

For example, the unique grace of constructivism at its best is clarity, purity, order, discipline, the resolution of its stated tensions. Even with no reference to Christianity, it represents, it seems to me, a unique part of the Christian vision. Symbolism is an intrusion, a dilution of the essential nature of the style without necessarily adding to the symbol. The dove descending, the tree of life, the cross are organic or dramatic. A constructivist dove is likely to be devitalized at the same time it is constructivism adulterated by the intrusion of an object foreign to its character.

A symbol (in this more limited definition of the word) if it is to have a genuine life among people must grow out of their living experience. It is of the essence of the modern styles, particularly constructivism, that they are far more intellectual than most people are capable of following in any sort of detail. Thus if these styles are to function in the life of the church it must be in terms of those qualities essential to them rather than by making them subservient to traditional symbols.

There is no return to a world which once was and is no longer, nor any significant speech in a language that is dead. Symbols in the more restricted, immediately referential sense of the word once had a life in the world and with men in general. Perhaps they might again emerge meaningfully. At the moment art must be taken as symbolic only if that can mean that it be taken in the essential existence of its being and its style. The church vitiates its life and its work by the reiteration of antique language. These things no longer nourish the world. This is a world which can be reached only by the actuality, not the shadow of reality.

III

ART AS

STRUCTURE

AND ART AS

EXPRESSION

Mrs. Langer's formulation has been attractive to many people and has received a good deal of emphasis, as it rightly deserves. As I have tried to show, however, it does not engage the work of art in its concreteness and hence it tends to be attractive to those of a primarily philosophical inclination who find in it the means for an intelligible ordering of the arts within their epistemological structures without the necessity for a very strong emotional involvement.

Paul Tillich, on the other hand, has been astonishingly successful in arousing more than just interest in a great many people but also a very strong concern. Furthermore, far from appealing just to the philosophically minded he has had a considerable influence among people in the arts, who find in his work as well as his essential respect for their work, a sense of restoration to the general body of the cultural enterprise. They have not fully measured the price they pay for that restoration.

Professor Tillich's greatest appeal, however, has been for those whose concern is for the communication between religion and culture and he has gone far toward establishing the terminology and the attitudes by which people in the church approach the work of art. It is inevitable that this should be so: in a fashion quite comparable to those who approach the art work as symbol he makes the art work an element in another enterprise and defines its language in the vocabulary of that enterprise.

This vocabulary overlaps Mrs. Langer's at one point, as he makes constant use of the word "symbol." He does not define this term with anything like Mrs. Langer's precision and he has been particularly guilty of leaving undefined his oft-repeated phrase "A symbol participates in the reality it symbolizes." (He probably means something fairly close to Mrs. Langer's "forms of feeling" by this statement.) It is not, however, this statement which has been so generally used but the various schemes (not always consistent with each other) which he has proposed in order to account for the relation of art to religion. It is not necessary to examine all these schemes, but at least one should be examined in sufficient detail to make clear the nature of his formulation. Unlike Mrs. Langer, Tillich's writings (which are usually speeches given on various occasions rather than systematic investigations into the problem) abound in concrete reference to many works of art.

Perhaps the most revealing, certainly a typical and symptomatic expression of his involvement, is contained in the chapter "Existential Aspects of Modern Art" in the volume *Christianity and the Existentialists*, edited by Carl Michalson. Here Tillich identifies what he calls the four levels of relation between religion and art:

"1. Non-religious style, non-religious content." At this level, "in secular style and without religious content, power of being is visible, not directly but indirectly." This includes the painters of the natural vitalities, such as Jan Steen and Rubens in his secular subjects.

"2. Religious style, non-religious content: the existential level." This is the level of style where the artist breaks through the surface appearance in an "attempt to see the elements of reality as fundamental powers of being out of which reality is constructed." The section is characterized by such expressions as "atomistic," "disrupted," "an attempt to look into the depth of reality, below any surface and any beautification of the surface and any organic unity" (expressionism, surrealism, cubism, and futurism), "the creative powers of nature" (Van Gogh), "emptiness... horror, crime, shock, that which is uncanny" (Munch), "the piece character" of our time which is horribly visible in Picasso, "the dissolution of the organic realities" (Braque). In this style the essential categories – time, space, causality, substance – have lost their substance. This is seen not only in contemporary style but in mannerism, some Baroque, Goya, Breughel, Bosch.

"3. Non-religious style, religious content." In contrast with the last section, treated in loving detail, this section is briefly dismissed. It is the level of conventional church art of today. It includes *also* Raphael ("a harmonious humanity which, of course, is indirectly religious, but is not religious in style") and Rubens (whose "Madonna and Child" "is wonderful to look at, but nobody would think this the Mother of God in the Catholic symbolism of this relationship").

"4. Religious style, religious content." This includes El Greco, Sutherland, perhaps Nolde and Rouault and, above all, Grünewald, whose work Tillich considers the very type and model of Christian art. "This form is generally called expressionistic, because it is a form in which the surface is disrupted in order to say something."

The first thing to notice in this account is the total failure of the terminology to correspond with best contemporary practice in art criticism. In each case the term is not "form" and "content" but "style" and "content" and content here is identified, not with form, but with subject matter. Tillich has ample precedent from the practice of many historians and critics. On the surface it would appear that there is no quarrel with a term whose reference is perfectly apparent. Yet it is always unfortunate to see two terms used for the same reference when another idea is thereby left unidentified. If "content" is used for subject matter, there is no term to use to refer to the human weight and significance and relevance of the characteristic art term, form. Thus, where the term is lacking, the idea is lost.

As a consequence of this basic terminological confusion, the decisive part in each case is subject matter. In fact, in this analysis, Tillich does not accept his own statement "The form which makes a thing what it is, is its content...." It is not possible to say even that he finds the defining quality in the tension between "style" and "content," for style in this usage is not so much a quality of form (as it should be interpreted and in fact is elsewhere in Tillich) but the manner in which a particular subject is presented. It is notable that the constantly repeated terms such as "disrupted" and "breaking through the surface" refer in each case, not to the form but to the subject, to the images of "real" things as they appear on the canvas.

The most striking thing about this is its curiously nineteenth-early twentieth-century quality. The chronological conjunction must be put that way for the manner of expression is not based on the categories of characteristically twentieth-century ways of working artistically but rather of the revolt of the twentieth century against the nineteenth or, more precisely put, out of the German section of that revolt. And it is a truism to say that a revolt is as much determined by what it revolts against as it is by what it works toward. Only the children of the revolutionaries can inhabit the land made by the revolutionaries, and Tillich is here perhaps too much concerned with Egypt left than the promised land ahead. For in nineteenth-century official art, subject was all. In Tillich's account, subject is still all, even if more powerfully and honestly seen.

The best test of his attitude is perhaps his brief account of Braque and Rubens, rather than Picasso and Grünewald, Tillich's most frequent points of reference in the arts.

Braque is his example of cubism, to which he applies the terms "dissolution of organic realities" and "disruptedness." Now, there is a certain amount of precedence for this terminology, for few styles have had as much rhetoric of this kind used about them as cubism has. Yet such expressions should be checked against two things: the nature of the act of painting and the actual experience of the painting of Braque.

Fig. 19

Only an understanding of painting that begins with subject matter can see a painting as *essentially* disruptive or destructive. In point of fact the painter does not begin with things which he then distorts but with a blank surface and paints (or other materials) to be applied to it. Thus the painting in its basic act is constructive, not destructive or disruptive. This is a practical truth of operation and an ontological truth as well. It is the way a painting comes into being, an object added to creation. In the pregnant words of Braque himself, "The goal is not to be concerned with the reconstitution of an anecdotal fact, but with the constitution of a pictorial fact" (*Artists on Art*, ed. Goldwater, p. 422).

If, in the light of this principle, the paintings of Braque are directly experienced, they will be seen not as disruptive but as profoundly constructive. Of all artists of the twentieth century Braque is the most profoundly ordered (with the possible exception of Mondrian who sought a point of stillness quite other than what Braque has sought). The experience of Braque is a deep quiet, an ordered relation that can be seen as disruptive only against a standard of Meissonier and Bouguereau. What he set out to destroy was not a false ontology but a false idea of painting. What he achieved was not an analysis or a symbol of disruption but one of the profoundest symbols of order in the whole enterprise of the twentieth-century mind. If words are necessary to supplement this account, his own will do again. "The subject is not the object, it is a new unity, a lyricism which grows completely from the means" (Goldwater, *Artists on Art*, p. 422).

Cézanne, to whom Tillich properly refers as the origin of cubism, could be called the artist above all others concerned with order and structure. It is quite simply impossible to experience Cézanne as "atomistic, disruptive" unless these ideas are superimposed on him. More than most artists, Cézanne was conscious of the structure of a painting, the governing integrity of its two-dimensional surface, and the structure of nature as he took it for a subject, the governing integrity of its three-dimensional depth and the quality of its environing atmosphere. Out of this tension Cézanne created his art and, in a sense, the art of the twentieth century.

Fig. 12

Is it correct, then, to say that Tillich is wrong in his analysis of twentieth-century art? Not altogether. For the things he says do apply to a certain range of art works – German expressionism as it developed prior to the time of the Nazis (and as it had been adumbrated in Grünewald and other earlier artists). Again the constructive work of these artists ought to be seen clearly, for they were not immune from the general law of making. But it is true that they construct their pictures out of an awareness of emotional life, of tragedy, the deep places of human consciousness.

That Tillich at his best speaks from the standpoint of German expressionism is not surprising, for the formative years of his work exactly coincide with this movement, and his obsession with its principles is not a limitation but a measure of his involvement as a creative element in a greatly creative situation.

The error comes, not in what he says of this area of art but in making its principles universal. Cézanne and Braque are not German but French. They worked toward a different goal and their relevance to the Christian understanding of culture must be quite differently defined.

Another test and another problem of definition is found in Tillich's discussion of Raphael and Rubens. Of Raphael, Tillich says (*Christianity and the Existentialists*, ed. Michalson, p. 142), "...a harmonious humanity which of course is indirectly religious, but is not religious in style." Now, "harmonious humanity" is a category of subject matter, not of form. It would be foolish to contend that the subject matter is irrelevant to an understanding of Raphael, for the subject was obviously important to him, and it would be the part of arrogance to deny it its proper place in the interpretation. Yet the humanity is a means to the harmony, and the harmony is a concretion of a felt quality in material and subject. Raphael's work is, perhaps, the most profound expression of an eloquent and deeply felt harmony, an expressive dignity of images, a calm and settled peace. Some of the finest artists of his time felt this to be the expression and statement of the peace of God. If this is impeachable it is on quite other grounds than the fact that its style differs from one arbitrarily chosen as the religious style.

Fig. 14

The description of Rubens is even less adequate. Tillich says of a Madonna, "It is wonderful to look at, but nobody would think that this is the mother of God in the Catholic symbolism of this relationship." It sounds a little odd for Tillich, of all people, to suggest that the proper function of painting is to imitate a theological concept (and bears out the notorious fact that a critic is at his worst in his negative judgments).

The *ad hominem* argument is relevant here. Rubens was a deeply, devoutly religious man. To make Tillich's statement about this work is to assert that Rubens did not understand his own faith or that he was incompetent to communicate it or that he pandered to popular taste. These would be difficult propositions to support.

Fig. 12

Furthermore, that Rubens had one of the finest intelligences among artists and was one of the most comprehensively learned, makes it likely that he knew how to adjust his style to his content. It is altogether likely that he knew that Mary was not a Flemish great lady of the seventeenth century. His subject matter was a part of the material he formed. It was a part of the grammar and vocabulary of his artistic speech. In the total communication of this language he established an image of such ordered power, of vital order, of exuberant vitality as has never been equalled in art. The balance and thrust of his rhythms in their ordered relation of parts and actions themselves communicate Rubens' vision of the nature of things, and in this language subject is a vital part – but only a part. This style, this formal language is not present in Rubens with the crassness of this verbal description but with subtlety, taste, and discrimination. These forms are the embodiments of Rubens' faith.

Tillich is not wrong in asserting the value of expressionism. There is ample biblical foundation for the principle of estrangement, the enmity of God, anxiety, emptiness, and brokenness. But the Bible is a comprehensive book, and Christianity is a comprehensive religion. There is foundation, too, for the sense of joy, peace, harmony, the glory of the earth. Not the least of these justifications are the parables of Jesus which transfigure with goodness the things that are. It is arrogant to say, "Mankind no longer feels at home in this world." Who speaks for all mankind?

It is not necessary to pursue the defense of Rubens in order to demonstrate the inadequacy of the standards by which he is being judged. It is of the essence of parochialism to make concepts limited in time or place into eternally valid standards. German expressionism is one of the essential aspects of the modern spirit. It is not the definition of the Christian faith or Christian art.

Then, following, "while the others are only indirectly representing the ultimate, the expressive element represents it directly." This kind of assertion is not supportable either in aesthetic theory or critical practice. It is evident that, despite the refinement of the vocabulary, the basic methodological flaw is still present. Incidentally, this leads Tillich, who is not an illogical man, into a curiously circular argument: "This explains two important facts: the dominance of the expressive element in the style of all periods in which great religious art has been created...." This is a fairly obvious statement – if we assume that great religious art is that which contains the expressive element! In fact, the statement is historically untrue.

The key to the difference between Tillich's definition of an art work and the artist's is found in Tillich's statement that an art work lacking form presents a "distorted reality and not ultimate reality." It is unsafe to generalize about artists, and certainly there is too little evidence to generalize about the artist's attitude toward his failures. But such evidence as there is indicates that no artist ever thinks of his failures as a faulty window through which reality is seen as distorted. As human beings, artists are as subject to sentimentality as any other men, and many an artist probably cherishes his failures as a parent may cherish a deformed child. But for the artist – as it is not for the parent – this is sentimentality. As an artist his attitude is closer to Cézanne, who abandoned his failures in the fields and walked away. Rouault burned his. Other, more frugal, artists save them for the sake of the canvas. As art works they have no existence. They are not imperfect representations or expressions of ultimate reality, they are nothing.

This is emphatically not the same difficulty that appeared in the earlier writings, arising out of the close and decisive attention to subject. In fact, this is another, more fundamental difficulty. It appears that, in Tillich's system, there is a reality to which the art work is subservient and secondary whereas, to the artist, reality is the art work. It is of the essence of this

39

argument that no general statement of this kind can be made about the artist and certainly Fra Angelico's attitude toward his work differs greatly from Jackson Pollock's. The one considers his work a means to a devotional end, the other considers his work an end in itself, a world to live in. Yet to the one as to the other the art work has an immediate physical existence foreign to Tillich's system.

The discussion, then, turns back into areas not the concern of this discussion – the problem of Tillich's ontology. It seems clear, however, that this ontology suggests that his primary or ultimate reality is something quite other than the world of experience and certainly other than the art work which can only, with a greater or lesser inadequacy, express or reflect it. It would seem, therefore, Tillich's basic position is fundamentally monistic and Platonic. It is, then, a singularly poignant revelation of the perpetual discontinuity between Platonism and art. Tillich's constant reformulation of his terms then appears less as a progressive sharpening of his tools than the desperate attempt of a man who loves art to save it from the rigors of a position which his ancient mentor so consistently faced. However valuable his insights as a man and however useful some of his principles, there remains a fundamental methodological flaw, and this flaw must be examined in greater detail.

The clue to the difficulty, the fatal flaw, may lie in an area which Tillich does not, to my knowledge, discuss at all, the question of the origins of the work of art. Why do men make these curious things called works of art? What does it mean to "create"?

To Tillich, ultimate reality, being itself, on which all finite existence depends, is out there, beyond man, beyond what man attempts to do and be. The art work has existence as any other human artifact only as it *partakes of* the existence of being itself. It is a response to an expression of ultimate reality. To the extent that it is original, creative, it is human and may therefore be a document of considerable interest and power. But as human, it is involved in matter and therefore in the darkness of matter. To the artist it is only as he can realize it in the material he has chosen that he has any vision at all. For Tillich there is a vision whose communication is obstructed by the very material which is the means of its realization. Thus all artistic expression which does not participate directly in ultimate reality is suspect, partial. With admirable rigor, he concentrates on the single notion of being itself and measures all man's creations against it. For him, only in expressionistic art does ultimate reality break through into the human experience and it is therefore only in expressionistic art that man can see the highest form of art.

Thus it follows naturally that the existential question is (by implication, never by direct statement) the only valid source of the work of art. The relevant man of culture confronts his condition and his times. Since man is always and by definition estranged from the ground of being, since he is sinful, there is always in his situation the element of tragedy. He is a victim of his finiteness, he bears the burden of his pride. Thus the clear and accurate contemplation of this situation must always see the void. "Often one gets the impression that only those cultural creations have greatness in which the experience of the void is expressed" (Tillich, *The Protestant Era*, p. 60).

In such a view it becomes logically inevitable that expressionistic art becomes the norm, for this style takes as its means and purpose the distortion and tragedy of human experience. The function of art as of culture in such a definition is to raise the questions, to show man in relation to the void. Only so can it be called "religious art." It can be Christian by suggestion if the subject is Christian and thereby suggests the Christian answer (which apparently is the responsibility of theology or homiletics and not of art). But it is respectably Christian or respectable for use in the intellectual life of the church only if it includes this sense of the void, this expressionist style.

The problem raised by this position applies to the whole existentialist movement and not simply to this aspect of it: is knowledge possible apart from tragedy? Is the experience of the void, the consciousness of man's brokenness essential to man's deepest life? Tillich asserts that it is, and it follows logically that only those works, which most clearly and powerfully manifest this experience and reveal being itself breaking through into man's experience, can be, in the fullest sense, great art.

No account which proposes to be a more adequate answer can ignore the problem just raised, for no problem is solved simply by identifying its fundamental philosophic roots (in this case Platonism). Existentialism would not be so live a movement were it not for its response to basic human needs. Yet Tillich has saved the arts for the modern mind only by the most grievous sacrifice. They do not create, they only respond. The larger part of their product is relegated to a secondary position. In contrast to Tillich, who begins and ends with the vision of ultimate reality, the artist and critic start with the individual work of art. The art work is reality, and the first concern is the integrity of the work. The theoretical problem then is how to maintain the integrity of the work and still make it relevant as Tillich does.

A further methodological flaw is uncovered in this very practical difference of operation and attitude. Tillich's monistic answer is virtually inevitable if the search is governed by *the* significance of *the* work of art. There is no such thing as *the* work of art, there is no such thing as "art" but only individual works produced by individual men for various purposes and from various contexts. Art is as varied as life itself, and no critical system that proposes to judge it by a single standard is generally valid.

Tillich assumes a single reality, and thus there can be a scale of art works showing their degree of closeness to that reality. Yet only in the most general sense can there be assumed one reality, for those who are not Platonists. Any man's apprehension of "reality" is both partial and distorted. His art work cannot, therefore, be taken as closer to or further away from "reality" than another work of comparable quality. It is, instead, the embodiment of this artist's relation to some partial aspect of reality. It is possible to make the degree of closeness to some significant element or reality the measure of the value or the quality of art works. It is not possible to make it a measure of their Christian or religious relevance.

Art is theologically relevant; even more, no account of man is complete or accurate that does not contain within itself a discriminating account of man's making of things. But the right questions must be asked. Tillich's question is basically the existential question, and the response to it would indicate that it is certainly one of the relevant questions. But the loss is too great.

The final impact of this discussion should not be the negative judgment on the work done by a theologian when the critics, whose proper job it is, have not done it. Out of this discussion should emerge the problems that must be solved and the theological issues relevant to them. A number of solid, practical problems emerge, whose solutions should call into relevance the theoretical questions.

What, for example, is the critical procedure for determining if a work is religious or Christian? What, if any, is the relation between this decision and the judgment of quality, or value, or relevance to the Christian faith?

What is the relation between form and subject matter? What is the origin of the form and of its characteristic individuality? What is the relation between form and verbal concepts?

These are the practical problems, the problems of operation that face the Christian critic. They raise the theoretical questions that intersect with the problems raised by Tillich's questions and his system.

The basic question is the essential or existential function of the art work. The world proceeds from the hand of God, and the artist is a part of the world. What then is the work of art? Is it an extension of the created order, an adding to it of an object that was not there before? Is it a transaction with the given reality of the world revealing its nature and communicating an understanding of it? Or is it truly an instrument whereby man seeks to penetrate or to control reality or through which reality breaks into the life of man?

Is this creation or intercourse good? Is it given to man to function as God or to be surrogate for God? Is the transaction with the reality of the world and experience a good thing, or is the desire for it a lust after falseness? Is the art work indispensable to man's quest and man's achievement, or is it so involved with the limitations of matter that, given the vision of ultimate reality, the art work must disappear as superfluous?

Does the art work reveal and uncover man's existential commitment, or does it express that condition?

Is tragedy essential to knowledge?

IV

THE

STRUCTURE

OF ART AND THE

ATTITUDE

OF THE ARTIST

While certain basic ideas have so far been continually reiterated in the discussion as a necessary consequence of the discussion of a variety of other ideas, it still remains true that examination of other people's positions can be no more than preparatory. I hope it has been clear during the course of this examination that I neither have the desire nor feel the need to repudiate the work of those who have defined art as symbol or as expression. In each case they are talking about an actuality and I differ with them only when they make a part into a whole. But it is not possible to assert that they have missed the sense of the whole if some account of the whole cannot be given. It is required of me, therefore, that I sketch out the case I shall try to demonstrate.

The most often reiterated remark I have made is that art is fundamentally a structure, with its own independent existence and value. The bulk of what follows must concern itself with that structure, the manner in which it can be apprehended and understood, its relation to the problem of communication. I can adumbrate that argument in the course of this chapter but my concern at the moment is with the source of the structure in the hand and mind of the artist. For the artist is not an abstraction but a particular human being making a particular object which stands in a peculiar relation to him and to his humanity.

An art work is a structure: before it is anything else it is a thing, an object. It is therefore inseparable from the material of which it is a part. It is generated out of a specific piece of a specific material. Further, the structure and the very act of manipulation which brought the structure into existence is an action by the hand of the artist. This is a truism so obvious it hardly seems worth mentioning yet vast quantities of aesthetics and criticism have been written as though this simple fact of operation did not exist. Yet it is the central fact of all art.

The life of an artist as an artist is lived in response to and in his command of his material. His training is from beginning to end learning how to handle his material for his chosen purpose. Thus the act of making an art work is an act of the sensibility, the response of trained nerves to the character and possibility of a given material and the response of trained muscles to the command which the sensitive intellect gives it. Again the simplest observation of an artist at work demonstrates how much a truism this is and yet it is just as often ignored as the primacy of the material was ignored. The act of the artist is an act of decision and the power to carry out that decision. The hand of the artist generates the art work out of the material.

The important question then becomes: what is the source of this decisive sensibility? If it be true that the basic act of art is the decisive act of the hand of the artist, it is equally true that the work of that hand is not infinitely various but has its own consistency and development which makes the whole body of a man's work his and not someone else's. The structure is inseparably linked to what he is as a person. This assertion is complicated somewhat by those artists who willingly sink themselves in the anonymity of a mass of workmen yet this constitutes no refutation: in these cases the individual workmen have so far allowed themselves to become instruments in the purpose of another man that they virtually constitute additional hands for another man's sensibility. Thus the question still remains: what is the source of this distinctive artistic personality?

Put this way the question may in itself act as a check against the tendency to think of one source for "art" as though art were a single thing. The distinctive artistic personality, the distinctive sensibility obviously has its source in the source of human variety; there is no ultimate accounting for the mystery of personality. Influences may be validly traced and they may be meaningful. But the amalgam includes influences and the uniquely human contribution of a living person. Only the disordered personality can be reduced to a simple diagnosis.

Thus the work of analysis which has been carried on in so many different ways is entirely appropriate and useful so long as one answer is not made to apply to all. All the political, social, religious, mythic, sexual, physical, environmental influences that have been variously identified might be relevant in this or that case. But they are relevant, not decisive. It is altogether possible that Freud is right in tracing certain characteristics of "The Madonna and Child with Saint Anne" to the ambivalent relations between Leonardo and his mother and stepmother; it is equally true that thousands of other men have had comparable experiences in their childhood and very few of them have painted "The Madonna and Child with Saint Anne." It is also quite probable that many genuine artists have had experiences of a comparable psychological intensity without being to any appreciable degree affected by them. Their sensibility, on the contrary, would have been formed by a different set of influences operating on a different intelligence.

None of these questions can finally be answered; the thing that makes them accessible to the observer who wishes to communicate with the artist is the structure which is generated by that sensibility. Thus the structure of the work of art makes it possible to get back to the attitude of the artist toward the world out of which he develops his work and this attitude now needs to be outlined.

The starting point for the artist's work is the sensuous qualities of the material itself, the material in all its uniqueness and specificity. The critical act of his work is his ordering of this material – which includes the subject, the things he might choose to include in the resemblance. The decisive act of analysis and understanding, therefore, must take place within this ordering, this making of forms.

The making of forms is not a casual act. The material, the physical substance of which the work is made, is formed according to its own nature and the nature of the work of art. The structure which results from the making is a system of relationships, of attractions and tensions, of forces which establish and maintain the particular state of equilibrium which characterizes this work and no other. It is with the imaginative and physical grasp of this system of relationships that the peculiar character of a work of art is fully understood.

It has been a part of the task of contemporary criticism to recover this sense of the unique structure of the work of art but too often the recovery was made only at the price of isolating the structure from its human significance. In freeing the artist from the burden of illustration it has been too often true that the critic has made the artist isolated and alone. Yet the structure of the work of art is determined by and satisfies some of the most profound beliefs, convictions, feelings, ideas, emotions of the human spirit. Access to these is achieved by the realization that they are not the beliefs and convictions which can be expressed in words but those which are expressed or communicated only by the forms of the work of art. That is, the language of art is a language peculiar to itself and access to the work of art is achieved by learning that language and not trying to reduce the art work to the terms of a language alien to its nature.

The achievement of a successful structure of this kind is a satisfaction and a completion in itself, not dependent on any extraneous relation the work might otherwise have. Why this should be so is not a question easily answered. The most probable answer is that the structure achieves order; not just any order but a system of relations which is peculiarly responsive to the sense of meaning held by the particular artist. Man is, from his earliest moments, besieged by sense impressions from the world outside himself. Achieving some sense of the meaningful relations of these sense impressions is the basic act of the most elementary type of maturing. It is only by these means that man can perform the elementary acts which are required of him if he is to maintain himself on the earth. To most men this elementary ordering of impressions is all they feel responsible for. There are others, however, to whom this is not enough, or not even particularly important. Their concern is with a more meaningful order. They receive sense impressions with a particular acuteness and seek to order them in ways which reveal their inmost nature. Some artists are content to remain at this level and their work becomes a revelation or an uncovering of the nature of things in the world. Others, however, feel a deeper union

47

between the sense impressions received from all kinds of stimuli and the nature of their existence on the earth. These men seek a structure and an order of forms which embodies, bodies forth, what they sense to be the deepest significance of this relation between the world of things and man's sense of the meaning of experience. This relation they do not interpret or express in these verbal terms (an artist's opinions, even about art, are not necessarily better than another man's) but in terms of his forms. Thus he does not stand ready to interpret something which the layman might call the "meaning" of the work of art but he nevertheless feels the sense of completion that comes with the establishment of order out of the chaos of experience. The search for order is the defining function of the artist.

This order, however, is not an inert or passive thing. It is an active system of relationships within the elements of the work of art. As active, it both expresses and communicates many things. The artist's relation with the world is as varied as any man's and within the domain of forms there is a wide variety of functions to which the structure of the art work lends itself. These functions are, in fact, as many as there are works of art but like all human activity they can be roughly grouped in ways which at least show the character of man's making.

Much of art, for example, is given over to a kind of celebration, a rejoicing in the nature of things. Again the popular consciousness of art tends to find in art the purpose of "beauty" and again the popular consciousness is wrong only in exaggerating this function and in identifying this beauty with the idea of subjective pleasure. Since the earliest days art has had the function of delight in the nature of things; first, perhaps, delight in the form itself, then delight in qualities of the natural world which can be translated into the work of art. This is not only one of the oldest and most elementary traditions in art but is still very much alive. The realist tradition which finds the natural world a constant pleasure to explore and interpret remains almost undiminished in its power and influence even when it does not occupy quite the central position it once held. The abstract tradition has not, however, departed from the principle of delight for a great deal of abstract painting is given over to a delight in the materials themselves and in the character of their combination and relationships.

Yet the artist's concern is rarely, if ever, given over wholly to the search for delight or the celebration of things. Certainly the whole of art has never been. There is simultaneously the constant pressure of the desire to understand, to penetrate into the nature and the meaning of things. This is not so primal a function of art as the expression of delight or the celebration of the beauty of things for it requires a degree of sophistication and objective self-consciousness which is generally beyond the primitive mentality. Yet it appears as one of the earliest stages in man's search for the meaning of the world. Neither words nor scientific forms are necessarily the earliest expression of man's search for meaning, although on occasion they might well be. But as often as not the search can be conducted only through the ordered forms of the work of art which condense into the symbol the sense of what things are essentially.

Just as the celebration of beauty could be directed both outward and inward, on the one hand toward the visible, natural world, and on the other hand toward the nature of the work of art itself, so the analysis can be directed in two ways. It, too, can be directed toward the understanding of the outward, natural world or inward toward the natural structure of the art work itself. In the first place, the structure of the painting must reflect what the artist sees and believes of the structure of the natural world. In the second place, the artist sees the structure of the painting as itself a significant part of the objective world which requires him to explore it with the same integrity of understanding and fidelity to fact which governs his exploration of the outer world. The structure of the painting itself, the ordered relations of its parts, have their own objective existence which must be respected and are not available for arbitrary manipulation by the artist's instincts. Once the preliminary situation has been established the work must proceed to its logically ordained conclusion.

The extreme development of the first type is an intellectually structured naturalism. The extreme development of the second type is the rationally ordered abstraction (technically termed non-objective art). The two can be combined and, in fact, usually are. The most self-conscious and rigorous attempt to combine them is the work of Paul Cézanne.

Obviously not all artists have approached their task with this kind of objective intellectual rigor. They have, rather, been concerned with their emotional involvement in the condition of man. They do not so much see and analyze, they feel, they react, and they manifest that feeling in the work of art. This is the artistic style generically called expressionism. Strictly speaking any work of art is expressionistic, since it expresses something. It expresses the artist's delight in the world, his act of celebration. It expresses his understanding of the structure of things, his act of analysis. Yet the need for distinctiveness of terminology and clarification of the ideas involved has suggested that the term "expressionistic" not be used to apply to these types of art (for which perfectly adequate terminology already exists) but that it refer to the style of art in which the artist's concern is his own inner state of mind or his emotional reaction to a situation outside himself.

Thus this is the type of art most intimately involved in human life. This does not necessarily mean it is the most accessible to the ordinary person. The ordinary person is likely to find the analytical type cold and inaccessible and for the most part responds most readily to the art of celebration, since that can be more easily reduced to easy decoration. Even though expressionistic art may state more accurately his own emotional state, it does so with an unpleasant vividness, it reminds him too forcibly of those things which he would like to conceal or escape from. It seems to assault him and he often reacts most violently against it. This violence of reaction reflects accurately the involvement of expressionistic art in the tragedy of the human situation. In some respects expressionistic art is the least "pure," the most literary of the major styles. Work in it requires that the artist not see the language of art as its own purpose or as an analytical instrument but as a means to the end of stating in visible form what he sees of the tragedy of man's life.

For expressionistic art is pre-eminently the art of man's tragedy. It sees the dreadful gap between man's possibilities and his failure, his hopes and his real fate. It sees the artist's own desperate grapple with his condition. These are the things that must be translated into the language of art.

Again, in a real sense, all art is a communication as well as an expression. Furthermore, there is no incompatibility between communication and any other category of art. That is, an artist might be commissioned to make a work for the specific purpose of communicating a doctrine or a political fact or any of the other innumerable uses which art might have, yet he can approach his task in a spirit appropriate to his own basic stylistic inclinations. Goya's portraits of the king of Spain are highly expressionistic while Velasquez's are coolly rational yet both serve the same purpose within the court ritual. At one or another stage in its development, medieval art can be wildly expressionistic or joyously celebrational within the same purpose of the communication of doctrine.

Nevertheless, communication as a deliberate purpose rather than an incidental occasion can affect the character of the work of art, and a considerable portion of the world's art has this deliberate function. It is understandable, in fact, that this should be so. A purchaser is often willing to invest in a work of art for the delight it gives him, but it requires a high degree of sophistication to share the artist's concern for analysis or expression to the point of investing in it and this kind of sophistication does not always coincide with the funds necessary to support it. Most art is commissioned or bought to serve a particular purpose and the work is expected to communicate some sense of that purpose, even if it is only to enhance the social prestige of the purchaser. At another level such art is expected to communicate a particular political ideal as it did with the art of Augustus, or the medieval German emperors, or Justinian, or Louis XIV. In its uses in the church such art may have a comparably political purpose in establishing hierarchical authority but it may also have the more humane purpose of teaching doctrine or inspiring devotion and guiding the devotional life. It can, in other words, not only indoctrinate and act as an instrument of power. It can also be an instrument of instruction and a focus for some of the most meaningful aspects of man's life.

An elementary, but necessary, observation must be made here. Performance of this function of communication does not insure significant quality. At the same time it does not forbid it. There are works which the professional critic must regard with contempt which have nonetheless performed their function admirably in an immediate and practical sense. Yet they survive beyond the occasion only if the artist has been able to rise out of the immediacy of the occasion to a sense of universal significance. There have been, in wartime, innumerable works of propaganda art which have vanished into well-merited oblivion once the occasion for their making has passed. At the same time, Goya's attacks on Napoleonic France or Picasso's attacks on fascism, which were intended to communicate as propaganda in the low sense of that word, live as major works of art precisely because the immediacy of the purpose did not obscure the human significance which gave meaning to the occasion.

Art has another function. This might be called the "discipline of imaginative creativity." Man has an incorrigible urge to make. It might be said he has an unavoidable necessity to make, for his life is full of things which must be made for survival, if for nothing else. His urge goes deeper than that, however, for man is not content simply to fulfill the utilitarian function. He both embellishes and expresses. His making goes far beyond what is required for the satisfaction of certain functions. When disciplined by a sense of coherent form, a sense of style, this compulsion to make can become an instrument of order in man's life. From this derives the coherence of common life which characterizes the form of many towns and cities of older cultures. When undisciplined by this sense of style, this compulsion to make expresses itself in a chaos of false or sentimental forms and the thing which should be one of the strongest forces for order and coherence in man's life becomes, instead, an instrument of incoherence. Either the outskirts or the center of any American town can provide ample documentation for this assertion. Nor is this a minor matter. This incoherence reflects a deep-rooted discontinuity in a people's sense of purpose and the function of the common life.

It would be a bold person indeed who would lay claim to comprehensiveness in any such listing as this and no such claim is being made for this one. It does, however, indicate certain basic types of approach to the problem of the function of forms in human life and thus can serve as a background for the study of the specifically Christian concern with the arts. A Christian might be content to accept the interpretation that the arts are congenial only to his general life as a man and not to his specific character as a Christian. If he is not thus content, he must determine that quality of the arts that is a part of his specific concern. This quality will here be termed the sacramental.

This is a dangerous use of terminology. The sacraments are by their nature specific and concrete and they have a specific function in the life of the Christian. To extend their function to those things that are not appointed to be sacraments is to risk dilution of the original idea beyond the point of usefulness. Yet the essence of the idea of the sacrament is the presence of God in human experience, the communication of God with man, the action of God on man. Wherever God acts through and by means of the concreteness of human life and human experience the sacramental is present. Conversely, anyone who asserts that it is proper to use the term sacramental to describe the arts is saying that in the work of art there either is or can be some communication from God, or even the presence of God and the power of God communicated to man.

It is possible to handle such an idea sentimentally along the lines of "finding God through nature." Such a sentimental conception of the sacramental denies the principle which is central to the whole idea of a sacrament: that the initiative is in the hands of God who may choose to withhold himself or reveal himself as he wills. Unless there is sufficient assurance that God has promised his presence (as there is in the gathering for the

Eucharist) it is not proper to impose on God the necessity for communication.

On the other hand, it is not necessary to assume that this sacramental communication is spasmodic or irrational. Perhaps the highest level of the sacramental is the direct action of God on man which is wholly within the initiative of God. But there are ranges of communication with the will and purpose of God which cannot be reduced to the instructional and can be described accurately as sacramental.

The working of this principle can be illustrated by applying it to one of the most delicate problems facing the critic who wants to define a specifically Christian attitude toward the arts: the problem of the place of non-Christian art in the life of the Christian.

There is the eternal temptation of man to divide people and things into good or bad, ins or outs, with the implied or stated assumption that he is on the inside. This is a particularly unfortunate tendency for the Christian to fall prey to for his call to come apart from the world does not suggest that he is superior to the world but only that he is called to a special function in the world ("You are the salt of the earth…"). There is no reason to think that the Christian artist is, as an artist, any better than the non-Christian artist or that there is any unusual merit as art in the body of church art. The Christian would come to such a conclusion only at the certain risk of impoverishing his life as a member of the common human community.

Yet to press this principle too far is to fall into the sentimentality of saying that all art is equally good or equally relevant or relevant in the same way. This is to obscure essential distinctions and clear distinctions are the basic act of the human intelligence. There are differences of value and of quality in the arts and there are different kinds of relevance.

Art has already been defined as the embodiment of man's response to reality and his attempt to order his experience of that reality. The Christian occupies no privileged position in reality nor does he have any special wisdom which qualifies him to speak with authority about that reality. The experience of reality – which includes defining what "reality" is – is a common human enterprise. The Christian can only hold that man is created by God and his response to "reality" is his response to God's creation. It is possible for man to misconstrue the nature of that reality and come to faulty conclusions about it and to this extent there are many works of art which are opposed to the Christian interpretation of the nature of things. Yet the response is always a uniquely human response. The assertions thus made may be true or may be false. In either case this is the way this living human being responds to reality and in this sense all genuine art is true and therefore deeply relevant to the work of the Christian. It is no distortion of the term to say of it that it is sacramental, for by laying hold of the work of art, apprehending its form and its order, the spectator is laying hold of one of the facts of human experience.

Furthermore, an art work is not a theory about reality (any such theory, which might be measured against Christian theories, are simply deductions or extrapolations), it is in its essence a grappling with reality. While the term reality (which has deliberately been left undefined) is one that will vary in its meaning according to the context of the particular artistic experience, it is, by the nature of art, an experience of the physical reality of the earth. Through a great part of the world's art this includes the experience of the reality of man and nature. Through all art, abstract or representational, the experience is one of the physical reality of the material of the art work and the reality of the ordering principles of that material in the work of art. Thus any work of genuine art is a meeting with one of the fundamental, elemental aspects of the human experience.

It is, therefore, a meeting with the center of creation. The experience of art is an experience of one of the defining acts of humanity. This includes all art, not the art in the service of any particular creed.

Thus, the sense of the sacramental is a dimension of all art as inherent in the human response to reality.

But, again, this principle must not be abused to obscure necessary distinctions. This would be proper neither for the intellectual integrity of the Christian, nor for the integrity of the artist, who has intentions for his work which must not in all charity and compassion be distorted to make them fit a pattern. It is not only proper but essential to clarify the nature of the different approaches to art and the different kinds of relevance they might have.

Not all art is religious in character or intention. Not all religious art is Christian by character or intention. All art may have relevance to the Christian's understanding but the character of the work must be respected. In respecting the character of the work it is necessary, however, to go beyond the artist's conscious and articulate intention to the implicit nature of the work. It is possible for a work to be implicitly as well as explicitly and deliberately religious.

There is, for example, art which can only be called non-religious (in a desire to avoid that ambiguous term "secular"). This is art which determines to do no more than record the facts of earthly experience, to stay wholly within the world of natural experience, of the quality of the material and of the natural human vitalities. This category includes the unqualified assertion of things as they are for the sake of themselves only.

The category of the implicitly religious would include the work of those artists who have approached reality with their imagination expanded to the edge of awe. There is no longer the simple assertion of the thing seen or the made object but a sense of something beyond, a sense of power or meaning not exhausted in the simple act of assertion or vision. This is what Tillich refers to as the sense of "being itself," if he would be willing to permit the use of his term to include more than existential expression.

A work of art would be explicitly religious if it included an authentic awe of the holy, the awareness of the *mysterium tremendum* at the heart of things. It would be consciously a part of the artist's intention, translated into the form of his work, to go beyond the merely naturalistic or humanistic and find the essential meaning of things in human experience.

The defining characteristic of the fourth category, the implicitly Christian, is the presence of the essential spirit of Christianity, righteous, holy love. It might be further characterized by saying it contains the religious awe before the ultimate plus a sense of humility. In theory, this is applicable to any subject, including pure abstraction. In practice, it is doubtful that criticism, at least at present, can be so discriminating as to identify this category without the aid of subject matter or the biography of the artist's intentions.

The last category, the explicitly Christian, defines an attitude toward art which is consciously incarnational and redemptive. Although it is true that there is no critical or theological justification for ascribing superiority to works by Christian artists or to lay a general claim to greater wisdom or insight for the Christian, it remains true that for the Christian, as distinct from the generality of mankind, there are works which occupy a special place and represent to him a closer path to the throne of grace. It is true to say that there is a sacramental quality to all genuine art. It is also true to say that in this last category are to be found the works with a special place in the Christian experience. These are the works that seek and communicate a special sense of the holiness of creation, works that are informed by the spirit and the purpose of Christ. Often there is in them a coherence of celebration, of instructional insight into the nature of things, a sense of tragedy and glory, of man condemned and man redeemed, which make them, beyond all other works of man's hand, fit instruments for the sacrament of God.

V

THE

STRUCTURE

OF ART AND THE

CATEGORIES

OF CRITICISM

It would appear to be obvious that the non-Christian or the non-religious critic might disagree with the definitions offered in the preceding chapter and it would certainly happen that such a critic would disagree with the inclusion of this or that artist under a particular category. Nevertheless it should not be difficult for a critic to accept the categories as such, since it would appear fairly obvious that artists would vary in the character and the extent of their religious concerns. It is equally probable that many critics would find the categories expendable, since the questions posed by them are not of particular concern to men who are not religious. Nevertheless the categories could be received into good professional acceptance.

To a degree, then, the categories have a real usefulness in providing the means for communication between the Christian critic and his non-Christian colleague. It often happens, however, that the means for communication have both the virtues and the vices of their useful neutrality. They are means for communication and not grounds for habitation. They do not suffice for the purpose of the Christian who wants to understand his work in the light of his faith. Thus it is essential to pursue the search for other categories which might provide a more adequate correlation between the various types of works of art and the major categories of the Christian faith. This analysis by its very nature has meaning only within the assumptions of the Christian faith and is acceptable to the non-Christian critic only to the degree that he is willing and able to grant that if certain assumptions are made at the beginning, then certain other things might logically and intelligibly follow.

If the search has so far proceeded on the basis of an examination of the operations and attitudes of the artists themselves, the discussion cannot proceed further without relating these operations to the fundamental interpretation of the nature of reality held by the Christian faith. At this point it should be possible to make this connection without falling into the trap already pointed out: deducing aesthetics and criticism from systems that do not take into account the fact of art and its operations. The task is now theological but theology of a distinctive kind, placing art theologically into the whole economy of God and thus defining theology as a dialogue with the experience of man and the reality of the earth. The purposes of this investigation could not be achieved without their theological foundation and justification but neither can theology properly grow out of systems that ignore the fact of man's making. Thus it is essential to start from the conclusions already reached and work into the essential theological principles.

The fundamental conclusion was that art is creative and constructive, not destructive and disruptive. Some artists concern themselves with the vitalities and the violences of human experience but they make up only one aspect of art, not the whole of it, and their overt activity cannot give an explanation of their own substantial work. If art is primarily constructive and the church wishes to speak relevantly to the arts, then it must be able to speak to the problem of man's making.

The basic act necessary to this communication with the visual arts is one the contemporary theologian is inclined to mistrust above all others: he must attempt to see man in his innocence and conceive the possibility that man's corruption might in his work be transcended and something analogous to primeval innocence be recovered. It is altogether reasonable that the theologian should mistrust this act. It is not only that he has the vivid memory of the rather pathetic history of liberal optimism and the falsification of human experience that came out of that optimism. It is much more the nature and the doctrine of sinfulness itself. It is of the nature of sin – and so his doctrine informs the theologian – that its corruption is general, pervasive. There are not areas of experience marked off as inaccessible to the compulsion to sin, and the pretense that it might be possible is itself an inalienable part of the sin. Yet even so, the theologian must be remorselessly consistent: sinfulness extends itself into his very capacity to formulate his doctrine. How sin is to be defined in its most primitive sense has concerned many theologians, but the various definitions seem to the non-theologian to have in common the sense of self-centeredness, despair, pride, a turning from God and the possibilities of God to the ugly facts of the self. If sin manifests itself most dramatically in those who invert values and make the evil good, it is not altogether absent from those who are obsessed with their own uncleanness. Out of this there comes and can come a preoccupation with the death of the soul and an obsession with the doctrine of the atonement or the various means of producing personal righteousness and personal salvation. Given the fact of the human condition it is inevitable that this should be so, and culturally speaking, it has enabled the church to carry on the conversation with non-Christians in contemporary culture who have passed through the stage of liberal humanism and seen its inadequacy against the condition of man.

It remains true that an obsession with self is of the substance of sin, whether it is the obsession that grows out of pride or the inverted pride that is the sense of despair in a Christian. Out of this condition much has been done in the imaginative literature of our time when it has been informed by the Christian faith. This literature is not without hope, for any work of man which is without hope is not of Christ. But the hope is hope out of the obsessed blindness of despair. It may reflect the culture of the times. It is not a universal definition of the Christian faith.

This despair can speak only partially to the culture of the times, for as a doctrine it has little to say to the visual arts and nothing at all to say to architecture. It can speak to the art of expressionism but it speaks to no other style and it does not speak to the problem of creativity.

The literary artist is more directly involved in the subject matter of his work and therefore more directly involved in the tragedy and the despair of the age. The work of the visual artist, certainly in a period dominated by abstract styles, is less involved in the tragedy of the human experience, and it is, therefore, less possible to resort to the criticism of subject matter and thus evade the fundamental aesthetic question. The basic aesthetic question is not the manner in which this or that style of art communicates intelligibly with a doctrine of the Christian faith but the meaning of the creative act itself. If theology derives its originative insights from the doctrine of sin, it has little to say to the artist and little to add to its own attempt to understand the ordering of things.

Thus the Christian intellectual might be required to surrender some of the most cherished of the contemporary theological shibboleths, particularly cherished because they have made possible the conversation with the non-Christian intellectual which has added much to the life of the church and its own awareness of its needs. He must surrender the exclusive devotion to a vocabulary that has fruitfully related the Christian concern for the abyss of sin to the concern of the contemporary non-Christian existentialist for the void or the absurd. That this conversation has developed is good in every respect. It has been of immeasurable advantage to the development of the mind of the church, for it has helped bring the church beyond its stage of a facile optimism into a deeper awareness of the full nature of man. Yet a price is being paid for this terminology, and the price is, again, another aspect of the wholeness of the Christian faith. The existentialist dialogue has led the spokesman for the faith to concentrate on the doctrines of sin and the atonement. Yet precisely here we have seen the problem of Tillich's aesthetic and critical practice. If critical thinking is focused on the existence of sin, then there is too little positive grounds for the construction of an aesthetic that will make possible the communication with styles other than expressionism.

The Christian, then, must enter on his total heritage if his commerce with his culture is to be complete. He cannot establish that commerce on the basis of his despair. Nor can he establish it on the basis of Christian hope, except for those who would listen to the most direct proclamation of the word. What he can do is live in the totality of his heritage, and his heritage includes not just the doctrines of sin and atonement but the doctrines of creation and the incarnation.

Some theologians have held that the whole of creation is involved in man's fall, that the created order is itself sinful and fallen. The critic comes to this doctrine, not from philosophical abstractions, but from the experience of the world and man's work within it, and there would appear to him to be no justification for such a notion in the actual facts of human experience. Furthermore, the doctrine has that quality perilous to any scholarly position: it does not account for a significant body of evidence nor communicate in any serious way with those engaged in a significant human activity.

This same difficulty arises with the corollary doctrine that everything man does is totally corrupt. This doctrine can be achieved and sustained only by the most adamant refusal to confront both the facts of human experience and the whole doctrine of the Christian faith. The part of Christian doctrine essential to the understanding of the creative activity of man is the doctrine of creation and the doctrine of the Incarnation: God created the world by a conscious act of his will and, therefore, it is to be seen as proceeding from the hand and the will of God; God not only created the world in the distance of time but entered it to inhabit it for a term. The world, therefore, can be understood as radiant with his presence and transfigured by his grace. The hope of redemption need not only be the sense of a completion in the fullness of time but a fulfillment of time in its present mode.

The consequences of this understanding of creation for the experience of man's art must be stated with utmost care else it becomes the occasion for serious error. One of the means of the expression of man's pride has been the doctrine holding that man is a creator on the model of God, that man creates as God creates, bringing into being out of chaos those things which would not be if he had not divinely acted. Such a doctrine is fatal, and both expresses man's sin and leads to fuller manifestations of that sin.

What is needed, then, is not to make man the equal of God. It is not necessary to flee the doctrine of despair into so injurious a trap. What is needed is to see the manner in which man's making, man's creating, is a commerce with that which God has done and a vehicle for man's fulfillment of the commands laid upon him. A further limitation on this task is the necessity for establishing this transaction on some basis other than the representation of the visible surface of the physical creation. It is essential to see the act of man as faithful to the commands of God and the products of that act as in some way fulfilling the nature and the functions of creation.

In order to avoid any monistic view of the art activity or of the reality variously handled in the work of art, it is essential that the varieties of motives and types of art be recognized and organized into some kind of coherent scheme. Aesthetic schemata generally suffer most from misplaced unity or dissolved diversity: they assume a single cause for the making of the work of art or else they unduly multiply the motives and the types.

I do not say that the account of art which depends on the doctrines of creation and incarnation is a reflection of the events of history. That art is essentially a part of the innocence of man does not mean that it began as an expression of innocence. No one can speak with authority on the problem of man's first creativity, but it is at least as reasonable as any other theory to say that art began as a consequence of man's fall, a magic attempt to hold back or to control the dark forces of the earth. Certainly its function as magic as well as its function as an expression or a tool of many another doctrine or hope lay at the beginning of man's creative activity. We are here being analytical and not historical. At the same time it is equally true that much art must have begun in innocence and delight, and even those who sought the magic instrument must have felt the glory of the matter he worked with in a way characteristic of the true artist.

Thus to understand how and why men make works of art we must begin with the essential nature of their activity, and no doctrine that begins by fitting the final product into an alien philosophical scheme is likely to touch the essentials of what takes place in the making activity of man. Only in so doing is it possible to take into account the reality of variety, the fact that art is not, after all, a reflection of philosophical abstractions but a truly human activity deeply involved in human experience.

Since art, then, is truly involved in both the depth and the range of human experience it obviously is involved in human sinfulness as well. From what has already been said it should be obvious that Tillich and the Tillichians are not wrong in finding that works of art can reveal the abyss in existence, and the ground of man's being. They simply limit art unduly when they find it ultimately significant only as a breakthrough of a supposed ground of man's being and existence.

Theologically speaking then, the source of man's creativity is found in his total humanity. The immediate source of his creativity is his response to the created order. The elucidation of both these terms must wait for a moment. It is necessary only to emphasize now that the reference of each major term is extensive rather than limited as Tillich limits it: "Response" varies as humanity varies; "created order" varies as the wholeness of creation varies.

For the moment, however, it is necessary to extend further the theological implications of this relation: if man is wholly corrupt is his creativity necessarily corrupt as well? In other words, is tragedy essential to knowledge, and is that art deepest which gets closest to the tragedy inherent in the human situation?

Any one at all conversant with theology must hesitate for a long time before offering the principle that some aspects of man's activity are exempt from the general corruption of man's acts. It is possible to do so, perhaps, only on the basis of the distinctive character of the act of making a work of art. (If this analysis is sound there is no particular reason that I can see why it does not apply equally well to other activities that involve a making or creating of some kind: scientific research, for example.)

The character of the work of art that most clearly determines the character of its making is its complete and absolute objectivity. The work of art is not the artist but something other than the artist. It is a thing in its own right living according to its own nature, obeying its own laws (which have nothing to do with the "perennial laws of great art" so beloved of the conservative commentator). This principle is essential to the aesthetic outlined here and it may be essential to the theology: if the work of art is something other than the artist, then it is possible to speak of the work of art as sinful only by the remarkably dubious theological doctrine that matter itself can be fallen. Since, on the other hand, the art work is not created by God and does not come into existence through any natural process but is a conscious product of the hand of man, there is a relation between man (and consequently his sinfulness) and the work of art which must be determined as a fundamental element in any system of criticism that might conceivably be called Christian. Sin may belong to the artist; if there is an intimacy of relation between the artist and the thing he makes, then obviously sin is relevant to the work of art as an element that may be incorporated into it through some principle as yet not defined. But sin does not belong to things, and, whatever their human relevance and weight, works of art are basically things.

Sin is an element of will. It is not a property of matter. All that partakes of the nature of the physical material of the earth is as pure and as innocent as it was at the dawn of creation. If Adam must be demythologized and made all men – as, of course, he must – and if we must therefore see that Adam is the heart of man in its innocence and its willed disobedience, then the creation story must be demythologized too. It is not an event simply in the past. God can not only look at Adam now and see the disobedience in his heart but look at everything he has made, and lo, it is still good. The goodness of creation is accessible to all men. What is accessible only to the Christian is the principle of created nature as the cradle of the divine, the locus of the incarnation. God sees that creation is good; he also entered creation to inhabit it for a time and fill it with his glory. On a level less doctrinal in its range it is necessary only to study the words of Jesus himself who sought in nature the full reality of the revelation. He never confuses nature with the revelation, but nature shares the quality and character of the revelation to a degree that makes it possible to explain the kingdom of God by the quality and structure of natural things. Furthermore, the life of man works with a kind of innocence in the life of things in such a way as to suggest that innocence may yet be within those places in the life of man which grow out of his life in nature rather than those places subject to his will.

In pursuing the nature and meaning of the creative act it is necessary now to define certain fundamental terms in order to lay out the limits within which the future analysis can take place. The definitions to be offered here are not original nor in the general literature of art criticism particularly unusual. They are not universally used, although many disputes in the discussions of the work of art might be avoided if they were accepted.

Basically, the work of art is composed of three elements: matter, form, and content. The character of a work of art is defined by its use of the three elements, the relations established among them as one grows out of the other.

The point of beginning is the matter, or the physical material of which the work is constructed. It is difficult for the layman in art to realize the overwhelming importance of the material in the work of an artist, yet it is fundamental to this argument that the work of the artist begins with the character of the material given to him.

The material of the work of art includes, obviously, all those materials which have been or might be used in the making of a work of art. This is not an obvious or elementary point: it includes these materials in an obvious sense, but it includes also all the particular qualities of the material in the most specific sense of the word, mass and weight and texture, color and volume, all those things that make a material what it is. Material is more, even, than that: it includes the relations which exist between things: space, light, tension, balance, rhythm. It is difficult – and unnecessary – to differentiate clearly between these elements and those relevant to the term "form," but it can be done for the purposes of the discussion. One aspect of space is relevant primarily to the discussion of artistic form. There is also space as experienced, as seen and felt, a part of what the vivid perceptions of the trained artist bring to his imagination and intellect as part of the material he works with. He experiences the natural rhythms and vitalities, movement, tension, balance, relation in the same way, since the whole of the sensuous world and the sensuous experience of the world is available to him, not simply the physical fact of a substance in its inertness.

The material, then, is the beginning of the artist's imaginative act and the focus of his creative attention. This must be true of all genuine artists. With some artists the concept of material must be extended further to include various aspects of the human experience and human relations.

The material is what is shaped by the hand and the mind of the artist. Form is the shape that results from the creative, making aspect of the artist's work. Again this may seem obvious, unless it is seen that the form is the locus for the full human weight and significance of the work. Form is that which is new, that which is created, that which comes into being by the act of the artist. Whatever the work of art has to add to the human experience or to say about the human experience is embodied in the form which he puts on the material.

That which is added to or said about the human experience is content. This is the most elusive term of all. Both form and matter are terms clear in their reference, at least in their surface meaning. Content, however, goes beyond the general experience and touches directly on the full substance of the work of art. It is not identical with form, but it is not separable from it. For the layman the confusion easiest to make is that between content and "meaning" in art. Content is all that a layman is asking for when he asks what a work of art "means," but it is not meaning in the sense of the layman's question; meaning does not exist apart from the work in its particularity and it is not then inserted into an appropriate vessel for the sake of transportation to the viewer. Content (to abandon as quickly as possible the useless word "meaning") is not something added to the form or existing prior to the form (other than in the adumbrations of it which an artist might generate out of his prior experience with the forming of material). Yet an exclusive reliance on the concept of form can lead to a serious separation of the experience of the work of art from the generality of the human enterprise. The art work must not be reduced to subservience to experiences other than that which makes up its essential act. But neither is it altogether *sui generis* and the concept of content links it to the totality of experience from which it grows.

Content is not subject matter. I say so, not because subject matter is unimportant nor even altogether because the mind of most observers makes subject matter all important. It is simply because subject takes its proper place in the analysis: it is part of the material the artist works with. It is not the purpose or the object of the work of art; neither, when it is present, is it unimportant or irrelevant as some critics have tried to make it out to be. It is available with the same impact and generative force of any element of the material. It might be made unimportant: this is one of the options available to the artist in handling any aspect of his material. Some sculptors, for example, sought to generate their work out of the specific character of stone. In their different ways this approach characterizes Egyptian, Greek, Renaissance, and much modern sculpture. Bernini, on the other hand, often ignored the specific character of his material and often seems to have ignored its possibilities. His concern was, rather, with the sense of space, movement, dynamic relations which could be transformed in his hands to a new and meaningful form. The material in the specific sense becomes less important in its specific qualities and acts more as a creative instrument in the hands of the artist. So with subject matter: it might be of supreme importance; it might be incidental; it might disappear altogether; it might appear less for its own sake than for its function as an instrument to the accomplishment of a different purpose.

Subject matter is part, but only part, of the means whereby the artist incorporates into his work reference to the general human experience, the life of will and emotion and action. The qualification deserves insistence: subject matter is emphatically not the only place where the general human experience appears in the art work. It may be faulty ontology, and it is certainly false epistemology to make concepts important and the logic and organization of sensuous experience secondary. Sense experiences, too, are a part of the general human experience, and there are few places in the study of history or philosophy so unhappily empty as the definition of their place in that experience. But if we use the terms in their more customary reference, it remains true and important that the general human experience as it is generally understood enters the world of the artist and of the art work by means of the subject. The artist is not, by terms of the definition here offered, required to have a subject; neither is it denied him, and just as he can with all parts of his material, he may make of it what he wills.

These definitions lay out the area in which the rest of this investigation must operate: the work of the artist as a man or as a Christian focuses on the quality and the nature of the things he does in the act of forming a given material; the work of man as a critic (extending that term to include all those who lay hold of the work of art according to its essential character) focuses on his apprehension of the content of the work of art through his apprehension of the form in its true depth. It is not yet possible to subsume both these activities under a single set of terms or describe them in such a way as would make them philosophically identical. It is possible, however, to relate them meaningfully.

A further quality of the creative act deserves attention. This is summed up in the answer to the question which initiated this discussion: is tragedy essential to knowledge? It is contained in the further statement: art is the morality of the imaginative life.

These questions direct the attention to those aspects of the creative act only suggested, or at most suggested but not described, by the definitions. The definitions establish the relations as they exist between the basic processes of artistic creation, but they do not touch on the problem of motive, the force in the artist that compels him to the creative act. There are rather obvious limits to the possibilities of finding these motives, particularly since it is integral to this argument that there are many different kinds of art and many different motives for making works of art. Thus it is necessary to look for the account that might make the variety of motives meaningful and relate them meaningfully. This search can be carried out only by generalizing from the actual experience of artists and their art works, not by a priori philosophical assumptions.

The first motive that seems to compel all artists is the elucidation of the character of his material. The material in all the fullness of its particularity is the object of the artist's entranced attention, and his work is in good part an uncovering of the nature of that material, a revelation of what it is essentially. The organization of the material into a work of art liberates its essential nature by subordinating the accidental or the unimportant to that which the vision of the artist has enabled him to see in it. It is significant and relevant to this particular context that Van Gogh, an extreme expressionist, has left record of the intoxicated delight which he felt in the materials of his painting and the world around him as a subject for his paintings.

The other principal motive refers to the second of the terms of the definition: the compulsive need the artist feels to bring his material into meaningful order, to penetrate it with his intelligence and rationality and create a new thing out of it. This is the process of forming and within this general description many more particular motives are to be defined. The artist feels this compulsion to order his material (including his subject if there is one) in such a way as to bring into being an object with its own existence and its own vitality. It is essential to emphasize that the work grows out of the delight or the passion of the artist with his material. It is essential, too, to see that the material is penetrated and transformed by the will, intelligence, passion, and imagination of the artist and thereby communicates with the human experience through him. It is essential further to emphasize that the work of art does become an object apart from the artist. Professor Howard Carter insists, "The umbilical cord is cut."

The art work, then, is a genuine commerce with reality. It uncovers things in the material, fixes them in a meaningful order, and reveals thereby aspects of existence and reality hitherto unknown or unrecognized. This is a knowing apart from tragedy, both a penetration into reality as it is and a bringing into existence something that had not been before. The sense of tragedy is perfectly possible and appropriate, but it is only one approach and only one of the forces that can be involved in the act of creation. The preference for one of these approaches over another is a matter of taste and philosophical orientation, not of objective judgment.

The course of this part of the discussion may have indicated why it is possible to liberate this activity of man from the general corruption that afflicts those things entirely subject to his will. At every stage of the creative process the will, the imagination, and the passion of the artist are subject to the requirements of his material and the structural necessities of his form. He is concerned to bring forth from the material a new thing with its own life and structural order, not his. The material and the order of the work establish their own requirements. If he does not live with innocence and integrity within those requirements he does not make a "sinful" work of art. He makes no work of art at all. He may be every possible kind of rascal in his personal life, but in his work he must have integrity, or there is a complete failure of achievement. Whatever may be its ultimate issue – and it remains involved in the corruption of man – the essence of artistic creativity is innocence, a revelation of things as they are in their most intimate particularity, the ordering of these things within the revelatory order of the form. Falseness, insincerity – immorality? – violate the nature

67

of the materials, violate the integrity of the forms, destroy the work as art. Art is the morality of the imaginative life because it is built up out of the principles that require respect if the work is to succeed. It is not a matter of a good act of will or a bad act of will in the ordering of common morality. It is an act that observes the essential principles of its own nature, or it is altogether fruitless. It is a moral act, or it has no existence.

This is not to say there is no such thing as a bad work of art or, to put it more consistently with the ontology implied in the definition, works which purport to be art but are not. Obviously the world is littered with them, and their presence is relevant. It must be said only that the apprehension of the art work, although more subject to abuse and misuse, is as moral an act as its creation. The work disordered in structure or profane in its material can be apprehended as a work of art only by a sensibility equally disordered or insensitive.

A truth involved in this is hard to keep under control; it is very difficult to distinguish in one's own judgment between taste and morality. My human limitations are such that I might judge to be bad a work which is simply foreign to my particular sensibility and this is the immorality of criticism. But this failure of apprehension does not affect the morality of the art work which has or does not have its order irrespective of my capacity to apprehend or to judge either. Such capacity for discrimination as a man ever achieves is both achieved and maintained only at the expense of as disciplined a humility before the work as was required in the making of it.

This accounts for the reaction to the forgery. The layman is inclined to ask the perfectly sensible question, "If this painting was precious when it was thought to be Vermeer, why is it less so when it is discovered to be a forgery by Van Meegeren? Is it not the same object? Is it not snobbery of name and antiquity to find it less valuable?" The critic can only reply that he may in time (and in fact, usually does) detect the falsity of the work. Yet the argument does not rest wholly on the capacity of the critic to overcome his own limitations; his eye may not be able to detect the falsity of the work, but once he knows it is a forgery he knows it is false, a lie. It may still have the qualities his mind once felt to be in it, but he knows that there is in it an insidious corruption that can only degrade his sensibility and obstruct every later act of apprehension he undertakes. His response is not snobbery but highly moral. It is the protection of chastity, a casting out of that which intrudes on innocence.

To communicate theologically with the work of art does not, then, require so Platonically remote a concept as "the ground of being." There is an immediate reality accessible to the artist and the analysis of the work of art must focus on this relation between the artist and his reality in order to define the theological weight and direction of the work.

Two aspects of this reality are immediately relevant to this problem: the constituent elements of the reality known to the artist and the distinctive character of his relation to them.

The nature of the reality is: the material in all the sensuous and emotional weight of its experience; the events and relations in the life of men insofar as they are accessible to the visual imagination; the life of the forms, those distinctively visual relations which grow out of the nature of the forms characteristic of the visual arts; the whole emotional and volitional life of the artist as he responds to the material and imposes shapes on it. Yet these are matters quite difficult to define theologically, as they exist in their own visual environment. They are to be apprehended by the eye, by the mind, and the visual imagination responding to the work of the intelligent hand. A fine painting is to be looked at, not debated.

Yet, just as morality grows out of choices, so the morality and the making of art grows out of choices. At every step of the way, the making of a work of art is a matter of leaving out something, of deciding among various possibilities, of making choices of every kind. Every artist knows how initial choices determine later choices, but this in no way alters the case. The initial choice is revelatory of the artist's intent, and his ability to follow out the logic of his own work is in itself of the substance of the understanding of all he stands for. As his material and his choices cohere into an intelligible structure the work of art comes into being. It is a thing made and it is a structure of relations.

These choices are made out of the totality of what the artist is as a human being and as an artist. The art work, then, is transparent, not to the ground of being which is inaccessible to man (as Aristotelians have never wearied of pointing out to Platonists) but to the faith and the human quality of the artist. No critic can say "This is ultimate reality, the ground of being," but he can say "This is the character and quality of this man's relation to the reality he knows." No man can judge finally the truth of these structures of meaning but only measure them against the structure of his own correlation to reality. He can judge what it is as an art work insofar as his sensibility permits him to receive it. Any judgment he makes beyond that is not a part of his work as a critic but part of his total human experience.

This analysis as developed is not peripheral. The art work is not just constructive in its technical means, it is essentially constructive. The act of construction, the choices and decisions that guide that act, the relation with reality that determines the nature of the choices, these are of the very essence of the work of art, and the proper definition of them lays hold on the essential substance of the work.

The making and the immediate apprehension of the work of art is an aesthetic act, defined in the visual intelligence. The act being analyzed here is the critical act, not fixing the forms of the work itself but undertaking the theological discrimination of the attitudes out of which the uniquely visual work grows. Thus it is essentially historical, the definition of the meaning of a distinctively human act in time. The making of the work of art is essentially constructive and therefore essentially innocent. The choices which go into that making grow out of the artist's involvement in the human community and out of his uniqueness as a person. This involvement in the total human enterprise sets the limits and the vocabulary of his expression, determines the range of his possibilities and establishes the area of the great historical styles. His unrepeatable singularity determines the choices that make up the singularity of the individual work, in art as in Christian morality the unit of man's intellectual consciousness.

It is the primary duty of the critic to define the structure of the work of art with all the precision and the integrity at his disposal. As a distinctively Christian critic he must stand within his own correlation of meaning and locate the creative act which he apprehends in his function as a critic. As a Christian critic he must participate in the act of mapping the Christian "landscape of reality." After identifying the artist's correlation with reality, he interprets that work within the intellectual enterprise of the church, the definition of what the world must be, seen in the light of Christ.

It remains, then, to sketch out the main terms of the critical methods whereby the Christian critic can carry out his responsibilities. There are certain clear limits to this enterprise: obviously this is not the occasion for exploring the full range of critical techniques appropriate to the work of art. The proper area for this essay is the categories of interpretation appropriate to the work of the Christian.

These categories must depend on and grow out of the propositions already set forth: the work of art is basically constructive, and the artist is constructing a work of art, not a theological proposition; the work of art as a structure incorporates selected elements of "reality" as the artist understands reality and the structure by its nature embodies the relation to reality in which the artist stands, again understanding reality to be that which is reality to the artist rather than reality *sub specie aeternitatis;* the constructive act is a giving of form to the material, including the subject matter; the act of analysis is directed to the form; subject matter, while often a vital part of the form, is never decisive; interpretation is the definition of content, which has no existence apart from form but is not the same thing as form; the content embodies a genuine commerce with reality and is communicable.

Thus the problem remains to outline the main characteristics of this constructive act in its relation to the Christian faith. The essential activity is to account for the relation of man's making to the creation of which his making is part and an extension. By this means only is it possible to establish some sort of working understanding of the generality of art without imposing a Christian interpretation where it would be unwelcome or losing the relevance of such a making to a Christianity that seeks to be comprehensive. It is equally important to avoid a rigid standard of style which would measure the degree of "Christianness" by the degree of conformity to this or that stylistic standard.

The essential meaning and significance of art must not be confused with any scheme or any set of terms contrived to explain it and account for its place in the human enterprise. It is perhaps safe to say that a variety of schemes could be constructed, each equally applicable. It is not only an affectionate disposition of the Christian to draw his scheme and his terminology from the basic events of his own faith but a necessity of his intellectual discipline. If the idea of the incarnation has the validity the Christian believes it to have, it reflects and embodies the essential meaning of man's relation to the created order: creation is good, and the structures of creation reflect the order of divine creativity. Genuine communication is possible within the structures of material reality and apart from man's tragic involvement with his own finiteness and his own sin.

Within the structures of created reality Christian man has several points of emphasis to provide his system of organization. The world and man are created by God, and man is placed in creation to rejoice in it. Man is created in the image of God and placed in creation to name its parts and have dominion over it. Man has fallen and sinned against God in his pride and in his lust and thus broken the goodness of his relation to reality. God has redeemed man, transforming the old into a new creation and transfiguring the relation of man to reality and to himself.

Each of these principles, with the possible exception of the last, manifests itself in art to the Christian and to the non-Christian. The difference comes in the degree of awareness manifested in each work. On the one hand man participates in these orders of creation conscious only of the immediacy of their relation to him. On the other hand, man participates in them with his vision illuminated by the incarnation, consciously or unconsciously, but in any case transformed by that which has been given to him in the divine charity. This separation is not, strictly speaking, a separation of the work of the Christian from the non-Christian, although in practice that is what usually happens. The artist, however, is uniquely concentrated on his work and is not always conscious of things which exist outside his work. Thus the artist whose posture toward experience is inspired by the latent Christ should not therefore be catalogued as "non-Christian" because he has not, overtly, made his allegiance or indicated it in the subject matter of his work. The function of Christian criticism is not to distribute tags but to define the essentials.

Thus within the range of art, types correspond to the principal events in the Christian drama: the arts of creation, the arts of man in the image of God, the arts of the fall, and the arts of redemption. In the arts of creation, man records the facts of creation or lives rejoicing in the process of creation. In the arts of the image, man probes into the structure of creation, explores its relations, seeks to understand its parts and its order. In the arts of the fall, man penetrates into the tragedy of existence and investigates the nature or the consequences of the fall, fallen existence itself, or the kind of world that results from the fall. In the arts of redemption, the artist is occupied with the redemptive act itself or the kind of world that results from the transfiguration of creation in redemption.

The listing of these categories entails certain responsibilities in two directions: toward their relevance to the arts and toward their refinement and their implications as theological principles. Both these responsibilities must ultimately, in this discussion, issue in the discussion of the arts. It might, therefore, be useful to specify the reference of the general categories first and then discuss the refinements and the problems they create in the understanding of the arts.

One of the obvious consequences of the doctrine of the fall is the conviction that no man can return to the state of innocence prior to the fall. Man is by nature finite and sinful and he can, in the final sense, see the world only through his finiteness and his sinfulness. In a real sense, therefore, there can be truly no such thing as arts of the creation. Nevertheless, it remains true that in the arts man can come closer to the purity and innocence of the Garden of Eden than he can in any other activity. It is the artist above all who can cultivate the innocence and freshness of vision which are associated with unfallen nature. In the arts of creation a singular kind of graceful, natural life seems to flow through the work. It is the joy of the Garden before the fall, life immediately under the grace of God. This is the peace and serenity, the order and harmony when the structure of God's creation constitutes man's peace. This is joy in the things that are, simply because they are.

Of the non-Christian concerns pure naturalism is the closest to the reality of this category. By the nature of art, naturalism involves a respect for created reality which puts it in a class other than the rape of nature so characteristic of materialism. Yet it becomes a religious work only when there is an element of awe, a sense of the numinous that lies beyond the immediately physical and it becomes fully Christian only as it becomes permeated with the sense of the incarnation behind the holy, not simply a generally numinous consciousness of the powers of life but the humility and the glory. The difference appears in a Dutch still life with its flat bourgeois materialism, a Chinese landscape with its sense of the numinous which appears through the physical, and a Chardin still life with its concentration of human weight and reference seen in the grandeur of material things. The art of creation is an art of rejoicing in the created order, the glory of things as they are, and for all that is revealed in them.

The art of creation includes much of contemporary art, curiously enough. This is to go quite counter to the expressed statements of some of the artists, statements which could only be described as demonic in their claim to a usurpation of the function of God the creator. The works produced out of this claim have various references, but many of them are most strongly characterized by a delight in the work as a thing, a delight in the act of making, in bringing into existence a structure that had not existed before.

There is no quality or characteristic of art which is more universal than this delight the artist takes in his material and in his enterprise. It is probably safe to say that a large majority of artists manifest it in their work and in their attitude toward their work. This does not exclude those expressionistic artists who are so deeply concerned with tragedy. The most noted illustration of this has already been mentioned. Van Gogh is the type almost beyond compare of the artist whose obsession with tragedy eventually destroyed

73

him. Yet his letters and his recorded conversations are full of his delight in the glory of the world and in his work as a painter. His tragedy is a personal one, the tragedy of a man whose mental stability could not meet the agony of his life. His tragedy is not that of the artist for in his art he found the fulfillment and completion he could not find in his personal life.

Delight in the world or in the work may be a dimension of nearly all art. Structure is an essential quality in all art for it is the very definition of art itself. Without an ordered structure, an organizing principle, there is no work of art. This applies equally to all categories of art works. Some artists make structure the aim and purpose of their work rather than a means to another end. It is these men whose work comes under the heading of the arts of man in the image of God.

Man is created and is a part of a larger creation. Yet he is not just another part of creation. He is created in the image of God, appointed in creation to have dominion over it, to fill the earth and subdue it. His art is an instrument of his dominion. Yet, if he is faithful to the Creator, and to the task which has been laid on him, he does not attempt to subdue creation to be an instrument of his lust for domination. This would be a consequence of his sin and belongs therefore under the arts of the fall. His art, rather, is an instrument for bringing creation to its full purpose, for making things more what they are in their nature.

Man is appointed in creation to name the things which have been created. This is his commission to understand creation, to order things in their true relation. Man is appointed in creation to tend it and to use it, to bring it to its full purpose and the fulfillment of its nature. This is his commission to make, to create, for his making is not only an examination of other things but is a fulfillment of the nature of his materials and a bringing of the work of art to the fulfillment implicit in its structure and its material.

In these arts man is self-conscious about creation and his place in it. He probes and tests. He is not content with the morning freshness of things as they might have been at the dawn of creation and he seeks to find their inner laws. For the sake of the deeper order of things he controls severely the external appearance. He imposes on the work the order of his mind which is controlled by his apprehension of the order of things in their essential being.

All artists must have this quality strong in their work if the work is to have any existence as art, for the only way the artist can make his insights evident is to embody them in the structure of a work of art. Yet there are men who use this kind of structure to make manifest their existential engagement with the vitalities of existence. Those men whose work belongs primarily under the category of the arts of the image of God are the men who seek the understanding of life that can give man meaningful grasp of it and dominion over it.

The art of the image is far more intellectual. Instead of a rejoicing in the thingness of things, there is an attempt to penetrate into their inner structure, to analyze them for what they are. It is often colder, less appealing than corresponding works characterized as the art of creation; a still life by Cézanne compared with the still life by Chardin. Again a distinction can be made. There are works of the Renaissance that are coldly intellectual, perfectly balanced, stating with entire lack of commitment that perspective structure which the artist was concerned to understand. Artists such as Raphael, for example, state this ideal of order with a perfection that approaches the numinous in the very purity of its presentation. There is, in the best of cubism, often a powerful sense of the strength that suffuses the order of things to hold them in their ordered place. Piero della Francesca, on the other hand, sees this order of things as part of the incarnated holy, the numinous power that proceeds from the throne of grace.

The category of the arts of the fall is perhaps the most complex of all, for its duality is more central to its work. Man is by nature fallen and his work, even at its best, is sure to manifest his fallen nature in one way or another. As a human enterprise it is inevitable that art should manifest the brokenness of the world and the rebellion of man. Yet even this direct manifestation of the fall is complex. Whatever the intent of the artist who manifests his joy in creation or his analytical grasp of the structure of creation, his work remains a symptom of his age, one of the deposits of man's pilgrimage through history. As such, then, it is a record of one of those moments in man's life which tends inevitably to its own destruction. History passes in its remorselessness. Man struggles painfully to synthesis and an order that he hopes will fulfill his search for meaning. Then he watches the order ebb away, since the order can be maintained only by the strength which has been consumed by the search for it and the value of order is never apparent to those whose energies have not been consumed in achieving it. They turn from it, therefore, and seek their fulfillment in other forms that dissolve the achievement. Thus, fifth-century Greece disintegrated in the softer isolated individualism of the fourth century. The balance of the thirteenth century gives way to the agony of the fourteenth- and fifteenth-century Gothic. Thus, the Parthenon and Chartres contain within themselves the seed of their own defeat and the brokenness and tragedy of man's life is perpetually manifest.

It is equally obvious that some works show forth this sinfulness more directly, for art, as one of the most flexible and expressive instruments of man's communication, can be exploited to the expression of man's lust for power or lust for any of the things that distort his nature and purpose. Art can be an instrument of his self-assertion, his arrogance, his power, his passions. Nothing human is foreign to the arts, including man's evil.

Even so it is probably safe to say that this category is most relevant to the concerns of the artist when he works with the fall and its consequences. There is a kind of purity about the making of a work of art which tends to impose itself on the artist, even if he is an impure person. The requirements of the material, the principles of its ordering, impose an integrity on his work which might not extend to his personal life. He violates this only at the peril of the quality or even the existence of his work. Thus it is probably safe to say that the arts are less amenable to abuse by man's sinfulness than many other types of his activity. What is relevant is his awareness of sin as part of the substance of the heart of man, built into his being. Or, if his faith is such that this terminology is unfair to what he stands for, his awareness of the tragedy and brokenness of human experience. These are the tragic artists, the great expressionists who find their concern in the passions, the cruelty, and the despair of man, trapped in his human dilemma. These arts are committed to the passion and the tragedy of man. Different men might vary in their sense of the source and issue of this tragedy, but this variation is precisely the kind of thing difficult to evaluate in the visual arts without the progression of events in time which is part of the subject matter of the verbal arts. Yet these arts have meaning only as they reveal the sense of the brokenness of man's life and work, and this is the reason for their importance in the eyes of the existentialist critics. They are the arts which open the abyss, which reveal to man the nature of his life and what he has made of it. This is the art of the great expressionists. This is the art whose knowledge does come only through tragedy.

Fig. 40   Yet the distinction, while blurred, does exist. The demon-ridden horror of the works of Munch is redeemed by nothing except the fact that they are fine works of art and therefore look beyond despair to their own order. Many overtly Christian works (e.g., the *Pietà*'s of the late fifteenth century) are similarly full of despair and are redeemed only by the liturgy within which they function, not by their own comprehension of their essential meaning. Only an artist like Rouault sees further than the tragedy to the redemption which lies beyond. There are additional characteristics of this category which must be explored. The work of art is constructive, not destructive. It is constructed in innocence of spirit and cleanness of intention, or it has no existence as art. Yet it must not be said to be irrelevant to the whole sense of man's tragedy and his sin.

Even though it is not required of all, some artists see reality as encompassing man's tragedy and man's sin. The problem is not particularly difficult when it is seen only as a problem of tragedy, for the very primacy of the constructive quality of art makes it dominant over tragedy. However deeply tragedy and despair may be felt by the artist and stated in his work, it is stated in a structure, a creation out of the deepest places of his humanity. If it is truly a work of art it comes into being in innocence and as created anew, and its very structure is a triumph over tragedy.

The relation of the art work to man's sin is more complex. It is even more complex in the actual practice of criticism than it is in theory. It might be possible to set up certain defensible critical categories but the application of them pushes perilously close to the kind of judgment not given to man to make.

In one dimension sin is like tragedy; incorporated into the work of art it is transformed into a higher unity. The artist observes and knows the sin of human experience. It is part of the reality he incorporates into his work. In the structure of the art work it is transformed into a vision of the meaning of human experience.

At another level it operates not to be transformed into the new unity of the work of art but to destroy it. An artist may properly turn his attention to man's lustfulness and make it the subject – part of the material of his work. If, however, his work becomes the instrument of his own lust, the essential unity of the work is dissolved in the muddy inchoateness of pornography. Similarly he can make the art work an instrument of power – his own or another's. If he has the capacity it can be a genuine art work as well as an instrument for an immoral purpose. Otherwise it is a brutal manipulation of the material exactly matching the brutality of the manipulation of persons, as can be seen in some Roman art or Nazi art. On the other hand there are many examples of art with a consciously political purpose which rank among the finest of man's creations. Some Augustan art, the mosaics of Justinian in Ravenna, many medieval works, many works of Rubens are examples.

None of this discussion invalidates the basic proposition that the art work is constructive and not destructive and that it is constructed in innocence of spirit. It is a part of the nature of sinfulness that man can corrupt his cleanness as well as indulge his lusts, but this corruption manifests itself more quickly in the disintegration that pursues the art work than in almost any other aspect of man's life.

The art of redemption is an art immediately under the grace of God. This art is not informed by the innocence of delight that characterizes the art of creation but by a glory transfigured out of pain. Tragedy here has been redeemed and transformed, not obliterated or forgotten, but caught up in a new meaning and a new life; the city of God is not given but is arrived at on pilgrimage.

Man cannot make a redemptive art, but he can make an art that communicates what he experiences of redemption as a man and what he knows of it as an artist. Only God is the Redeemer, and the artist who sets himself the task of creating an art of redemption only manifests further the art of the fall, the setting up of false gods as idols. Yet the artist works in a world where redemption is the key act in the ordering of life. No Christian who takes his work and his faith seriously can go on acting as though the order of the world is one thing and the act of redemption is an act like all others, of relevance only to the individual who might take note of it.

It isn't sufficient for the artist to describe the redemptive acts as his subject matter. His work must embody the structure of events out of which the work of redemption could proceed and within which it still acts. This means encompassing the great tensions that are the Christian description of the order of things: matter and soul or, better, inspirited matter; sin and sanctity; tragedy and triumph. No purely tragic work can be in the order of redemption, for it is only tragedy transfigured that can be fully loyal to the redeeming Lord.

These categories are, as categories always are, mental abstractions to which the vital reality must not be compelled. Those who know the work of **Fig. 12** Cézanne intimately know that a depth and passion of commitment entirely belies the seeming intellectuality of the surface. Grünewald is an ex- **Fig. 35** pressionist often seemingly obsessed with the tragedy of man. Yet he has caught perhaps more precisely than any other artist the glory of creation in the light of the incarnate Christ and the transfiguration of matter in the **Fig. 4** light of the resurrected Christ.

There are also ambiguities. In Byzantine mosaic the Christ triumphant is one of the great achievements, the majesty of the incarnate God towering over the earth. Yet is there not in this sometimes a touch of the hierarchy of power, the injection of man's political order into his vision of the sacred?

These ambiguities only emphasize that in any living phenomenon, categories are tools to be used with discretion. But they are nonetheless tools for the opening of things otherwise shut off. No category can say all there is to say about the living work of art and after the proper categories have been determined there is still the arduous work of apprehension, the essential act of criticism. Nevertheless there is the hope that the categories can make intelligible the order in the multiplicity of phenomena which can give some meaning to the orders of the earth.

It is all too obvious that a list of fundamental theological principles such as this must be highly selective. The list can be defended as containing the basic elements of the Christian experience, stripped to the bones, and any attempt to be more specific or detailed in describing anything that could be called "the" Christian experience runs the risk of being parochial and thus cutting off the discussion from some important aspects of Christian history. Yet an awareness of this danger does not remove from a writer the obligation to carry forward his theological concerns as far as they can usefully go.

Just as the doctrine of the incarnation is fundamental to the work of the artist so it presses in on the critic of the arts with peculiar insistence. It is not enough to say that the incarnation is the means whereby the redemption is made actual, for incarnation is too central to the human experience generally and the experience of the artist in particular to be dismissed as a subheading. It is not only relevant to the action of the artist with his work, it is in many ways the principle by which his work is justified. This last statement can also be turned around, for theology grows out of life, not life out of theology. The existence of art makes incarnation part of the structure of existence. Art makes a Manichean or a Platonic universe unthinkable, as Plato very well knew. The fact that man can find his completion in the matter of the earth opens to his understanding the reality of the presence of God.

It is the critic rather than the artist who needs this justification but this does not make the justification any less important. The attempt to order one's ideas in intelligible and legitimate forms makes the justification highly relevant. Man needs to know why he acts and why he can rightfully respond as he does to the things and events of his life. The existence of a meaningful art opens to his consciousness the possibility of incarnation as a part of the natural order of things. The record and the experience of the incarnation as an historical event sustains him, then, in the work or the experience which engages him.

It must be, however, that he not only sustains himself on the fact of the incarnation but that he should respond to it as a part of the reality which he experiences in and through his art work. That is, the response is a part of the obligation of the Christian seeking to express the reality of his work. The fact of the incarnation becomes then a test or a measure of those who are not Christian and the treatment of it becomes a symptom of the quality and the character of the Christian's faith.

The doctrine of the Incarnation would hold that God has seen fit to accept the ordinary and the contingent. Thus the world in itself and as itself can never be rejected as illusory or evil. It has been, and therefore perpetually can be, the vessel of the divine work with men. No one to whom this is a living fact and a reality can ever again look at the reality of the visible world with quite the same attitude.

This principle must not be interpreted as applying a test to all kinds of works at all times. No art can be wholly comprehensive, and the concerns of a particular artist at any particular time may be such that there is no feeling for the goodness and the glory of the physical world. The aspect the physical world bears in a particular work may, in fact, approach the monstrous simply because this is the form in which the artist can embody his consciousness of despair or ugliness or the monstrousness of existence. No one artist is responsible for all things at all times in each work. The artist, as other men, is often trapped within the limitations of his own world. When, as in the life of our own day, it appears that sentimentality has cut off the possibility of expressing the goodness of the earth, then the artist, too, might find his honest posture only in the general malaise and mistrust of things which afflicts his society. This does not alter the fact that the characteristic Christian attitude toward the ordinary facts of existence is to accept them in their glory as once having touched the hand of God. The artist whose work is a response to this fact can see the goodness of the earth with an attitude beyond the naïveté of the Garden of Eden. It is not the morning freshness of things newborn he sees but the glory of the sacramentals which have been graced by the presence of God.

There is, too, the whole area of man's response to the great acts of God. Man's sinfulness is a response of sorts but it is more a part of the order of things which man manifests or seeks to understand than a conscious response. Man's response is his attempt to obey and adore, his service and his worship. This appears in the arts in the artist's explorations of the moral life and in his creation of the whole body of devotional and instructional art. The type of mystical art, for example, may be a statement of the nature of God's redeeming revelation but it is also man's response in his record or his visual equivalent of the vision itself. It includes also all the numerous attempts man makes to control the divine, the magic arts that attempt to make God an instrument of man's will.

The analysis of man's moral life is not as amenable to treatment in the visual arts as it is in drama or the novel, yet it is not altogether absent. There are many narrative paintings where the narrative is an occasion for the painting. There are also many that make the human dilemma embedded in the narrative the principal function of the painting and art has a significant contribution to make to this analysis.

VI

COMMUNICATION

IN THE VISUAL ARTS

There remains one critical problem of inescapable importance which must be treated before the evidence can be rightly submitted. Much has been said in the previous chapters about the nature and purpose of the work of art and the various categories of thought that might be applied to them in order to incorporate them intelligibly into our general experience. The claim has been made that art is a genuine knowing, that its commerce with reality is real and purposeful. The questions that remain to be answered are: How do we know these things? How can we speak of them with some hope that our speech validly represents the object? How can we hope that our analysis is true and accurate?

These questions are the practical expression of the general problem of communication in the arts. Under the interpretation developed here, the general question would have to be formulated in the artist's direction first: How does the artist communicate with "reality"? Then it must be asked:

How does the artist communicate with the spectator? Only by answering these questions can any validity be claimed for the interpretations. Unless there is genuine communication there is no possibility of doing anything beyond responding emotionally to the work and no possibility of submitting one response to the whole community for a check of its validity. Unless this can be done there is no real possibility of validating the categories that have been suggested or the claim for relevance of the arts to the Christian life.

Unfortunately there is no general theory of communication to which allusion can be made with the conviction that it is adequate to the purpose and generally acceptable. There is a large professional literature on the subject and much of it is directed to the kind of problem that imposes itself here. But most, if not all, of this literature is organized around the philosophical problem. Many important attempts have been made to extend this concern to the "language" of the visual arts and many useful contributions have been made. The bulk of these seems, to the artist and the critic, to share the quality of conceiving that which is communicated as something discrete, to be transferred by a vehicle. This tendency is being dissolved in the concern for the proper understanding of myth and symbol, of sacrament and ritual, and of art, but it is a hard prejudice to overcome.

So the task remains: to define the general nature of communication as it appears to a Christian to be consistent with his faith; and to indicate how the critic can apply this understanding to his work with the arts. The basic problems are these: In what ways can fundamental attitudes toward the problems of existence and experience be embodied in the physical material of a work of art and what are the procedures to follow for identifying them? In what ways are the arts relevant to man's understanding as distinct from his appreciation? In what ways are the arts relevant to man's knowing rather than just his sense of "beauty"? In short, on what grounds do we take the arts as contributing to understanding and communicating that understanding rather than simply reflecting or illustrating understandings which have been attained by other means?

This way of putting the problem involves two related problems which are interdependent in the context of this discussion. Both are essential to the Christian's attempt to understand the world he lives in, in terms of his faith, although there are no reasons why their implications do not have relevance for the non-Christian as well (and, indeed, they must have such implications if the Christian is not to claim special wisdom or commit himself to a coterie truth). The first is the problem of the definition of communication as it is essentially. This, to the Christian, must mean initially, how he believes God communicates with man, how God acts on man. The second is the problem of man's response to the word and act of God by means of the formed material which makes up the work of art and the related problem of how men communicate intelligibly with each other by means of the arts.

In following up these questions it is necessary to reiterate a definition already made, else a semantic trap would open up and prevent the further development of the argument. The temptation at this point is to speak of art as communicative and art as expressive. The temptation is real, for the distinction does reflect two of the divergent claims that an artist might feel pressing in on him. It is true that his material is, to one artist, the means for stating and even resolving his feelings. It is also true that to another artist, his work is a statement of his understanding which he makes for the sake of communicating it to others.

Yet the use of this distinction would prevent the pursuit of the principle which is fundamental to the critical method used here. Art is not primarily either expressive or communicative. Both of these are aspects or emphases of art but they do not define the essential act. The essential act of art is constructive and before it is expression or communication art is meaningful construction. Expression and communication are products of the structure and are embedded in the principle of construction. Both expression and construction are to be identified insofar as the principle or organization which informs the construction can be identified and accurately described. Thus it is necessary to find and describe the sources of the constructive principle as the first act in apprehending the work of art.

The problems of relativity which always pursue the human enterprise are particularly forceful here and require a careful discrimination of the elements of art. For constructive principles are not amenable to casual handling or spasmodic invention. They proceed only from the deepest places of the spirit of man, they are inherited by the successive generations of man. They can be modified only by major effort and the course of their natural development is not easily deflected or even influenced. The Christian is first of all a man born to the condition of men. His forms and the structural principle of his forms is a portion of his inheritance. He is born into a landscape and into a tradition and he can discard neither without grave peril. The question, then, is to determine which parts of his principles belong to his general heritage as a man and which to his specific faith as a Christian, and which part of the general heritage is determined by the character of the Christian faith.

It is in this context that the question of the language of the arts and communication in the arts must be pursued.

When Christian men want to understand any event or relation, they have two characteristic ways of working: they can study the nature of God's act and God's work and they can study the actual material they seek to understand.

Both ways have real dangers. Man in perfection might be able to grasp the fullness of God's working, but man in his sin remakes God in his own image and seeks to make God's work an instrument of his own selfishness. Hence he can never claim to have mastered God's way of working so as to understand it fully.

On the other hand the material itself is never enough alone to give him truth. When he looks at it alone he sees it alone. He seldom sees its relation to all the rest of things which give it meaning.

Thus man should start with the material without imposing his own wishes upon it. He must approach it with the attentive humility which he learned from knowing that creation is from God.

He must study the ways of God's work with man, of God's communication with man, trying again in all humility to understand enough to make sense out of all he studies in the material.

It is necessary first to remember some of the things already established or stated. Initially the word sacramental was used in relation to the arts. This was previously stated in the Prologue, but this overture was not intended to be an edifice of sound making an ornamented entrance to the principal structure. It was intended to provide the underlying theme justifying the whole work. The human reference of this theme was the agony of spirit with which certain men have tried to find meaning in the disorder of their existence, a meaning which would not be that of the rational intellect but of concrete experience. The ethical mind of the modern liberal found it originally in the assertion of a living physical reality (and, at the end of the play, in a restored relation of persons, which, in the limits of ethical liberalism, can have no source or reference but only the reality of its existence). Job could not be content with this answer alone nor could he be content with the rational assertion of the source of the life of physical reality but only with the living experience of that source. This is the reality of the sacrament against dogma. Job needed, not theories about God, but the actuality of God himself. Dogma may be essential as the attempt to formulate conceptually in the realm of rational discourse the meaning of the essential relation but the spirit of man is not nourished on dogma but on the sacramental. In fact, the history of religious intolerance suggests that the sin of man and not his spirit is nourished when he lives on dogma and seeks the protection of dogma rather than life within the total relation which is the life in grace.

It remained, then, for Hopkins to voice the passionate desire of the artist to make the form that is sacramental. It is to this same end that the subsequent chapters have attempted to establish certain essential conditions for understanding the arts as "sacramental form." Of these conditions the most important are: the art work is primarily a physical thing constructed by the mind and the hand of man; this physical thing is constructed out of a thirst for meaningful order and as a response to certain chosen aspects of the created order; this response is a commerce, a communication, a genuine knowing of the nature of reality. If these things can be taken as established it is necessary to turn next to the examination of each in greater detail to the end that it may be understood, not just as the assertion of a general principle of interpretation but as an instrument of critical analysis. To keep things in their proper order, before turning to the necessary account of the critical understanding of the work of art, it is necessary to speak further of sacramental communication. The task is to determine how an artist communicates. It is essential, then, to pay the most careful attention to the art work to understand what happened in its making. It is necessary also to study God's communication with man to see if there is something to be learned about human making from what can be known about God's creation. There is much material for such a task but space permits only two: the gospel and the parable, each of which bears directly on the most general aspect of biblical communication – the nature of "prophecy."

The writers of the gospels were faced with a problem that appears not of insuperable difficulty. They needed to tell the story of Jesus to those who had not known him. They went about this task so simply that it is usually assumed their work has no literary value, that it is not literature (and, of course, is thereby not art). Quite the contrary, the gospel is a distinctive literary form, unlike any other, quite irreducible to any other. It is an art form of great subtlety and great effectiveness.

There are at least three ways the life of a great teacher can be told. First, it can be a history concentrating on the whole structure of events of which his life was a part. Second, and closely related to the first, it can be biography concentrating on the events and the inner development of the subject. Third, it can be handled from a completely different direction and the teaching itself expounded systematically, with subject and events subordinated to the teaching.

The gospel writer chose none of these methods exclusively but made use of all three.

The gospels are obviously not a history. The life of the large world is there but only as it impinges on the subject. Yet in a deep sense they are historical. The events are events in history: "...in the days of Herod, the King of Judea," "now in the fifteenth year of the reign of Tiberius Caesar...." In the gospels there appears the fullness of life in occupied Palestine, the governor Pilate in his dealing with the Jewish officials, the tax collectors and the centurions, the restless rebelliousness of the Jews. The historical quality of first-century Palestine is there, but not its full history.

Nor is it a biography. There are none of the familiar characteristics of biography, none of the details, none of the description. We have no idea what Jesus looked like, how he grew up, what his family was like, where and how he lived. Instead we have in careful detail the events of his birth and the time immediately following, one event from his twelfth year, then the events of his ministry in considerable detail but not much attention to the time or order of events (we do not even know whether the events of Jesus' ministry took place in one year or three), then the events of the last week in loving detail.

This is not a biography as we know it. But the life of people fills the book. Jesus dominates, of course, but all kinds of people pass through the account. This may not be conventional biography but it has the sense of the common life of men such as few books can show.

Similarly the teaching is present but never as a system, never as a detailed and developed program of action or belief. There are few connected discourses outside the Gospel of John. Instead the teaching appears in flashes, in brief pithy statements, in pointed replies to questions or situations, in words inseparable from the acts which accompany them or the person who speaks them.

Thus the gospels are human without being biography, historical without being history, full of orderly teaching without being systematic philosophy.

87

What does this mean for communication and for art? Working back from the evidence of the work itself, the gospel as we have it, we can see what kind of goal each writer had, and how, in his creative process, he went about it.

His goal differs considerably from the goal of the novelist, the poet, the biographer, the historian or other form of writer. He had to embody in words a person, yet not just the uniqueness of a person as in a word portrait or the sort of thing found in Plutarch's *Lives*. The person had a purpose in life which had to be represented in its full vitality in his historical life yet had to be shown forth to be operative in the life of the reader.

Thus the writer had the distinctive purpose, not just of carrying information to the reader, but of making the subject manifest in the world of the reader.

To do this he confronted the subject, the person Jesus, in his wholeness. In humility the writer responded in a kind of total experience. From this experience he took (abstracted) the elements necessary to carry, not just information about Jesus, but the living presence of the Lord himself to the reader.

This is not done through a neat, orderly, exquisite structure. There is much of the disorderly vitality of life itself. Yet over this natural life there is a powerful shape which points the whole to the crucial event of the crucifixion-resurrection. Each builds up to the climactic event in its own way but a way determined by a single view of a single meaningful life.

The unique significance of this life, could not, by the nature of things, be carried in a single conceptual statement. Only an art form would suffice to the purpose. It is of the nature of other forms to be of the rational intellect, and things that are of the intellect alone shift with the shifts in the intellect.

A rational explanation of the meaning of Jesus is open to changes according to shifts in the working of the mind. Conceptual statements are tools good for their purpose but their purpose is served only within the area of agreement on the meaning of their terms. Outside this area of agreement the terms get spongy and the meaning is obscured. The whole idea becomes changed into something other than its original self.

It is the nature of man to try this transformation with anything. Men certainly do it with Jesus. Through the centuries he inevitably is given, in the minds of men, the quality of their own period, whether a feudal overlord, an eighteenth-century rationalist, a nineteenth-century liberal or a twentieth-century salesman. This does great harm to our ability to see Jesus and many people remain victims of their own partial views. Concepts can be the victims of such a process and, being comparatively inert, can be remade by such handling. In contrast, the picture of Jesus in the gospels has the capacity of enduring such treatment untouched. The prejudices of a period or a person become a screen between the person and the living reality. The picture itself lives with the compelling reality and power of great art which translates the power of the original into its chosen medium. Therefore it retains the ability to cut through the screen. Because there is a reality and because that reality is alive in the work, each person has the ability to confront that reality newly made. Thus the art form of the gospels is an instrument of redemption.

From this purpose spring the characteristics of the gospel and what appears to some to be disorderly becomes meaningful. Without being history it is historical, without succumbing to the conceptual it is pedagogical, without being moralistic it establishes a coherent morality, without being bio-graphical it is human, without being materialistic it lives in the substance of this earth, without being subjectively individualistic it preserves the personal, without succumbing to the mass it creates community.

All this and more is the end to which the gospels move and they move thus, not because the apostles were creators hovering as God over chaos making a new reality or because they see this or that in reality and wish to describe or explain it. These are not the ways of the artist. Rather he looks in humble receptivity at the reality that confronts him.

However, humility, an essential ingredient of the artistic act, is not the only ingredient; for the artist is not a passive instrument recording a kind of spirit writing. Rather, the reality which he received (in the case of the gospel writers, the reality of Jesus) interacts with all he is as a person and an artist to make the art work. Thus the irrepressible individuality of the apostle is part of the structure of the gospel. The dictation theory of the fundamentalist breaks down at this point. It assumes a God apart from His creation sending over a pre-formed message. The fundamentalist asserts that modern man rejects this interpretation of biblical inspiration because it offends his rationalist prejudices. In many cases this is undoubtedly true but there is a better reason for objecting to the theory. It violates the structure of creation as revealed in the Bible itself, and violates it precisely at the point which is most important in the understanding of artistic creation and communication. This is the doctrine of the Incarnation, which means the inextricable involvement of God in the very fabric of earthly existence. This establishes very clear and definite limits to man's ability to understand God. Man sees God only in God's revelation of Himself in creation and incarnation and so is limited by the extent of the limits of the created world (Jesus said, "Why do you call me good? There is none good but God"), but man who truly sees creation and the incarnate one has seen God (Jesus also said, "He who has seen me has seen the Father").

Incarnation is an essential element in revelation. God became man and was fully man without being exhausted by his manhood. God was fully in the man Jesus yet Jesus was not all there is of God. Similarly, Jesus is incarnated in the Bible yet he is not a prisoner of the Bible. Similarly, Jesus is fully in the church, in the word and sacraments which are the heart of the church. Yet the church is not Christ and in the presence of the reality of Christ, gospel, Bible, church and sacrament fade away (there is no temple in the celestial city of the Book of Revelation).

Still more evidence is needed before the outline of this biblical theory of communication is clear. The best evidence to use is the most characteristic and original means of communication used by Jesus: the parable. For the parable is one of the greatest of the biblical art forms.

The best way to misunderstand the parable is to compare it to the sermon "illustration," as though Jesus were making a point which had to be livened up by a pseudo-dramatic form or simply making an abstract principle concrete. This, too, is what is done in allegorizing a parable. An allegory can be defined as the personifying of ideas. Ideas are uncomfortably abstract and seem dull, hence they can be livened up (often very effectively, as in Bunyan's *Pilgrim's Progress*) by making them persons in conflict with each other. Allegory, however, is a form of communication which requires its terms to be translated back into the original idea if it is to have any meaning. Therefore it is a relatively inert form and a very limited one.

A good example of what happens with an allegory as against a parable can be seen in Mark 4:1-21 where Jesus is described as explaining a parable. Attacking this text is risky business. To doubt the authenticity of this passage is to raise questions about scripture which cannot be discussed at the moment. This should not be done lightly, and Jesus may have meant something that eludes us by such an explanation. It has some usefulness as an illustration of characteristic reaction. On the face of it, however, the explanation is quite inadequate to the nature of parables and falsifies the very parable it explains. It appears to be the work of some scribe who thought he knew more about the necessities of communication than Jesus did.

The explanation, which allegorizes the parable, turns it into an inert thing. There is a one-to-one correspondence: word on stony ground = people who hear but soon weary. The futility of such a procedure can be seen by the fact that this allegory applies equally well to a philosopher or, indeed, any leader of men. Not only the life but the uniqueness of the parable is gone.

Compare this explanation with the parable itself. There, in so brief a passage, is all the fullness of life, sun and rain, the beaten places of the path of men, the disorderly weeds of natural growth, the growth and fading away, and the abundant life. This is not an allegory of the gospel, this *is* the gospel, which is of the very stuff of life itself. The gospel is alive: not an object to be possessed, but a different order of life. This is not to be grasped by the intellect alone. This is a world which has to be entered, to be lived in if it is to be understood.

This is the clue to those enigmatic sayings, "He that has ears to hear let him hear," and "...that they may indeed hear but not understand." This sounds as if Jesus were a teacher of mysteries for a spiritual elite and this is what the scribe with his "explanation" assumed. The gospel is not the possession of a few enlightened ones but neither is it to be played with like a gross toy, or cast like pearls before the insensitive and obtuse. Explanations can be misunderstood so easily and, in fact, they almost inevitably are. Many people have had the disheartening experience of hearing someone say, "yes, I agree perfectly that..." following with a wholly garbled account of what was said. That cannot be safely done with a parable for you do not "agree" or "disagree" with it. You either enter and live in it or you do not.

And to enter it you must be a different person. You might have ears but unless those ears are related to a receptive person the parable remains a meaningless noise. A parable speaks not to the elite but to the converted or those ready for conversion. At the same time, it consciously keeps out those who are not willing to pay the price.

By this time God's ways of communicating with man become a little clearer. He does not communicate by precept, concept, or law although each of these is used to the fullest as instruments of biblical communication. He communicates by revelation, by the uncovering of that which man's finiteness and sin have covered. Precept and concept are given, not as systems to be mastered by the rational intellect, but as training, as preparation. The law is not laid as a whip on the backs of men but is a discipline to make possible the reception of the revelation.

The characteristic tone of New Testament preaching is not instruction nor command nor exhortation nor condemnation but proclamation. The gospel is the good news of the Kingdom of God. The New Testament is not the new law but the new covenant, the thing which is done between God and man. The word is about the new birth, the new life, the new world, the Kingdom of God which is within the world but not of it, like a fourth dimension. This kingdom is not to be argued about nor used as a club nor given as a bribe or threat but is proclaimed, presented, and re-presented.

From this derives the nature of inspiration as describing God's communication with man. To the Christian the Bible is divinely inspired, it is the word of God. Yet how irrelevant are the arguments about verbal inspiration! It is not a matter of one or the other side's being right. Both sides ask the wrong question so the answer is bound to be irrelevant. Each side assumes that words and the ideas they stand for are things and the question is whether these things originate with man or with God.

This quite clearly misstates the nature of divine communication. It is not a question of the writers of the Bible acting as scribes or as agents for the transmission of a divine word-thing nor of their writing their own conception of religious truth. It is a matter of God transporting the spirit of these men into the new life. They return, shaken, broken, and transformed to report what they saw there and what they now know.

It is a process which can be traced in some detail. The apostles, even in the presence of Jesus were men as other men. They were quarrelsome, often obtuse, misunderstanding of the teaching before them, fumbling in their attempts to heal, obstructing access to Jesus, seeking advantage over their fellows, craven in crisis. The resurrection brought them together again but it was the descent of the Spirit at Pentecost which made them the new men who turned the world upside down.

This was a shattering process. A man chosen to be God's stenographer or even God's translator might be honored and pleased above other men but essentially undisturbed. A man who writes his own interpretation of the nature of things may find it exhausting labor but he is not broken by it. The consistent reaction of those chosen by God in the Bible is that they wish they were dead. They are men blinded and shaken to the center of their being by all they have experienced yet impassioned with the need to proclaim that which they now know.

They are shattered and remade, but not destroyed. Their own massive individuality is always present so the proclamation comes in the passionate anger of Amos and the tenderness of Hosea, the matter-of-factness of Matthew and the vision of John. What happens is that the totality of the divine communication is seen through separate lenses, heard from separate tongues. Men who are transported into the presence of the Kingdom of God interact with it to make their work, which is then the means for re-presenting the reality of that kingdom to the rest of God's people.

On this foundation is built our understanding of art as communication. But it would be a fatal error to assume man is as God and man's communication is as God's communication. Man is created in the image of God and his communicating is in the image of God's communication but determined by his own character and his own limits.

This use of the character of biblical communication as a model for understanding the nature of artistic communication should not suggest that the connection between them is mystical or that the pattern of one area of experience is superimposed on another. Whether or not models of this kind are laid up in the providence of creation is a fascinating problem but it is not the problem at issue here nor does the issue of this investigation depend on the establishment of the validity of such general structures of experience. Both the theory of biblical communication, the theory of artistic communication, and the transition from one to the other, must claim no privileged status but submit to the appropriate test of all intellectual work: they must increase the understanding of the material at hand. Nor does the relation between them and the transition from one to the other impose any special sanctity or authority on either. Rather the one can illuminate the other, particularly when the relationship makes possible the more precise definition of the word "religious" in the study of religious art.

The point of interaction lies not so much within the process of making as in the process of receiving, which is the purpose of the making. The biblical record has God communicating, not by specified bodies of information or insight but by a translation of the person into a different context of meaning. In this sense he is born again, born into a new world that is a new vision of the world always known. Then the biblical writers communicate by forming a body of material in such a way that full communication with it is not possible unless the reader or hearer is remade in order to enter the world of what he reads. Although there are vitally important differences, the work of the artist proceeds in the same essential way:

he makes a form which requires of the viewer that he submit to the world and the laws of that form in order to see intelligently.

This is a principle of the most fundamental and far-reaching importance. Like many fundamental principles, it is one of the most elementary truths of operation. Any teacher of art, teaching an elementary class, very quickly learns it. The best students are immediately at home, responding to a work in its own unique terms. Others come only very laboriously, haltingly, to an awareness of that distinctive combination of intelligence and material that constitutes a work of art. A beginning artist develops within the same limitations. Some respond to the material with a vibrancy born of love. Others coldly and awkwardly push around the material, drawing lifeless and inert lines that are hardly, in any effective sense, lines but are, rather, narrow smears of graphite on the paper. Some of these latter persons never really enter the new world. Their skill may increase with practice but they do no more than impose their strength on the material, they do not have their intelligence and their sensibility cohere in a work representative of a new world. Their work is skillful, accurate, and inert, showing no quality of love or passion that is the true communion with the formed material.

The true artist is the one who can submit himself to the structure of his material and bring forth out of it the revelation of a new meaning. The difference between the true artist and the amateur, even the most talented amateur, lies in the completeness of the living in the new world. With the amateur, the world which is not that of the art work constantly intrudes. When a true artist has a failure of taste it is usually a breakdown in the lines of his own internal communication, some violence or falsity in the handling of his material. The failure of taste characteristic of the amateur is usually an intrusion of an idea foreign to the work he is actually making, particularly when it is foreign to the idea of art.

Thus the artist is a creator and his creation, too, is a kind of revelation, a way into a new world.

The crucial difference is this: God creates out of chaos; his communication with man is an unveiling of the reality of his creation. It is the revelation of his own being, his actions, his work. Thus in no sense is God the "Master Artist," for his work is not simply different in degree. It is different in kind, unique. God's order is not made like man's but is the source of all order.

Man makes the art work. His freedom to make it is of the substance of his freedom as a man. In this sense he does create. Yet he does not create from nothing. He creates (makes is the better term) in response to, in creative interaction with, the reality which is the wholeness of God's creation. His act is not revelation but re-presentation. (It is necessary to insist on this hyphen. Art as representation is too closely linked to the ideal of a crude naturalism. Re-presentation is a clearer definition.)

With God all things are whole and present. With man nothing is whole and all things are broken into time. Hence God's communication is total. The fullness of God's word to man, the acts in history, the Bible, the Incarnation, the word and sacraments in the church, contain all man can know or need know, either explicitly and in detail, or implicitly with detail to be developed by man in his work.

Man's communication is partial and proximate. He can apprehend only part of creation and respond only to part of what he apprehends. His ability to record his response in the work of art is determined or conditioned by his technical ability, his available material, the culture which formed his way of seeing and working. What he makes is conditioned by his finiteness, his pretension, his pride and ambition. Man is man and not God.

At this point the argument requires a clearer definition of art as the whole of things man has made.

Art is the embodiment in a formed material of the creative interaction between the artist and reality, thus setting forth the substance of the artist's apprehension of the nature and meaning of that reality.

Such a definition can be no clearer than the description of the process which it defines.

Begin with the term "reality." The most cursory acquaintance with philosophy shows how loose, imprecise, and open to dispute the term reality is. There never has been and certainly never will be a commonly accepted definition of reality, yet the search for that definition constitutes the whole of philosophy.

For once, however, a definition can get along quite happily with a term which is imprecise and subject to dispute because it deals with the artistic problem and not the philosophic problem. We are not here concerned with what reality is but the way the artist "thinks" of reality in terms of the "language" of art. Therefore, within the terms of the definition it does not matter what reality is but how the artist's conception of reality participates in the making of the art work. Thus, the definition could refer to both the Christian and the non-Christian, and the differing interpretations can contribute to clarification of the term reality.

This accords with the Christian doctrine of man. Man is created in the image of God and in his sinful rebellion has fallen away from God. Since man is in the image of God, there is a point of contact between man and God in the creation of which he is a part. (This is a much disputed theological point, since some theologians contend that man's sin has broken the contact or so dirtied it that it is meaningless. The artistic evidence would appear to be opposed to this point of view.) Since man is created and is not the creator he is within reality and not master of it. Therefore, his processes are part of the processes of reality, and inevitably his reflections on the nature of reality are complicated by their participation in the reality reflected on. Partly because of this, partly because of the simple fact of being created, man is limited and finite and his understanding of the nature of reality is correspondingly limited, partial, confused, and imprecise.

Furthermore, man is a sinner. This refers, not to moral misconduct but to a disposition or attitude or habit of soul away from God to himself and his own interests, a choice of disobedience over obedience, of self over the other, of selfish gratification over selfless service. Thus his apprehension of reality has not only the quality of finiteness, of limitation, but it is also corrupt and distorted.

Three affirmations develop from this analysis: there is a reality which is here identified (but not defined nor described) as the whole of the created order including man living and acting within it; contact with this reality and some knowledge of it is possible to man, a contact and a knowledge which can be modified and enriched by man's participation in God's redemptive act (being a Christian) but is not dependent on it (Christians are not wiser than other men); this contact and this knowledge are real but limited and distorted and never ultimate. A fourth could be added: man is able to judge the true and the false, the real and the unreal, the genuine and the distorted; but such judgments are subject to the same limits and the same sin.

Thus there is a reality, and it is available to man but man can never fully know what it is nor which of his apprehensions of it are closest to the truth. This affirms a middle way between absolutism and relativism. There is an ultimate truth but man can never really know what it is. It also affirms a kind of tolerance. All men are subject to the same sin and no man or groups of men are made sole custodians of the truth.

This discussion of reality and man's participation in it and reflection on it has nothing exclusively to do with art or philosophy. Everything man does manifests either his place within the created order or his attempts to lay hold on that reality and understand it.

At his lowest and most primitive level man eats, sleeps, drinks, eliminates, protects himself from the weather, makes love, feels fear against danger, fights, all as simple and direct manifestations of his place in creation. At his highest and most sophisticated level man constructs complicated social systems, develops intricate political organizations, makes paintings and machines, develops complex philosophies, all designed to control the disorder of primitive existence or to understand, and communicate the understanding of the nature of reality and the meaning of existence within it.

Somewhere there is a dividing line. Somewhere man ceases to exist simply as a vegetable and begins to reflect on his existence. Where this dividing line comes can be argued. Man at his most sophisticated level is profoundly affected, but not determined by his most primitive needs and emotions. At the same time, the act of reflection appears at the lowest level and is not a possession of the civilized only. It is a part of man's nature to reflect, to seek to control and command, to apprehend and understand.

It is impossible to say finally what is the cause of this mental activity but the dividing point between the bestial and the human comes with the development of language in the broadest possible sense. It comes at the moment when man goes beyond simple existing and attempts to act positively on and within existence. He tries to articulate and make manifest what happens in the contact with reality. He very likely is not, at first, communicating with anyone else, but with reality itself or with himself. But language is the pivot on which man turns from brutishness to some rudimentary civilization.

He is aware of needs and relations with other creatures like himself and constructs social organizations and law. He is aware of powers beyond himself and develops his religions. He is aware of quantity and number, senses there are relations among them and develops mathematics. He is conscious of color and shape and arranges them into art works. It is the same with the other manifestations of his experience, including philosophy – the attempt to put into concepts the nature of the primary reality.

These manners of expression develop at different rates; some presuppose certain prior developments or certain conditions of mind. For example, so long as nature is made up of malignant personal powers to be placated by abject worship or appeased by sacrifice, there is not likely to be much by way of a meaningful physics, which depends on a certain coolness

97

of attitude as well as the accumulation of certain data and the presence of certain physical and conceptual tools. Until man can stand off from himself there is not likely to be a real philosophy. Yet all are ways of taking hold of reality, of embodying that apprehension in the appropriate form, which constitutes the proper language of that portion of experience.

Anyone familiar with some kinds of discussions about the nature of art can see where this treatment is headed. For the arts have often been treated as part of man's play, as a way of using the surplus of time and energy and therefore as a luxury. On the contrary, in all the ways man has of apprehending reality the arts are among the earliest and most determinative. Man is born into a world of color, shape, weight, volume, texture, rhythm, space. He takes these inchoate elements and for some purpose or other organizes them into art works. So compelling are these organizations that a good case can be made for their having a determinative influence on the imagination, which then decisively influences the development of other forms of mental activity.

There is one other quality of reality which needs to be indicated before going further in the discussion. Man never confronts reality as though he were the first man in the dawn of creation. He is always a member of a particular society accustomed to its order and its rhythms. He is present in a particular landscape conditioned by its light, color, shapes, and the quality of its activity. Particularly, he is aware of the work of other artists, the shapes they have imposed on the material they have at hand. His own vision is controlled by this background to a greater or lesser degree. Thus art works, which are a response to or an analysis of reality, become a part of reality for subsequent artists.

This schematic arrangement needs to be developed a little further although the manner of this relating cannot be made clear without analysis of the works themselves. Yet the analysis itself cannot be made clear without indicating what is being analyzed and why it should be.

The basic nature of the scheme has already been indicated. The artist comes into relation with reality, and out of that relation produces the work of art. The spectator can then reverse the process. This process might be a little clearer if reduced to a diagram, beginning with a diagram of the more usual understanding of the way an art work is made.

The usual understanding of an art work is "realism" in the sense of "look like." The artist is considered a kind of lens with recording hands and a diagram would look something like this:

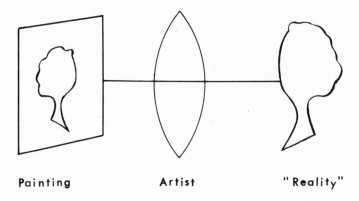

Painting   **Artist**   **"Reality"**

Thus, in this view, the artist looks at the object and reproduces it as exactly as his skill permits.

But to those who consider the problem further a question immediately occurs: what does anything look like? On even the most elementary level of visual experience this is a difficult question.

A tree, for example, is a complicated arrangement of solid matter, of certain colors. This is the sort of thing a good craftsman can reproduce on his canvas. But a tree is more than this. It has weight and solidity; even a small tree has massiveness. It is also alive, growing out of the earth, tense, with branches that spring. A painting might "look like" the surface and still be a fluffy, empty thing.

There is much more to say. A tree is not an object in a studio. It is in the light and air. Every color and form alters subtly as the light changes. Which is "the tree itself," the solid, immobile form or the ever-changing play of light and shadow? Is a leaf truly a leaf when it is petrified in a "realistic" painting or when it glimmers on a tree?

As a matter of experience, both of these attitudes have appeared in first-rate art, for both aspects of the tree "are" the tree. Yet both cannot appear in one painting, and the choice is made not on a basis of greater or lesser "realism" but on a view of what "reality" is.

It is difficult to realize in an age when so great a range of visual experience is before us that much of this view of reality is a matter of visual experience. Most of us actually see very little of the visible world. We see only what we are accustomed to see. The history of painting is in part a history of the slow conquest of the visible world. Each object, tree or leaf or plant, was a distinct and separate thing until Leonardo's great eye and hand brought them into a single landscape with a single order. One of the real by-products of close study of the arts is the manner in which the spectator becomes sensitive to aspects of the world he has never seen before (Oscar Wilde once quipped, "Have you noticed lately how nature has set herself to look like the landscapes of Corot?").

Even yet only the surface of visible reality has been mentioned. The branches and subbranches and twigs of a tree are disposed along the tree in a certain rhythmic ordering. The tree itself stands in a certain rhythmic relation to other trees or other objects forward and back or side to side in space. So the tree becomes involved in space and rhythm and tempo, all abstractions but all inextricably involved in the "reality" of the tree.

These qualities of a tree or any object, are only in part a matter of simple visual experience. That is, they are not at all times available to the full free choice of the artist but are determined by much of what lies outside him and what he believes. What he sees is in good part determined by what he is, what he knows, what he believes.

Thus the relation between the artist, the art work, and "reality" is far more complex than the idea of the artist as a recording lens would indicate. Reality is, for the artist, in part what it is and the artist can truly see it. It is in part what he makes of it in his total personality. Thus the artist is painting some aspect of himself.

Thus the diagram would have to be changed somewhat:

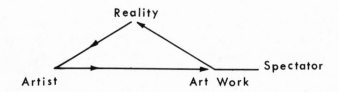

This is an improvement on the original diagram. It indicates a more active role for the artist. It indicates that there are two things that go into the art work: the artist and some aspect of "reality" as selected and modified by the artist. It indicates that the spectator can apprehend something of the artist and of the reality as they are incarnated, given bodily form, in the art work.

Still, it is not adequate. In the first place, the diagram would indicate that the artist has some conception of reality which is then put into an appropriate art work. (This is implied by the common question, "What does that painting mean?" as though there were a meaning apart from the painting.)

In the second place, it overlooks the manner in which the artist works. He works, not with "reality" but with paint, or stone, or ink. Just as a tree has its qualities so paint or other material has its qualities and the work is made of these. Further, a work of art has its own qualities, made in part of the qualities of the material that are inherent in the work.

Consequently, the artist does not have an idea of "meaning" which he then puts into an appropriate form. Rather the form is the means for achieving meaning. In a sense it is a window through which the artist sees reality and only with clarity and coherence of form is there any clarity of meaning.

Thus the relation can be more accurately represented in this fashion:

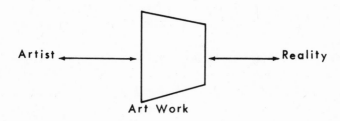

That is, the art work is not only the product of the creative interaction between the artist and reality, it is the means whereby the artist takes hold of reality, it is the arena where the creative encounter takes place. It *is* the relation and without it the artist is struck dumb. In a kind of ascending spiral, reality and the art work depend on each other in the consciousness of the artist. Only as each becomes clear can the other be clear and manifest.

This must be followed further, as this analysis touches the heart of the creative act and the language of the arts.

The place of the material in the making of the works needs to be made clearer. The material is not only the locus of the embodying of the artist's vision of reality, it is one of the most fundamental ways in which reality presents itself to the artist. This is primary. The artist may have an imagination full of intimations of meaning and reality but it is only as these images begin to take form in the actual material that they can be handled in any way. In the other direction, the material itself can give rise in the artist to images which carry much of the weight of meaning. There are various legitimate ways for the artist to handle his material but when the artist becomes brutal or insensitive to materials his work turns vulgar or false. For examples of this see the sentimental slickness of most magazine illustrations, the glossy sterility of most drugstore fronts, the assertive vulgarity of filling stations.

In all the infinite complexity of "reality" the artist is not limited to that which he can see and touch but his major concern is with the material and the sensuous. This is his door into reality. Any abstract idea must be embodied in a physical form if it is to be his. For example, an artist coming at human reality through the human body, that most expressive of all instruments, can do a lot toward the expression of emotional states. Yet the static quality of his material prevents him from doing much with change in emotional states, whereas a poet in the fourteen lines of a sonnet can analyze very subtle changes and developments in emotions. Thus the material can establish both the possibilities and the limitations of the art work.

Next, reality for the artist begins with the visible world but does not end with it. That is, he is concerned with any and all aspects of what he sees. It is not only the external physical appearance of the tree that concerns him but also its massiveness, or its springy strength, or the pattern of light through its leaves or any of its other qualities. Then, if he wishes to concentrate on some of these elements and eliminate the tree which first caused his awareness of them he has a perfect right to do so. This often happens, not only in "abstract" painting, but in decorative forms which have the sinuous vitality of organic life.

There is one major exception to these observations about the rootage of art in the visible natural order. There exists in reality relation and rhythm. These appear in all sorts of natural forms and are a prominent part of the language of any artist. They also appear alone and thus create most forms of decoration as well as much very intelligent abstract painting (e.g., Mondrian or Kandinsky). The decoration of pots in bands or repetitive design, the design of a rug, the ornament on a building all grow out of rhythm and the relation of one element to another.

There is a further complicating factor in the artist's relation to reality: it might be called his emotional and intellectual distance from it. There is art, for example, which quite simply and frankly revels in the joy of making and observing the things which are made. In a real sense this is art which simply participates in the structure of reality.

There is the art which stands apart from reality, examines, and analyzes it. This art is far more objective and intellectual. This is a much more self-conscious art.

There is the art which moves into the artist and records the effect of the chosen aspect of reality on him. This is a highly subjective art which takes two forms. If the concern is with the effect of the sensuous aspects of reality on the sense organs of the artist it is called impressionism. If the concern is with the emotional reaction of the artist it is expressionism.

This is an analytic description with little relation to the realities, for all these elements are present in nearly every work. This sketch does say something about where the center of gravity of an art work might lie. And it also says something about the complexity of art works which so many people have considered simply as pictures of something.

Always this complexity of relation is carried on in terms of the material. The relation is manifest, embodied in what happens to the material. This that "happens" to the material is the forming of it and the form is the imprint of reality on the material by the mind and the hand of the artist. The form, then, is the crucial aspect of the work of art. It is not simply the gateway for the spectator into the work of art. It is the substance and essence of the work of art. It is the heart and spine and muscles of the work of art. It is what makes an art work what it is.

Therefore, any grasping of the art work is taking hold of the form, any understanding of it is by the analysis of form. The whole purpose of this argument has been to affirm that art is a way of knowing and that one of its aspects is the communication of that which it knows and asserts as well as the manifestation of all it is. If this is true its language is the language of form. Its communicating depends on sensitivity to all which is in form.

All that is communicated by means of form is content. From the foregoing analysis it is evident that content is the term for the artist's conception of some portion of reality as he can embody it in the work of art.

Content is not subject matter although the term is sometimes used as referring to subject matter. In fact, this whole discussion has been developed deliberately without reference to subject matter, except for a passing reference, since the popular view of art reduces it to a representation of subject matter. This popular view makes impossible the conception of art as communication or, for that matter, art as anything important. To indicate the real nature of art in its capacity as a way of knowing, it is essential to move as far from this as possible.

This does not mean, however, as some critics have asserted, that subject matter is of no importance. It does mean that subject matter has been misplaced in the study of art. As the name indicates, subject matter is a part of the material the artist works with and is therefore a part of the reality the artist is looking at. Subject matter is not the content, which is the artist's interpretation of the reality he sees through his work. This reality might be, in part, an identifiable subject matter. It usually is.

The subject matter might be all important. It might constitute the area in "reality" of primary interest to the artist and both material and all other relevant aspects of reality – color, gesture of body, space – might exist for the sake of manifesting and embodying the artist's conception of the subject.

The subject might be of little interest to the artist and be present simply as the occasion for the setting forth of the things which do concern him.

Going still further, the subject might disappear altogether, as in contemporary abstract painting or much decorative art. It would be more correct to say subject matter as overt reference to something in the world outside the work has disappeared. The painting or some aspect of painting has become the subject. In some abstractions, color relations are the main concern of the artist, in others it is relations of space or movement. In a different type, the artist expresses his own emotions directly and they constitute the subject matter while there is nothing identifiable represented.

An artist might paint a Madonna and Child using his wife and son as models. If he wants consciously or unconsciously to make manifest the meaning of Mary and the Infant Jesus in his understanding of them, and all the complex relations of form necessary to manifest this, then the subject matter is the primary area of reality for him and its interpretation is the content. Again he might be indifferent to the religious ideas while still representing the subject (since that is what he is paid for) yet his main concern is the human one of the mother and child. The subject is unchanged but the content is the formal structure which manifests the human relation.

Again he might use the subject yet be concerned primarily with the complex relations of two human bodies in space.

Or he might use the subject but reduce it to patterns of color or line on the surface of the canvas. In this case the subject has no meaning or even usefulness except in its reference to tradition, as modern artists sometime use it to testify to their link with the problems defined by their predecessors.

In each case the subject is the same but the content is different. This can be determined only by awareness of the form and by careful analysis of it. The locus of artistic communication is form.

This preliminary survey of the language of the visual arts has laid out the general categories applicable to all art forms. It is necessary now to consider the specific character of the "vocabulary" and grammar of the visual artist.

There should emerge, from this discussion of the nature of the artistic language, a connection with the account of biblical communication. No communication, particularly artistic communication, can be considered a trucking job. A "meaning" is not loaded on the communicating vehicle (language) and carried to the other person where it is deposited. Rather meaning and vehicle, message and language, form and content are inseparable.

The "meaning" is clear to the speaker (or artist or scientist or mathematician) only as it becomes embodied in the appropriate forming of the proper material. The student who says, "I know the answer but I can't express it" is, quite simply, deluding himself. It is quite possible to be unable to articulate the meaning in words for there are meanings which can be expressed only in the language of music or mathematical formulas, or colored shapes. But unless what is in the mind can be articulated in some language it is formless, foetal, of no significance for life or understanding.

It is a superstition of a word-obsessed civilization that all meanings can be put into words. Words are perhaps the most flexible and versatile of all instruments of communication. Words are the primary instruments for the preservation and transmission of culture, words are the precise instruments of analysis, words set the limits and determine the controls. They also function as a high instrument of form. Yet there are areas of meaning and understanding which words cannot enter.

Content in the visual arts cannot be translated into words nor is there any verbal equivalent of artistic content. Even in the verbal arts content cannot be translated into other words because content and form are inseparable. Any change in the form changes the content.

Thus the understanding of artistic content requires the spectator to enter the world presented to him. It is more than simply responding to the formal relations; it is an entering into a world which has its own structure and its own laws. The preceding sections have tried to show there is a connection between the world of the art work and the world of "real" meaning. It is a connection which finally can be judged for its adequacy but not until the world of the art work has been lived in.

The artist responds to those aspects of reality which are available to him and organizes them according to his own understanding of the nature and meaning of that reality. This organization can range all the way from slight works with no great cargo of meaning or pleasant things aiming only at delight for the senses to complex works manifesting and embodying a total view of the nature and destiny of the world and of man. It is a debatable question whether a man can finally participate in a work unless he shares that same total world view. Certainly he can participate in it to a significant degree for it uses the common language of art and shares the common human act of responding to the common human situation. So, given humility, charity, and diligence, the world can be entered.

Words can be the key to the door into that world. In a world where the characteristic language of art has been lost or obscured, the recovery of it may need the guidance of words. There are other functions for artistic criticism (having to do with the place of art in the study of history) but certainly one of its major functions is to lead the untrained observer into the world of art, to point to the unique character of the artistic language and open the door into it.

That such a door must exist needs to be asserted if art is to be truly communication and not simply manifestation. The difficulty with speaking of things like "reality" in this abstract fashion, is the implication that art is esoteric and mysterious. There is certainly more to the world of art than any one person can finally grasp and in that sense it is mysterious. With ever greater knowledge and increasing refinement of sensibility the arts remain inexhaustible with the inexhaustible vitality of life.

Yet the beginning is not so esoteric as all that, for the point of contact is with that which is common to all – things in their solidity and earthy reality. Reality has been left undefined, for it has widening ranges of meaning like the stone thrown in a pool. But the center is the most pervasive reality of common experience, the objects of the two senses, sight and touch. An art work is not first of all a reflection of the meaning of the universe, although a conception of that meaning may be condensed into it. It is first of all a physical object characterized as physical objects are in the common experience. It has no quality not found in the world as it is known by every person from infancy.

The difference is that the world of sense impressions is so unbearably varied that the senses of most people are drowned in it. They do not survive as sense organs except in the most rudimentary manner. To the insensitive eye nature is a masterless chaos held together by little more than the law of gravity.

The artist is a man who sees the same chaos but in some way makes sense out of it. He might eliminate much but magnify a few characteristics (which under the artist's guidance we can then see, where before we were unable to single out the impression). Or, while still eliminating much (the artist of necessity eliminates much) he might clarify a wide range of things in order to give a sense of the meaningfulness of the whole range of things in the visible world (e.g., Van Eyck and the whole of Flemish art). Or he might use those things and those qualities of things which present coherently the order and intelligibility which exist at their heart. With any of these, but particularly the last, the world's chaos becomes meaningful because there now exists in it an object, a thing with a meaning, an order, a coherence, a unity of its own which has distilled into itself some qualities of the order of the living world. An art work is communication between artist and spectator because it is first of all a communication with the essential life of the world of things.

Bringing the language of art back to its rootage in the physical and sensuous makes it somewhat more available to the layman than it would be if too exclusive emphasis is placed on the high "spiritual" or intellectual realities to which it points. Yet the world of art is still almost as bewilderingly variable as the world of nature. This is particularly true in this time because the eye is constantly assaulted by forms from every time and culture. Magazines are full of illustrations of authentic examples of art from all times and places. The things we use or live in or work in or see have been influenced by great numbers of other things so there is no continuity of style to give coherence of vision.

Thus, to be presented with the whole multitude of artistic forms is a little like being presented with the alphabet or at least a set of dictionaries and told that these are the languages. The comparison is not complete for the isolated letter and even the isolated word have thinness and insignificance whereas isolated colors or shapes have a certain independent meaning and often carry in themselves real pleasure. It is only in meaningful relation to each other that words make a language and that relation is according to laws appropriate to that language. It is only after this preliminary organization of the original raw material that individual creativity takes place but this creativity depends altogether on the use made of the language which exists.

Corresponding to the organization of sounds into words and words into language is the selection of formal elements and their organizations into styles. Not all the infinite possibilities of sensuous reality relevant to art are available to the artist, any more than all words in all languages are simultaneously available to the writer. Rather there are groupings of these elements into styles. There are a few basic stylistic attitudes subdividing (in a very disorderly and unsystematic manner) into the major groupings of styles, which contain chronological division into period styles and the regional (or national) styles, the local or even city styles and finally the styles of individuals. This last, obviously, is the crucial aspect of style for it is the only locus of the others.

Simply identifying a work as belonging to a particular style doesn't say the important things about it. But intelligible ordering of things is necessary to human knowledge and styles form the skeleton for supporting the work of individuals. Therefore, the beginner can begin by becoming aware of the gross differences, and as he trains his sensibility he can come to see the more subtle differences which make up the life of the arts.

The determinative origin of style is lost in the beginning of things, and it is no part of the purpose of this book to enter the controversy about it. It might help, however, to point out some of the possibilities, both to make the phenomenon more intelligible (since we see style mostly in the highly refined products of a sophisticated art) and to indicate how close style is to the most elemental aspects of human existence. Style is essential to life rather than an idle and luxurious ornament.

Of all aspects of style perhaps the most basic is space, for man's existence is inseparable from space. He begins in the tight, warm, all-sufficient space of the womb and other such confinements as swaddling clothes. He lives in the great hot spaces of the desert, the intricate congestion of the jungle, the alternation of open and closed space in forest and plain, the solidity of the earth in the mountains.

A more personal influence is the form of his first dwelling. Does he live in caves in the earth? Does he pile up stones to make a shelter? Does he weave brush or reeds into a tent? The first enters into matter and conceives of space as interior. The second builds and therefore emphasizes the solidity of matter conceived as mass. The house becomes an object in space with a useful interior. The third emphasizes volume, and the material is a membrane acting as a boundary between inner and outer space.

Closely related, indeed interdependent with space, is mass. In fact, as the preceding paragraph shows, there is no space effect without mass, or some material to define the space. Yet mass is an effect in its own right. The sense of mass is less apparent to people of a machine age where there is little effort involved in doing anything but it imposes itself coercively on the man whose existence is carried out only in struggle with the substance of the earth.

How, for example, does he make his containers? He can hollow them out of stone or wood. He can model them out of clay, building them up with his hands. He can weave them out of grass or reeds. The process is different and the psychological effect is different. In the first, matter is solid, massive, to be entered only with a kind of violence. In the second matter is plastic, submissive, more easily coerced. In the third, matter is pliant, willful, but easily subdued.

Then there is the climate and the landscape, whose effect has often been exaggerated but which is nonetheless fundamental. It makes a great deal of difference whether a man's vision is informed by the vast expanses of desert sand, yellow, blinding and empty. Or by the stony mountain, solid, sculptural. Or by forests green and brown, open and closed, crowded with summer leaves, empty in the lacing of winter branches. It makes a difference whether he is accustomed to seeing objects clear and sharp or softened by mist and rain.

These are samples, not a catalogue. Yet they may point to the ways in which artistic styles flow from elemental experiences. Even so, elemental effects do not determine the styles of a high art. They may determine what is possible but ultimately the style is determined by the controlling idea in the mind of man.

As an indication of this, the same soil of Greece produced the most corporeal of all arts in classical Greek sculpture and the most incorporeal of arts of the body in Byzantine mosaics. A Greek temple is all outside. Its interior is the home of the god and appropriately treated but its important artistic function is its external relation to mass. The Byzantine church is all interior space and its outside is a scaffold. There is a demonstrable relation between these two phenomena and between each of them and the land of

Greece. But it is a fairly subtle relation and the differences are fundamental.

The difference is made by the mind of man. Primitive man can be defined as primitive by his involvement in natural processes. He responds to or, better, submits to the processes of nature and so his art is to a high degree determined by these influences and these necessities. This is not entirely true, because man as man always exercises his intelligence on what he makes, but there is relative truth in it. Out of this submission there develops the major stylistic attitudes which are found at the heart of all later styles just as the most primitive desires and urges are found in the motives of the most sophisticated person.

Yet these stylistic attitudes, these basic attitudes toward space and mass, time and movement, line and color, become a true style only when intelligence manifests itself in and through them. In primitive art there is a response to the natural order, a communion with it, but less of the genuine relation which constitutes communication. In art as such, intelligence interacts with the physical reality and thus in the embodiment of this communication in the appropriate form there is the possibility of communication with other persons.

In primitive art there is repetitiveness, slow changes which fail to affect the fundamentals. This is because man is for the most part simply responding to the necessities of his situation and most changes are on the surface, subject to fashion. When intelligence communicates with that which is given in the human situation then the style takes on order and direction. Then history begins. The manifestation of each insight into reality creates new problems and possibilities. Man asserts himself in this new order and embodies his new insight in new forms which then create new problems and new possibilities until exhaustion sets in.

Thus there are not only the primal types of stylistic attitudes to use to sort out the multitude of visual impressions. There are also the linked changes in each style which, with all the breaks, incursion of other influences, speed-ups and sterile periods, provide an intelligible and orderly sequence of phenomena. This sequence carries in itself much of the meaning.

Little more can be said here in any systematic way about styles or their sequential development, for this is neither history nor textbook. So brief a sketch may indicate something of what must be done if the language of the visual arts is to be learned. It may serve further to indicate an essential aspect of this argument: that human relation and human communication are rooted in the human situation; that man is never wholly free nor wholly bound, since the conditions and the elements of his language are imposed on him yet he can respond creatively to the conditions; that to understand the communication it is necessary (and possible) to enter the true relation, to enter the world of the art work, to apprehend its particularity and its order, live within it, and grasp its essential quality and meaning.

With the deeper entry into the language of the visual arts the concept of communication in the arts ought to become clearer. Again, communication is not a trucking job. The "meaning" is not a thing to be transported. It is rather the order and the essence of a world, related to but not wholly of the world of ordinary knowledge. It is grasped, not as an object that can be purchased but only in living relation.

"He that has ears to hear, let him hear." The essence of communication is relation. The essence of relation is communication. In each case the essential act is to sit where the other sits. To use the most important distinction in modern theology, the essential act is to establish the I–thou relation. If the art work is treated as an inert thing, if the relation is I–it, then there is no relation and no communication. There is only exploitation.

The I–thou relation presupposes the living reality of the other. "I sat where they sat and I sat astonished among them seven days" (Ezekiel 3:15). To love another as myself is not to love him instead of myself, committing a kind of spiritual suicide, but to love him as though he were myself. To love is to know, to enter his condition of manhood, to think as he thinks, to see as he sees, to be a part of the world which radiates from him as a center.

This is the nature of communication, of any communication, including the arts. The price is creative submission to order oneself for a time according to another's work, to see with his eyes, and through the form he has imposed on his material, submit receptively to the laws of the work he has made in the image of what he thinks the world to be. Unless this is done he who has ears will not hear nor will he who has eyes see or understand. He will contract within himself, into his naked solitude, eating his own flesh, and passing into ultimate oblivion. For "all real life is meeting" and he who is not in relation, who sees the world only as an "it" will become an "it" among the inertness and become as nothing.

To do this, to live in relation to the fullness of man's creativity is to enter many apparently alien worlds. There is no true relation just to one's own, for what profit is there to love only those who love us? To enter into the wholeness of the world's art is to enter the wholeness of the world's attitudes. This means entering alien places and many of them will, finally, remain alien, for communication can be of the evil as well as of the good. Many others will remain worlds which this person or that cannot live in permanently. But all are the articulation of the humanness of man and the experience of them gives dimension and meaning to life.

FIGURES

FIG. I. THE RESURRECTION

By Piero della Francesca. Galleria Comunale, San Sepolcro. Courtesy of Alinari-Art Reference Bureau.

FIG. 2. RESURRECTION

By Donatello. San Lorenzo, Florence. Courtesy of Alinari-Art Reference Bureau.

FIG. 3. RESURRECTION

By El Greco. The Prado, Madrid.
Courtesy of Anderson-Art Reference Bureau.

FIG. 4. RESURRECTION (detail)

By Mathias Grünewald. Musée Unterlinden, Colmar. Courtesy of Bildarchiv Foto Marburg

FIG. 5. ADORATION OF THE HOLY LAMB (detail)

By Jan van Eyck. St.Bavon, Ghent. Courtesy of A.C.L.-Art Reference Bureau.

FIG. 6. SAINT FRANCIS IN ECSTASY

By Giovanni Bellini. Copyright. The Frick Collection, New York.

FIG. 7. NUMBER 10

By Mark Rothko. Courtesy of Collection,
The Museum of Modern Art. New York.
Gift of Philip C. Johnson.

FIG. 8. NUMBER 1

By Jackson Pollock. Courtesy of Collection, The Museum of Modern Art. New York.

FIG. 9. THE TRIBUTE MONEY

By Masaccio. Sta. Maria del Carmine, Florence. Courtesy of Alinari-Art
Reference Bureau.

FIG. 10. THE ADORATION OF THE THREE KINGS

By Peter Paul Rubens. The Prado, Madrid. Courtesy of
Anderson-Art Reference Bureau.

FIG. 11. THE FLIGHT INTO EGYPT

By Giotto. Arena Chapel, Padua. Courtesy of
Anderson–Art Reference Bureau.

FIG. 12. LANDSCAPE WITH VIADUCT

By Paul Cézanne. The H.O. Havemeyer Collection. Courtesy of The
Metropolitan Museum of Art. New York. Bequest of Mrs. H. O. Havemeyer, 1929.

FIG. 13. LAST SUPPER

By Leonardo da Vinci. Sta. Maria della Grazie, Milan. Courtesy of
Alinari-Art Reference Bureau.

FIG. 14. THE SCHOOL OF ATHENS

By Raphael. The Vatican, Rome. Courtesy of Alinari-Art Reference Bureau.

FIG. 15. THE ADORATION OF THE SHEPHERDS

By Ghirlandaio. S. Trinita, Florence. Courtesy of Alinari-Art Reference Bureau.

FIG. 16. THE MADONNA OF THE CHAIR

By Raphael. Pitti Palace, Florence. Courtesy of Alinari-Art Reference Bureau.

FIG. 17. THE FLAGELLATION

By Piero della Francesca. Ducal Palace, Urbino. Courtesy of
Alinari-Art Reference Bureau.

FIG. 18. CHRIST HEALING THE SICK
By Rembrandt. Courtesy of Bildarchiv Foto Marburg.

FIG. 19. OVAL STILL LIFE (The Violin)

By Georges Braque. Courtesy of Collection, The Museum of Modern Art.
New York. Gift of the Advisory Committee.

FIG. 20. PHILEMON AND BAUCIS

By Rembrandt. Courtesy of National Gallery of Art. Washington.

FIG. 21. S. SIGISMONDO AND SIGISMONDO MALATESTA (detail)
By Piero della Francesca. Malatesta Temple, Rimini.
Courtesy of Alinari-Art Reference Bureau.

FIG. 22. CARDINAL DON FERNANDO NIÑO DE GUEVARA (detail)
By El Greco. The H. O. Havemeyer Collection. Courtesy of The
Metropolitan Museum of Art. New York. Bequest of Mrs. H. O. Havemeyer, 1929.

FIG. 23. GATTAMELATA

By Donatello. Padua. Courtesy of Anderson-Art Reference Bureau.

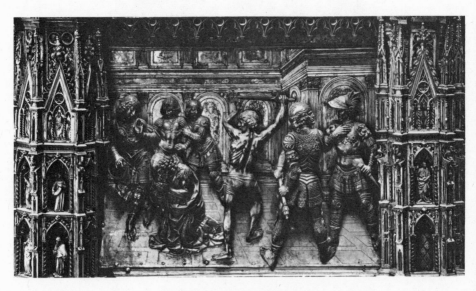

FIG. 24. BEHEADING OF JOHN THE BAPTIST

Attributed to Verrocchio. Duomo Museum, Florence. Courtesy of
Alinari-Art Reference Bureau.

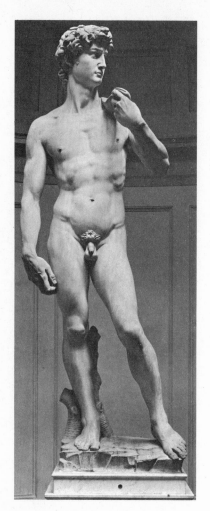

FIG. 27. DAVID

By Michelangelo. Academy, Florence.
Courtesy of Alinari-Art Reference Bureau.

FIG. 28. RONDANINI PIETÀ

By Michelangelo. Sforza Castle, Milan.
Courtesy of Alinari-Art Reference Bureau.

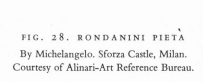

FIG. 29. VENUS AND THE LUTE PLAYER

By Titian. Munsey Fund. Courtesy of The Metropolitan Museum of Art. New York.

FIG. 30.

CHRIST CROWNED WITH THORNS

By Titian. Altepinakothek, Munich.
Courtesy of Bruckmann-Art Reference Bureau.

FIG. 31. BATHSHEBA

By Rembrandt. Louvre, Paris. Courtesy of Bildarchiv Foto Marburg.

FIG. 32. DANAË

By Titian. National Gallery, Naples. Courtesy of Alinari-Art Reference Bureau.

FIG. 33. THE JEWISH BRIDE

By Rembrandt. Rijksmuseum, Amsterdam. Courtesy of Art Reference Bureau.

FIG. 34. NIGHT FROM TOMB OF GUILIANO DE
MEDICI, MEDICI CHAPEL

By Michelangelo. San Lorenzo, Florence. Courtesy of Alinari-Art Reference Bureau.

FIG. 35. THE CRUCIFIXION

By Mathias Grünewald. Musée Unterlinden, Colmar.
Courtesy of Bildarchiv Foto Marburg.

FIG. 36. DEPOSITION

By Pontormo. S. Felicita, Florence. Courtesy of Alinari-Art Reference Bureau.

FIG. 37. ELEGY TO THE SPANISH REPUBLIC, 54

By Robert Motherwell. Courtesy of Collection, The Museum of Modern Art. New York.

FIG. 38. MARY MAGDALENE

By Donatello. Baptistry, Florence. Courtesy of Brogi-Art Reference Bureau.

FIG. 39. PIETÀ

By German School, around 1300. Courtesy of Bildarchiv Foto Marburg.

FIG. 40. ANXIETY

By Edvard Munch. Courtesy of Collection, The Museum of Modern Art. New York.

FIG. 41. MADONNA

Cemeterio Marius, Fourth Century, Rome. Courtesy of Alinari-Art Reference Bureau.

FIG. 42. APSE MOSAIC FROM SAN APOLLINARE
IN CLASSE, RAVENNA

Courtesy of Alinari-Art Reference Bureau.

PART TWO

THE EVIDENCE

VII

STRUCTURE

AND

EXPRESSION

IN CHRISTIAN ART

In turning to the evidence from which these theoretical principles have been derived and by which they must be proven, the safest thing to do would be to look at those styles generally recognized and accepted as Christian. Having sought a certain common denominator among these it might then be possible to work out principles applicable to other works.

In many ways, however, this convenient device is misleading by the very reason of its simplicity. The reason for this has bearing on the course of the argument.

Different periods look to different points in the past as their golden age. It is humanly probable that most Christians, as most people, have looked back to an immediately preceding generation as in some ways normative for the statements of Christian art. But beyond this natural human inclination, certain other periods stand out with particular importance as central to the Christian experience.

For example, the poignant naïveté of the catacomb paintings has real appeal for those who know them. Perhaps the period most often looked to as normative in recent decades is the Gothic. This is not unnatural since it was during this period that the church reached its greatest range of social and cultural influence and most nearly dominated the major expressions of culture in a creative period. Thus many people look to it as the Christian period without parallel or equal.

In recent years, largely through the eloquent voice of Paul Tillich, German expressionism (as a style rather than a distinct period) has become normative for many leading Christian thinkers: those, in other words, who might be aware of the writings of theologians and critics of culture. For Tillich, this expressionism is centrally important, for he says, "...while the others are only indirectly representing the ultimate, the expressive element represents it directly" (Tillich, *Theology of Culture*, p. 73). To Tillich, expressionism is not simply a moment in the past which has become normative, it is an indispensable ingredient of all truly religious art.

This preference for certain periods of the past tells a great deal about the theology and the faith of those who feel it. It can also tell a great deal about the preferred period, since a passionate fondness for a period or a style often enables a person to speak with particular eloquence of its merits and to be particularly sensitive to its important characteristics which less affection might ignore.

Yet such preference remains misleading, even if used as a point of departure. Such norms take for granted a principle that is false to the whole body of evidence: that one style is somehow in itself more Christian than another. Such a principle violates the evidence and falsifies the approach.

Style is a creation of man, not of God. It cannot be said truthfully that one man or one body of men has any privileged position in the sight of God or any unique means of access to God. Style is the locus of the formal statement of their apprehension of the meaning of God and of God's creation. It can reflect the different degrees of their piety and insight and these might differ from one man to another. But they differ, not by the inherent quality of the style, but by the integrity and the profundity of the man who makes and uses the style. Style is a part of the whole human enterprise and to select one style as uniquely favored in the eye of God is to make the grievous error of taking the part for the whole. It is only as the wholeness of the relevance of man's work in the styles of art is understood that man can determine the full nature of Christian art.

The other main objection to the procedure which makes a particular style normative is a corollary and the consequence of the first. If one style or one period can be given any unique position in the life of the church, then it follows that other styles and other periods are to some comparable degree inadequate or even false. The period to suffer this fate most acutely has been the Italian Renaissance which, among many intellectuals in the church, has fallen from the high estate it once held, to a position of condemnation and rejection. Such judgments share the falseness of the selection of one period as normative, for they involve, not this time a privileged position, but an outcast position for a powerful human enterprise. Any Christian sits in judgment on his fellows only at grave risk to his integrity. Every human act has relevance for the deeper understanding of his faith and of creation if he approaches it with charity and compassion. Further, the rejection of a whole period or a whole style means arrogating the right to judge the work of dedicated and devout men. The necessity for judging a man's work to be false often becomes an unavoidable requirement for a Christian put to the point of judgment. But the study of history is not properly a hunt for heresy and condemnation must be reached only after most painful and intimate consideration. To reject a period or a style as basically unchristian or inadequately Christian is to commit an offense against personality of major proportions.

To choose, then, one of the periods or styles popularly identified as peculiarly Christian might make the demonstration simpler but would distort certain essential principles of the case here being presented. It is not a matter of rejecting the popular solution, for such a procedure would have no more merit. These selected periods have a relevance equal to any other expression of the Christian faith in art. They must not be taken as normative and to use them expediently would be to encourage the inclination to see them normatively. They must appear in their proper place. The case will be successfully proven only if it is made in other ways. There would appear to be no better way than to accept the challenge offered to the Renaissance and set forth the relevance for the Christian faith of the work done by Renaissance artists.

It is neither necessary nor possible to reject or weaken the case for certain periods which are taken to have a particularly obvious relation to the work of the church. It is equally unnecessary and impossible to pretend that evidence does not exist for the widespread feeling that the Renaissance was an age characterized by many beliefs and acts that are incompatible with Christianity. It is not necessary to review all the evidence which points to this impression for it is a part of the general consciousness. According to this case, the Renaissance was worldly, materialistic, sensual, humanistic.

In truth, the case is often stronger than it is generally made out to be. A case which rests solely on the overt acts of powerful individuals, the crimes of despots, and the corruption of the papacy is still dealing with symptoms and paying too little attention to the essential causes. Morality is not measured by acts but by the fundamental disposition of the soul and it is possible to find in any period of human history an enormous quantity of evil acts at all levels of the social and political order. This kind of moral arithmetic, which would measure the amount of evil in high places and judge the Renaissance to be an irreligious phenomenon, is not convincing.

Yet the peculiar quality, as distinct from the quantity, of the evil of the Renaissance makes it a truly singular phenomenon in the history of western civilization. Much of the evil committed in the Renaissance was the simple human evil which is inevitably a consequence of man's humanity. Much derives from this inevitable evil because of the particular concatenation of circumstances that gave to man's ancient evils a singular opportunity for manifesting themselves. Much of it, however, was an inevitable consequence of the basic assumptions about man and the world by which Renaissance civilization developed and for which it must be held morally accountable, in the deepest sense of the word morality. This is no place for an extensive examination of the structure of Renaissance morality but it did manifest itself in Renaissance art, and therefore its impingement on that art must be discussed.

It is rightly felt that a major concern of the Renaissance was the discovery and development of the individual personality – of which more must be said. This search was central to the Renaissance experience, to the point that it is one of the defining characteristics of Renaissance art. If a work does not manifest this sense of individuality, it is, to that degree, not a part of the Renaissance. Yet it wholly falsifies the evidence to take it in two dimensions only. The search for individuality was not one thing only but several things. Yet, again, the existence of this multiplicity of attitudes does not permit overlooking those among the attitudes which are counter to the Christian doctrine of man. There are works of Renaissance art that, in their overt reference and in their fundamental rhythms, set forth an image of man as wholly autonomous, responsible to nothing outside himself, with no morality or experience that can set limits to his personality. There are, for example, works of Pollaiuolo with tense and violent rhythms out of which emerge images of men of appalling ferocity or self-indulgence. Cf. Fig. 24

At other levels, there is the pursuit of sensual realization, of materialistic luxury, or ostentatious display. In many ways the most inhumanly subversive of all the Renaissance ills was the trivializing of the sacred, the slack rhythms and mindless naturalism of Ghirlandaio, for example, leading Fig. 15
ultimately to the sentimentalities of Raphael's minor Madonnas. Fig. 16

These things exist and there is little purpose in trying to explain them away. They exist, not because of any peculiar perversity of vision in Renaissance men, but as a part of their life and enterprise. Renaissance men must, therefore, be judged not solely by the aberrations of their enterprise, even when those aberrations are logical consequences of the basic act. Rather, the main concerns of that enterprise must be identified and judged and then only can those acts be properly accounted for that here are called aberrations from a central line of concern.

The integrity of this Renaissance enterprise can be seen most clearly when set off against the particular virtues and characteristics of the time that preceded it. The medieval period is felt to be so distinctively Christian because of the soaring aspiration of its architecture combined with the mystery of its darkness colored by the glass (the terminology and description are cast in the conventional terms, which only in part distort the reality); by the calm and serene grace of the sculpture, untroubled by passion or personality and obedient to its place in the whole structure. Serenity in order, grace under hierarchy, charity within comprehensiveness: these are the qualities loved in medieval art.

It is a matter of wry amusement to the historian that these qualities are found only in the limited range of the high Gothic, and other medieval monuments are amalgamated to that ideal only with considerable difficulty. If the concept of style and historical periods is to have any meaning at all, then the idea of the medieval is equally responsible for the awesome terror of the Romanesque style and the fearful abandon and death obsession of the late Gothic. These two are part and substance of the medieval enterprise and equally a consequence of its assumptions. It is one of the perversities of the historical consciousness that they are ignored or explained away, whereas forces in the Renaissance no more prominent in the character of

"Renaissance man" are taken to be the defining elements of his character. Yet the high Gothic stands as a major type of the Christian consciousness in the purity of its expression.

What this Gothic stood for was a great thing and there was great quality in it even in its decline. In its decline however, it was no longer a fruitful insight but a codification of rules which lay as a smothering weight on the spirit of man. Having worked out what could be worked out within the terms of these principles, human creativity had to turn to new expression and new knowledge. The Renaissance turned to the search for the reality of the world and the reality of man's mind.

One of the principal motives in the criticism of the Renaissance by some churchmen is the unwillingness to accept this search as a religious act. The critic tends to set apart piety and knowledge and the search for knowledge becomes an impious act.

It is true, and should be stated, that many a Renaissance man seeking after knowledge in his own realm consciously felt this search to be an obligation on him as a Christian and a faithful servant of God. It is also true that many of them made such avowals of piety out of convention or (as a later artist was to put it) as a kind of insurance policy which leaves a man free to pursue his own work independent of such protestations. It would require an appraisal of each individual to measure the depth and quality of his sincerity and its actualization in his work. This argument will not be pursued, not because it is irrelevant but because it is distracting: what is needed is not an excuse for the enterprise of the Renaissance man but a validation of it in its own quality and character. If a case is to be made for the involvement of the Renaissance task in the unfolding of Christian consciousness, it must be on the inherent worth of the task it set for itself, not simply because some of the participants in that task consciously intended it to be a work of piety.

God made all things and saw that his creation was good. Therefore, it is given to man to rejoice in creation and take delight because of it. God placed man in creation to have dominion over it and name the parts of it. Therefore, it is given to man to exercise his intellect on the world he lives in. Since the art of man is involved in the fall of man it is not surprising that Renaissance art should have manifested man's general sin in the particular forms it had chosen for its own expression: that Renaissance art should on many occasions exaggerate delight into materialism or sensuality; that he should extend the individuality of his intellect into unrestrained self-assertion. Yet out of sensuality and assertion there developed the tragic dimension of the Renaissance consciousness, the awareness of the depths beneath the overt life of man. Out of this sense of tragedy and awareness of man's tragic imprisonment there developed the sense of the redemption that lies beyond despair.

In short, the Renaissance manifested the full range of styles earlier characterized in this study as relevant to the Christian understanding of reality: the celebration of the arts of creation, the rationality of the art of the image, the tragedy of the art of the fall, the fulfillment of the art of redemption. Because of the singular intensity of personality in the Renaissance each of these types is seen with unusual clarity and strength. What the true Renaissance man did, he did to the full extent of his powers and this gives to his work a paradigmatic quality that makes it particularly appropriate for a study of this kind.

Out of the full life of the Renaissance, then, there comes the full stream of human endeavor which can serve to introduce the evidence of this study.

It is always too simple to attempt to sum up the main intention of an historical period in a few handy phrases but the attempt can serve as a guide through the maze of events. This is particularly the case where the defining concerns of the Renaissance intersect so meaningfully with the concerns of Christian art.

One of these defining concerns of the Renaissance was space; not so much space as such, since nearly all western art has sought a relation with space, but the rational construction and control of space. In that space they sought to present the natural world as they saw it and felt it and believed in it. In and through the space they sought to present the action of human drama; not just man as a part of nature but the distinctively human quality of man in action or in function. Laid over all these as both creator and instrument of control were the characteristic Renaissance proportions and rhythms. Thus out of their rhythms they established space, nature, man, and the human drama.

The particular character of these concerns has been at the root of many of the attempts to stigmatize the Renaissance as non-Christian or even anti-Christian. The cool rationality with which many of these problems were analyzed, with each element pursued to its logically inevitable conclusion, and their characteristic independence of mind, conspire to give to the Renaissance enterprise the flavor of opposition. This is particularly true when the Renaissance is contrasted with the highly romanticized idea of an Age of Faith that preceded it. It is beside the point that this picture of the medieval period is highly oversimplified for it has become fixed in the imagination, not only of the popular student but of many people who should know better, that in the Middle Ages work of the hands and of the intellect was wholly at the service of the faith. Thus it is not so much the rationality of the Renaissance which is found objectionable as the independence of that rationality. Laplace's "I have no need of that hypothesis" is a statement originating in a Renaissance attitude. Even though there is no necessary conflict between such a statement and personal piety (at least no conflict was felt to be implied at the time) it asserts the work of the mind as independent of prior assumptions derived from the formal statements of the faith. This has always been disquieting to those whose faith has been closely dependent on ecclesiastical institutions.

It would not be fitting at this place to undertake a full scale theological justification of the use of the intellect independent of prior assumptions and exercised on the evidence and the logical structure of the method alone. The possibility of such a defense is assumed and is implicit in the course of the argument. It is more fitting, however, to touch on the theoretical theology only incidentally and undertake the defense by means of the evidence of the arts, since it is essential to see the arts developing in their own theological right and not by sufferance of formal or systematic theology. Thus the proof requires the statement of the assumption, the description of the course of development which, even in its independence, can serve the purposes of the Christian faith (if not always the formal Christian community), and finally show that this enterprise issues in works which manifest some distinctive quality of Christian art.

It must be said, then, that the theological enterprise is more than the work of formal or systematic theologians and does not always serve the overt interests of the institutional church or start with the doctrinal assumptions of the institutional church. It is not only possible but essential for the health of theology that it be conducted through the total work of the mind and the creativity of man and not simply through verbal and conceptual statement. It is of the essence of the Christian faith that it transforms the total human experience and must find its expression in the total human experience. This means, further, that the theological problem can be worked out in other forms and in other terms than the purely verbal, that the essential theological dialogue involves the whole work of man. Theology is not given to man (what God gives to man are the acts of redemption and the grace of faith to apprehend those acts). Rather theology emerges constantly fresh from the dialogue which grows out of the essential conditions of the human experience. Theology is nothing if it is not constantly renewed out of the shifting condition of man and since the understanding of his condition is never complete in man but only partial and changing, theology is dialogue or it is a rigidly dead system. And in a dialogue both terms are alive, both terms are essential to the dialectic out of which emerges the sense of truth that lies beyond the changing apprehensions of man.

Thus the validation of the Renaissance as part of the Christian experience requires a recognition of the dialogue with the period which preceded it and also involves a recognition that what it did was a dialogue within itself. It is possible to see even those elements of the Renaissance which most strongly asserted their independence of the church or their opposition to the church as fundamentally involved in the essential work of the church. This cannot be assumed out of simple generosity of spirit but must be demonstrated in terms of a genuine dialogue which issues in a theologically valid position.

The dialogue with the period that preceded the Renaissance established the conditions of its development. The whole concept of periods in cultural history is a debatable one. There are qualified persons who deny that history ever divides itself into such compartments, which appear to exist only for the convenience of the historian. Certainly the process is far more intricate than the simplifications of historical writing often indicate, with whole combinations of overlappings, survivals, anticipations blurring any dividing line that might be set up. Nevertheless, there are differences and these differences are important.

A stylistic period (leaving aside the Spenglerian attempt to relate all aspects of a period to a single style) is defined by its primary concerns and works itself out by the solution and the statement and consequences of those common concerns. Of these elements of periods perhaps the greatest attention has been given to the first two: the statement of the central and defining concern of problem and its working out to the classic solution. Nearly every period of study has suffered from the tendency among historians to see only this part of the development and to treat the remainder as a mannerist decline, a slackening of energy, or a failure of nerve. This is bad history and, what is more to the point, it is bad theology. In part this is so because preoccupation with one body of evidence to the point of rejecting another eliminates much that is important in human history.

It is so in part because the one grows logically and inevitably out of the other and thus reveals characteristics of the earlier stage which would not otherwise be so evident. Any style bears the burden of responsibility for what grows out of it.

The general understanding of the Gothic period as the Age of Faith is not wholly wrong for the classic Gothic statement. It is perhaps not too great an oversimplification to say that in any period of Christian art one concern dominates even though others are always present. If this is the case, the classic Gothic style is above all the period of awareness of the Incarnation. God had seen fit to enter the material world. The material of the world was irradiated with the glory of God and it was the true service of man to celebrate the glory of God in the material of his art. Thus Gothic art soars, not just in the conventional romantic reference to the architecture (not all of which soars to quite that degree) but in the sense of ascending with the sense of the glory of God and the radiance of the world. All elements of Gothic religious art contribute to this sense of the radiance of the incarnate God and the world which contained that Incarnation. The supreme serenity of the sculpture patiently fixed to the cathedral, giving individuality to the impersonality of the stone, the harmonious verticality of the architecture, and the perfect harmony of the colors in the glass all establish this radiance.

It is necessary to feel this statement in order to feel what follows. There is no real tragedy in the classic Gothic. Man had emerged from the often nightmarish world of the earlier Romanesque style into the radiance of God's peace. Yet tragedy is of the substance of the human experience, no less in the medieval period than in any other. The moment of harmony was short-lived as the "classic" balance always is. The sense of the tragic thrust itself into the consciousness of the artist. Yet his artistic instrument was not equipped for the deeply rational exploration of tragedy or the sensitively self-conscious statement of it which is a part of still other styles. His style could only respond expressively. This response took different forms, the frivolous, if delightful, decoration of late Gothic court art, for example, or the flamboyant mannerism of much late Gothic architecture and decoration. Most relevant to these concerns is the passionate, almost Fig. 39 hysterical, obsession with death and suffering which is found in so much late Gothic painting and sculpture. These are the expressions of outraged innocence, offended naïveté and are a coherent part of the Gothic style as such and an outgrowth of its fundamental attitudes.

There is more to the medieval period than its side of the dialogue with the later development, yet this suggests the contribution made by the precursors of the Renaissance to the dialogue out of which the Renaissance arose. These precursors turned to asceticism, to the symbolic, the other worldly, the denial of the earthly. The radiance of matter transformed by the Incarnation became befouled by the sense of sin and evil which was considered to lie behind the tragic suffering of a society riven by war and plague. Works of singular loveliness were made by men who could submit themselves to this arduous human discipline. But creativity had become an unworthy thing, the world was an offense and a burden, piety was defined through the sense of death and tragedy.

It was the responsibility and the privilege of the Renaissance to recover the humanity of man.

This is a generalization and historical writing is too full of generalizations which do not endure the light of detailed criticism. Men there were in the Middle Ages and the humanity of man is part of the experience of man, which is not restricted to time or place or a particular religion. But whatever qualifications must be made for the fullest picture of the Middle Ages it is nonetheless true that they are qualifications to a main line of development. There is a difference between medieval and Renaissance and this difference is measured in part by the recovery of the sense of the distinctive humanness of man as man. This humanity of man was not felt as a dogma illustrated by art for it extends beyond the art work itself. The artist himself became distinctively human in a way which differed from the position of his predecessors. The work of the artist became a work existing for its own good and because the making of a work of art was a good thing in itself.

Thus the recovery of the humanity of man in the painting and the humanity of the painter is paralleled by the recovery of the sense of the humanity of the Christ. Christ was no longer simply the tortured symbol of redemption or the triumphant symbol of divine rule. The sense of his full humanity became truly a part of Christian art.

It would not, of course, be true to say that this process of dialectic recovery was carried on without the payment of a heavy price nor can it be said that the Renaissance was purely Christian in contrast to the older fashion of stigmatizing it as purely secular and pagan. No human enterprise is without fault. The recovery of the humanity of man required seeing man as he is, as a man, neither a theological fact nor an element of an institution. This meant that the temptation of the Renaissance was to the exaggeration of man. The Renaissance as a historical phenomenon and an artistic style is marked by the most intense development of the autonomous individual ever seen. That this is not Christian (since the Christian faith rests on the interdependence of men in charity and humility) is a truism. Yet it is a price which, in the pain of history, had to be paid for the recovery of that which is truly Christian: the integrity of man in the world.

The predominant emphasis of the Renaissance is on the "arts of the image," for it was the cool rationality of their artistic instruments which enabled them to accomplish what they did. But the purpose of their art puts it into the area of the arts of creation, for the celebration of the existence of the world and all that is in it was the principal purpose of their work. Man makes no development without exaggeration and it is not at all surprising that the peculiar interest of the Renaissance should have been carried forward beyond the bounds of orthodoxy. On the other hand nothing human is bought without a price and this price had to be paid in the tragic dialectic of history. The Renaissance is not all the Christian vision of man. But the Christian image of man is a poor and impoverished thing without the achievement of the Renaissance.

The sense of the humanness of man is a part of the doctrine of the Incarnation. Medieval art celebrated the Incarnation with an innocent delight. Renaissance art pursues the awareness of the Incarnation with a sense of its full human implications. It is a touching thing when the medieval sense of delight is combined with Renaissance rationality (in the work of Fra Angelico, for example), but generally Renaissance art moves past even informed innocence into a more self-conscious rationality. And this rationality led them to see the consequences of the Incarnation: that the world as the world is not fallen and evil but proceeds from the hand of God; that man is created in the image of God; that Christ is the fulfillment of humanity. This led them to the abuse of a kind of nature mysticism; the abuse of making man divine; the abuse of making Christ only human. This is the price that had to be paid for what they had to accomplish.

These movements, these ideas – visual ideas – are found all through the Renaissance, although the internal logic of the process means that the manifestations of the principles at the end of the Renaissance differ significantly from those at the beginning. In the creator, or anticipator, of the Renaissance style, Giotto, there is fully present the sense of the humanness of man engaged in a moral existence in a real world. Giotto's figures have weight and solidity, they move with an organized muscular existence, they occupy three-dimensional space, they act in the morality of human

Fig. 11

drama with their fellows. To the critic, perhaps the most important thing to say about Giotto is that he has with fullest success translated these into the language of the art work, and the stately rhythms of his forms give artistic reality to what might otherwise have been merely verbal ideas. Giotto's theological principles are stated in the language of art, not in the verbal concepts of the systematic theologians.

It was Masaccio's responsibility to work out the implications of Giotto's style and bring it into the mainstream of the Renaissance (for a variety of reasons Giotto's immediate successors turned back from his contributions). The space in Masaccio becomes deeper, the action of the figures freer. Very little of the greater depth of the painting is actually used for the action portrayed and the figures have much the same gravity of bearing and deliberation of movement which were so much a part of Giotto's style. Yet the enlargement of the space does not reduce man proportionately (as it does in some seventeenth-century landscapes) but enhances the dignity, which is almost grandeur, of the human figure.   Fig. 9

It is a quality held in common by Masaccio and Giotto that their paintings are not excuses for abstract studies (which is hardly likely to happen at this time) nor simply narratives, but statements of the moral drama in terms of the abstract structure of the painting. In every case the painting grows out of the central core of the act, all motion or gesture in the painting is immersed in the slow, steady, powerful rhythms across the surface which give stability and meaning to the act.

In this pairing of effects neither element is more central to the whole thought than the other. If the Renaissance is characterized by "the discovery of the world and of man," it is only at a late stage, if ever, that it can be said they saw the two elements separately. Drama is human and space is natural but the space becomes an instrument in the dramatic conflict and the drama becomes a means for establishing and controlling space. Later in the Renaissance the center of gravity of the artist's interest seems to shift toward one or the other and almost invariably when this happens the resulting art is less than completely satisfactory. The interest in drama degenerates into anecdote when the firmness of space construction is no longer felt as essential to the action. In Ghirlandaio, the absence of any serious control of spatial effects (which are handled with the technical proficiency of a well-trained student) either accompanies or causes the loss of any serious sense of the moral dimension of the action portrayed and the action becomes simply entertaining narrative.   Fig. 15

On the other hand, interest in space alone tends to move into experimentation without human or moral impact. The term "degenerates" is not quite so appropriate. The process is one that often has the most serious professional purpose and the resulting constructions are often of the greatest importance in the process of development. There is difficulty in making this judgment, for the space constructions of the fifteenth century are peculiarly congenial to the eye of twentieth-century man conditioned by the development of cubism. Yet their aim is not the same as the cubist painters nor does their work have the same significance in the analysis as the cubists do. Within the terms established by their own day, not the twentieth century, the loss or absence of the dramatic seems to carry with it the loss of the creative moral center of the work, that point from which the real vitality of the work seems to grow. So these experiments remain an important part of the development of the language of Renaissance art, yet still slightly apart from the main line of concern.

The question of cause in any historical process is the question that is most difficult of all to answer. It would be too much to say categorically that the distinctive quality of the Christian faith made the development of the Renaissance possible or caused it in any way. Some find the motives for much of the Renaissance development in St. Francis but this is by no means universally held as the source and mainspring of Renaissance spiritual and intellectual development. A Christian critic, above all, ought not to reduce Christianity to one of the competitors in the arena of historical study. The Renaissance has suffered enough from such claims and counterclaims. It remains, then, to study the results, to see when and in what way the general process is either compatible with the Christian faith or contributes significantly to it.

It cannot and must not be asserted that the process of development so lightly sketched above is Christian in any single sense or developed by Christian artists or for Christian purposes. Much of the development takes place for wholly professional motives, without overtly religious purposes and is constantly branching off into streams that move away from the concerns of this study. It would be false to attempt to baptize all this work. At the same time the very fact of the appearance of this type of work is theologically of the greatest significance. A fully developed "theology for work" is not possible here but one is clearly adumbrated in the work of these men. The independent mind working solely on the basis of the evidence and according to methods which appear to the man himself (with all his chronological limitations) to be most appropriate to the evidence at hand; this is what the Renaissance brought most actively into the mainstream of modern thought and this is a fundamental ingredient of the Renaissance rediscovery of man. Only a mind incorrigibly devoted to ecclesiasticism can object to this. This independence of mind was essential to the full humanity of man and the recovery of man's humanity was not an act of rebellion against the omnipotence of God but an act of respect for the integrity of God's creation.

If Giotto and Masaccio set the tone and establish the basic principles for so much of the Renaissance development, that development is not always in their direct tradition. The intensity of the moral drama in these two men and the artistic power to state this drama in visual forms is not granted to every man and many of their followers fell off into the byways. There was one man, however, the most austere of the Renaissance painters, who brought to fulfillment all they had earlier done: Piero della Francesca.

The consequences of the work of Giotto in the high Renaissance are yet to be observed. So far the discussion remains within the fifteenth century. Piero is the crown of the main effort of the fifteenth century in Italy.

Piero's work poses the question of a Christian style with peculiar intensity. There has been in recent years an increasingly strong movement to identify Christian style as the existential engagement with the tragedy and the vitalities of life. Of this there is nothing in Piero and so strict a reading of Christian making would have to exclude him. Much in his work does not yield to easy rejection, and this is the dimension he inherited from Giotto and Masaccio and then transformed.

In Piero the rhythm has become more than a tool. It has become the major element in the work, quieting the drama to absolute stillness, circling in on itself so the fulfillment of the work is within its own structure. It is no accident that Piero finished his career as a mathematician, for the rhythm is not dramatic or existential but mathematical.

On these grounds it may appear improper to present him as the heir of Giotto, to whom the moral drama was the purpose of art. Yet at the center of Piero's work there is no contradiction, despite the impression he has so often given. It is the lesser men who develop one element only of their predecessor's work, eliminating all which gives richness and variety to a style. Piero is not a lesser man.

In Piero's work the drama has not been eliminated in favor of the rhythmical geometry. Rather he has refined the drama to its essence and sees the work in terms of the essence of his drama. There is no hint of the anecdotal in Piero, only the concentration on the essence of the human situation and the presentation of essence in terms unmarred by any action or movement. It is the most precise statement of pure humanity in all art.

Fig. 17   Perhaps the clearest illustration of this interpretation is to be found in the most enigmatic of all his paintings, "The Flagellation." In this painting there is no drama, despite the representation of the subject, and no reference for the curious juxtaposition of the scene of three men related to Christ and the soldiers. Historians dispute the interpretation and where the specialists cannot agree, others would do well to seek their sense of the picture in something other than its historical allusion. Possibly a look into the mind of the artist would find an explanation but it is perhaps healthier that it should be as it is. It is true that many works of art can be explained by their reference to things outside themselves, the story or the event they illustrate. Yet both the making and the reading of such an object is easily done and cheaply bought. The loss of the explanation or overt reference – if in fact there ever was one – makes possible with this painting what is too seldom done in painting – the understanding of the thing in itself. Thus the only way to take hold of the painting at all is in terms of its existence as pure painting.

The painting, then, is a puzzle only because it refuses to open itself to the usual instruments of art historical research. When seen for what it is, pure painting, its reference becomes more apparent. Pure painting is a term more usual in application to the abstractions of the twentieth century where there is no subject reference at all. Nevertheless, it is relevant to Piero's work for his genius lay in reducing not only the forms and the rhythms to pure expression but the human reference as well. Most probably the picture represents the young Count of Urbino flanked by the treacherous advisors furnished him by the despot, Sigismondo Malatesta. As such it might be a memento or a votive offering from the Count's successor. Other explanations have been suggested. It does not matter. Piero only starts with something specific and concrete. He does not rest until he has pursued the event or the relation to the essence of its meaning. Just as Giotto isolated the essential moral dimension of the narrative which concerned him and then bent every means to the attainment of a structure which could contain that dimension, so Piero isolates the essential nature of a relationship and embodies it in a structure.

The disturbing thing about Piero's achievement is that his art is not so decisively moral as Giotto's. In this the Renaissance generally differs from much which went both before and after, and it is, perhaps, the dim awareness of this which causes much of the discontent with Renaissance religion. It should not be necessary to say that morality is a great deal more than a code of conduct or a set of rules to distinguish between right and wrong. It is rather the fundamental disposition of the soul from which conduct proceeds. It presupposes an order of things to which man can conform himself. Obviously the awareness of the existence of such an order will encourage certain kinds of minds to assume the possibility of codification but true morality goes far deeper than any such code can ever reach. Giotto's work cannot be understood apart from the moral structure which lies behind it. This moral structure is deeply Christian, dependent as it is on love, compassion, humility, as well as on the awareness of all those emotions which are by nature part of man's being. To say, as many have said, that they could look for hours at Giotto's paintings being aware only of the fineness of his formal language without noting the subject is simply to misread Giotto's intentions and misunderstand his work. The moral order, which Giotto saw with subtlety and precision and yet with the directness and passion of a child, is the very substance of his achievement.

No such moral order can be detected in Piero's work. His world is a world beyond the awareness of normal human drama. His figures are the quintessence of Renaissance individualism. They are wholly self-contained, realizing their own action and its reference alone. It is as though man had passed beyond the stage of morality, either for it or against it, and into a realm where only his own humanity counted, and this humanity developed to its fullest.

Piero was one of the most deeply Christian of all painters, and the fulfillment of this aspect of Renaissance Christianity in art. Here he becomes the fulfillment and final statement of Renaissance humanism. Never before or since in man's art has there been so clear a statement of the essence of man in a world where only his will and his nature are the code of his living.

To make of such an art and such assertion a Christian thing is no simple or obvious accomplishment. Piero had no thought to judge the world he lived in or remake it but to do with it what an artist could. "The Flagellation" is not a pure statement of his Christian faith for his intention was different. But the elements of his Christian language are there. His record of Renaissance humanism is not simply a record. It is that humanism stripped to its unadorned and unfalsified essence and embedded in the purest of all painting styles. The anecdote does not matter. The essence of man's agony, human and divine, is presented as though in a crystal, the one assertively forward in the consciousness of the spectator, the other back out of history and time at the end of one of the most perfectly proportioned spaces ever painted. The transfiguration of tragedy takes place not in drama or rhetoric but in space and color, a pure harmony of each which transcends earthly experience.

Fig. 1   The purest statement of Piero's faith is his "Resurrection." Here there is no need for allusion to drama or tragedy but only pure presentation. Of all the subjects in Christian iconography the Resurrection is the one most in harmony with the essential nature of Piero's style, for it is of the essence of the Resurrection that it be pure presentation. The Resurrection has been represented in other manners – see for example, Michelangelo's great drawing – but many artists of different temperament have found it necessary to resort to pure presentation in order to communicate the

Fig. 4   Resurrection. Grünewald, in all stylistic qualities vastly different from Piero, made his painting of the Resurrection a pure manifestation. The figure floats weightless in the air as Piero would not have seen it and the primary instrument of his means is light and brilliance of color. In Piero, the color is equally important in the coolness of its harmony but his principal instrument is space and the purity of his geometric rhythms. Every element of grace and serenity which is to be felt in the idea of Christ is summed up in this figure.

It is of the nature of Christian art that there is no one single way of representing any of its subjects; there is no uniquely "Christian style." This is true of Grünewald as much as of Piero. Grünewald's expressionism is one of the indispensable aspects of the Christian spirit in art. It is not all of art. In Grünewald's painting the interpretation points to the triumph over Good Friday. The body, which in the crucifixion panels was heavy, anguished, torn, and green, has become all light, transfigured into color and weightlessness. It has overcome the flesh to the point where, were it not for the panels of the crucifixion, it would be heretical. The emphasis is still, however, on the rise of Christ out of darkness and night. In Piero, the Resurrection has been accomplished, all that is not Christ has been destroyed or silenced, there is no more drama and no more suffering, only the statement of the fulfillment of the purpose of God. This is not the triumph over Good Friday but the fulfillment of Easter morning. The earth, itself symbolizing the change from winter to spring, has been transfigured by Piero's color and light and provides the setting for the body of Christ which dominates the whole painting and the whole imagination of men who see the painting.

Thus the indifference of Piero to the moral drama which so concerned Giotto and Masaccio is not the indifference of the autonomous man asserting his right to the control over his own destiny according to his own will. It is rather the transfiguration of morality, superseding it by the new order which is so crystalline in its purity that it can stand as symbol for the peace of God.

The structures that Piero extracted from Giotto's work and brought to completion did not end with him, but never again did this structural system perfectly embody so sensitive a Christian vision. It flowered again in Raphael, who found such harmony of space in the action of his figures and produced what is perhaps the finest statement of the dignity and glory of the human body outside the art of fifth-century Greece. He did this in terms not at all irrelevant to the Christian ideal which still so fully informed society. The harmonious humanity of his figures is handled with such grace and dignity that they communicate the sweetness of an earth newly seen. But this gentle personality was torn too much by contradictory influences. He was constantly seeking a dramatic expression not congenial to his style and therefore many of his Madonnas degenerate into aimless sentimentality. There are others of the high Renaissance who grasp this sense of harmonious dignity and it is one of art's grand styles. But they work without the sense of drama transformed which gives to Piero's work its most meaningful tensions.

It perhaps would accent the real nature of Piero's achievement if it is compared with others who have a comparable tension of presentation. There is nowhere else in the Renaissance any parallel to Piero's stillness and quiet. The main stream of Renaissance art is, rather, intensely dramatic. There are, however, works which match his tension in terms of the inner psychology of the figures and the turning inward, the coiling inward of the formal structure. Such a work, for example, is Verrocchio's silver relief for the cathedral showing the beheading of John the Baptist. Such a relief is not a narrative since the narrative is simply one element in it. It presents, rather, images of painful sensuality or appalling ferocity and presents them for no narrative purpose whatsoever but simply for their own presentational value. They simply exist, outside morality, developing one or another

Fig. 14

Fig. 16

Fig. 24

aspect of human psychology to the most intense possible attitude, stated in forms of exquisite craftsmanship. Yet, since the artist sees them in this isolation there is no restraint on the expression of what they are. In the work of Piero there is always the controlling harmony of light, color, and geometry. Behind the stillness there lies the tension of man's passion and man's tragedy. Yet this dimension of the tension is in the past, it is transfigured but never lost. The power of tragedy is so great that only the most powerful structure can control it and Piero's art is a search for that structure. Thus Piero's art never shows the naïve pleasure in the world which characterizes certain late medieval paintings. It cannot be classified under the category of the arts of creation for there is too much awareness of the tragedy which is a part of the human experience. Much of his work is given over to an exploration of the geometrical order underlying the dynamics of human experience and therefore belongs as a part of the arts of man in the image of God. But Piero's Resurrection is the vision of the earth redeemed.

In the understanding of the expression of the Christian spirit in the Renaissance, Piero's work represents a major tradition and one which has been unduly neglected both as an element in Renaissance spirituality and in its own right as a part of the Christian's awareness of the order of things. It is not, however, the only part of the work of the Renaissance artist. It is in fact so austere a style, requiring so ascetic a discipline, that few people can attain it in anything like the same purity. A more general concern of the Renaissance artist, with Giotto again the great forerunner, was the human drama, the drama of human emotion and relation.

The interpretation of this type of art in the context of this study is both more difficult and easier than the interpretation of Piero's. It is easier because its drama brings it into the context of the more customary Christian attitudes toward the nature of things. The Christian sense of the moral order can more easily handle the shape of drama than the shape of space, which is less amenable to the discipline of concepts formed out of the interchange of normal human relation. Constructivist art (and, while it is stretching the term, Piero's art can be described in part by that peculiarly twentieth-century term) is more metaphysical than dramatic, and the interpretation of it has all the dangers which accompany the attempt to make the Christian faith more dependent on some one metaphysic rather than another. This difficulty becomes particularly acute in the twentieth century when constructivism is divorced from all human reference, and is overcome in the interpretation of Piero only because he remains a man of the fifteenth century and not the twentieth. His constructivism is rooted in his sense of the drama and is designed to extract from drama, not the narrative and certainly not the anecdote, but the essence of the relation which makes the drama significant.

The interpretation of the dramatic art of the Renaissance presents certain difficulties, however, which were not present in the interpretation of Piero's art. A constructivist art is outside the normal work of the human mind and is, therefore, difficult to grasp. But, once apprehended, it states its fundamental being with such clarity, such completeness, such wholeness that it can be fully grasped, entire and immediately. On the other hand the very incursion of the other style into the murky and uncertain realm of human relations makes the picture diffuse and complex. The proper understanding of these relations has given rise to complex systems of casuistry and still there is no generally acceptable answer. This is the case with human conduct as such and the statement of that conduct and the relations arising out of it in literature. Both the actual events and the literary events, however, change in the course of development and this is a singular advantage for the interpreter. The whole event can be seen, from beginning to end, and the direction, pace, and quality of its movement can be appraised as a vital ingredient, if not the most important ingredient, in the whole structure. The visual arts, even in their serial forms, are incorrigibly presentational. One moment and one moment only out of the dramatic action can be chosen and the direction of that moment can only be suggested, never fully described. The choice of the moment to be used is relevant but not nearly so clear as the shape given to an action by the dramatist. The work of art, no matter how quiet, has its own movement and the rhythms which of necessity accompany that movement, but these are internal rhythms which move within the language of form, not the language of common morality.

Thus it develops that the interpretation of the quality and character of a dramatic art cannot rest on the understanding of the drama alone but must revert to the problem which now appears to be fundamental both to dramatic and constructivist art: the uniqueness of the language of visual forms. At the same time it must be reasserted that this conclusion does not change the fact that the dramatic relation is one of the vital ingredients of the painting and the work cannot be fully understood without the adequate grasp of the drama. The rhythms, the structure which all art must share

with constructivism if it is to be art and not illustration, remain the primary
locus of the analysis.

The strength of Giotto's achievement in the convincing portrayal and
analysis of the structure of the human drama lies less in action or in character
than in gesture. Gesture is a complex word in criticism as it must include
both that which is normally referred to as gesture, the action of the limbs
and the attitude of the body, and the attitude and disposition, the emotional
or expressive quality of any object or element in the work. It can with
safety, however, be used with its more restricted designation in the study
of Giotto, for he excels as a master of gesture and of the translation of
expressive action into the language of art. Gesture is only in part representative of dramatic action and more directly reflects that inward disposition
of the soul which is the proper definition of morality. If, then, it can be
taken for granted or demonstrated that Giotto's work contains an effective
use of this gesture within the strictly artistic structure of the work of art,
there would be established a more immediate and more apparent relation
between the whole body of his work and the Christian interpretation of
life. This is in marked contrast to the style of pure space, the other great
stream of Renaissance style.

The demonstration of Giotto's singular sensitivity to gesture is perhaps –
or certainly? – conducted better through the visual materials directly
rather than by verbal account, for it is a matter to be grasped most immediately. It would be too much to say that he covers the full range of human
feeling and their expression in human action but he would come as close
to it as any single artist. This comprehensiveness marks him, for some
historians, as the major figure of the Renaissance, since the working out of
the psychological insights first stated by Giotto was a major preoccupation
of the significant Renaissance artists.

Giotto's themes are exclusively those of the Christian story. Thus his
gesture and his dramatic action are worked out in the context of the
Christian history. This would not be enough to insure the Christian
quality of his work were it not for the gestures themselves. But in these
gestures Giotto sets forth an image of man profoundly informed by the
Christian faith. There is no hero except Christ. There is no grandeur or
dignity except under the reflection of Christ. There is the full range of
emotions which make up an awareness of the total character of man,
anguish, fear, shame, ecstasy, compassion, love, tenderness, longing. There
is no idealization involved in his view of man and this willingness to see

all of humanity is a characteristic of his work hard to imagine outside the Christian view of man.

Such a position is both difficult to assume and dangerous for it is seriously damaging to Christianity to assume it gives to its adherents special wisdom which does not belong to non-Christians. The purposes of this study would not, in fact, be achieved if it did not make clear the degree and the kind of debt owed by Christians to the work of those who have worked outside the Christian faith. Yet the nature of Christianity is such that certain things are possible in the light of the Christian faith which are not possible under any other conditions, or possible only under such conditions that it might be said the person is almost convinced.

This characteristic of Christianity arises from the fact that the major spiritual investment of the Christian, alone among men, is not in himself but in the act of another. To secure his own confidence or hope he does not have to picture himself other than he is and should, in fact, see himself complete. The Greek can acknowledge himself to be an offender against the will of the gods and even see a certain grandeur in the offense. Only the Christian can acknowledge that he is silly or trivial.

There is in Giotto the fullest possible sense of ordinary humanity in all its dimensions and in the context – only in the context – of the redemptive act of Christ. The formal language in which this interpretation of man is presented is well adjusted to the subject. Giotto has a predilection for noble, dignified figures but a trivial or ignorant or stupid person in one of his stories will be unbalanced or unsteady. Yet the fundamental rhythms of his paintings are steady, quiet, firm, and clear. A painting by Giotto performs its function with dignity and grace, with no false note or superfluous touch. The balance is alive but firm. The color harmonies are deep without being somber. All the drama, all the humanity of Giotto occurs in a world of deep serenity, majestic calm.

There were those among the many who learned from Giotto who could see only the touch of ordinary life in his work and so there stems from him the anecdotes which are a constant element in fifteenth-century painting. These are usually charming, often decorative, and occasionally rise to the level of an art of real rhythmic vitality. Yet Giotto's humanity without Giotto's depth of understanding of the context in which humanity stands can be little more than anecdotal and the anecdotes of the fifteenth century are the direct ancestors of the sentimental illustrationism which has been the plague of the church's making for many years.

It is not surprising that this should be so. Giotto's achievement depends on a degree of artistic and intellectual integrity and perception that is granted to very few people. Fortunately there were others.

Masaccio was the only one who sought a balance between drama, character and structure which is comparable to Giotto's. Piero shifted the center of gravity to the side of structure and rhythmic harmony. The other giant of the fifteenth century, Donatello, shifted the center of gravity toward drama and created perhaps the most intensely dramatic art of the Renaissance.

Just as the emphasis on drama in Giotto cannot be understood apart from the moral order out of which he developed his art, so the drama in Donatello's art cannot be understood apart from his particular moral vision. A consciousness of this moral vision must not, however, be seen as something independent which shines through the work of art. That would not only violate the essentials of the theory here presented (a doctrinaire judgment) but would violate the substance of Donatello's structural achievement. It is not only that the moral vision is incorporated into the formal structure of his work in a distinctive fashion but that the moral style of his work was generated in a distinctively personal fashion and a fashion that is very important in the understanding of the Renaissance achievement.

What little is known of Donatello's personality outside his art would indicate that he was a rather gentle, friendly man, generous to his friends and altogether rather naive. Nothing of his personality dominates his art. For all the passionate drama that characterizes his work from beginning to end, his is pre-eminently a rational style, passion and drama controlled to a rationally chosen end. In this he is fully worthy of his great contemporaries, Brunelleschi and Masaccio.

This is nowhere more clearly seen than in his use of his sources in past styles. Influences are necessarily a consistent element in all art history, so much so that André Malraux has said that an artist owes more to past art than he does to the study of nature. With Donatello it is more than a matter of influence, it is a matter of his using past styles as a source for his work. It is dramatically fascinating in itself to see a great creative mind moving sensitively over the body of material available to him and taking from it, with precision, what he wanted and needed. Much is assumed in this kind of description; it is obviously impossible to know precisely the nature of his attitude or work. But the results would appear to bear out the description. Donatello had no hesitation at all in making explicit allusion to the models he studied and at the same time, with few exceptions, these models are fully incorporated into his own work in his own terms.

The major influences on his work were classical sculpture (available to him primarily in the form of rather ordinary and even debased Roman works) and the late Gothic sculpture of Giovanni Pisano. The Pisano influence is speculative and is included here as a guess on the basis of stylistic analysis; it might represent no more than a common stylistic attitude within a reasonably common stylistic milieu. The classical influence, however, is clear, easily documented, and extensive, ranging as it does throughout his career.

This is an interesting art historical bypath but none the less a bypath for the purposes of this analysis. The manner of his use of these sources is not incidental. Giovanni's work is for the most part intensely dramatic, carrying out one medieval attitude in this sense. It is also medieval in another sense – it is structurally architectural rather than anatomical. The figures act dramatically but they do not live independently.

Roman sculpture, and the classical idea still manifest in the rather ordinary, routine Roman work Donatello knew, is necessarily more diverse but the common element which Donatello extracted was the consciousness of human anatomy, the ability to construct an anatomically coherent form. Donatello used Roman sculpture for other purposes not germane to this discussion. This one is germane for, by means of this study, he could weld the medieval idea of the figure in relation to the classical idea of a coherent anatomy. The result was perhaps the most powerful sense of an existing individual yet seen in art. He freed the figure from architecture and thus freed the figure into individuality.

The manner is, perhaps, as important as the result, for the manner was, above all, rational. Donatello's work is not in the least an adaptation of the classical nor does it contain unabsorbed elements. He analyzed with precision to determine what he wanted and with comparable precision welded what he selected into his own work: the rational control of technique to a chosen end. This chosen end was the realization of the full humanity of his figures as feeling, acting subjects in all the fullness of their individuality.

Donatello, in his preoccupation with the dramatic, moved away from the solemn hieratic dignity of Giotto and Masaccio and consequently he shares with Piero the distinction of creating the most significant body of secular art in the Renaissance. Piero's portraits of Sigismondo Malatesta   Fig. 21

Fig. 23 and Frederigo da Montefeltro and Donatello's Gattamelata are indispensable documentation of one of the most essential aspects of Renaissance political and social thought. These works were possible, not simply because of Christianity (although Christianity was involved) but because of the whole process of emancipation of man's mind which developed during the Renaissance. Other works of Donatello, as well, manifest the secular humanism of the Renaissance. Many of his narrative reliefs, for example, portray a sacred event, but emphasize more the event than the sacredness of it. The act takes place and the whole human comedy develops around the event in focused concentration on it. Furthermore, there is in his work a strong element of the moral ambiguity of the Renaissance, in his famous bronze David and his innumerable *putti*.

These latter are not works of "Christian" art even though done by a man who created works of Christian art from the beginning to the end of his career. To attempt to baptize all art, created in whatever independence of mind and spirit, is to commit an offense against history and human personality. As a movement of the human spirit, the Renaissance set itself the task of exploring certain aspects of the human personality and of power. This exploration depended entirely on the personality and the power of the artist and was conducted without conscious reference to any assumptions, particularly principles deduced from theological assertions, and without conscious reference to any religious purpose. The integrity of the enterprise depended on this independence and could not have been attained without it. Furthermore, for all the price which was paid, the work done by this secular Renaissance was a good work. If part of the purpose of Christianity is the fulfillment of man, then part of that work is owed to the Renaissance which was enabled, by its independence, to contribute much to the understanding of the nature of man which has to be fulfilled. In this enterprise, Donatello had a major place. He went a long way toward the definition of drama in art, the passionate interaction of human will and purpose.

Thus, if Piero can be said to anticipate the modern concern with structural geometry, Donatello is almost equally modern, almost equally able to communicate the expressionistic reality of the inner life of man. Donatello's technique was rational but his art is more comprehensive, for his is the rational and passionate intellect. His work is in good part the statement of the wholeness of isolated man (thought to be a modern insight) ravaged by time, act, and passion. The vision of man which informs his art is a fusion of Hellenism and Hebraism, the intelligent vision informed by prophetic passion – which is a kind of definition of Christianity. This work culminates in his pulpits.

Fig. 2

As did Michelangelo after him, Donatello sums up in himself the course of the development of Christian thought in the Renaissance. His earliest works of significance were the prophets for the campanile, passionate individualists seemingly consumed by the intensity of the message within them. Just as these figures thrust forward from the architecture which supports them and provides their spatial context, so the major part of the work of his middle period deals with the passionate action of the human drama. In his final period, particularly in his "Magdalene" and the pulpits for San Lorenzo, the human drama becomes inseparable from the Christian tragedy and the individualism which the Renaissance, and Donatello in it, so strongly developed now brought almost unparalleled vividness and sensitivity to the vision of the redemptive sacrifice. The importance of this work in the understanding of the Christian ordering of things is a prime example of the significance of the independent "secular" research into the meaning of mankind which lies behind the style of the pulpits. This work is one of the great possessions of the church and a theological document of major importance.

Fig. 38

The development which Donatello illustrates so vividly is almost exactly paralleled by other great Renaissance figures, Botticelli, for example, and the greatest of them all, Michelangelo. Botticelli's art, in good part, represents the quintessence of Renaissance secularism, a sophisticated court art, hovering in a dimly defined area between an innocent delight in the glory of things and a thin-blooded sensuality toyed with in the area of human indulgence, not analyzed in the power of man's desire to know. But Botticelli's conversion was a real thing and his late work contains an authentic vision of Christian meanings.

Michelangelo's development, because it was a part of the intensity of his personality, is more dramatic and better known. He, too, recapitulated the spiritual history of the Renaissance, from the powerful humanism of his early works, such as the "David," to the tremendous essays in frustration and despair as seen in the Medici Chapel, to the final vision of the redemptive tragedy in his last works. This is one of the most important and most significant documents in the whole history of man's theological thinking in visual forms.

One of the distinctive Renaissance problems comes to a focus in Michelangelo's work and has a good deal to say for this argument. An argument is not a history and the evidence chosen to support an argument is necessarily selective and partial. A general account of Neo-Platonism in Renaissance thought or art belongs to a general account of the Renaissance. It does intersect with this argument for it is undoubtedly true that, to Michelangelo and to others, Neo-Platonism as a vision of the order of the world became an ordering principle. There is always among the artists as well as the philosophers, an air of the artificial about this attempt, but even – perhaps particularly – the artificiality has significance for this argument.

Almost any philosophical system can influence the kind of fundamental attitude toward the world and the things in it which are the primary concerns of this study. Similarly almost any philosophical system, even some very foolish ones, can provide subject matter and programs for valid works of art. Difficulty arises only when an artist allows his imagination and his sensibility to be dominated by philosophical definitions rather than growing and working according to their own character. By its nature, Neo-Platonism (which is an overly complicated but certainly not a foolish account of reality) lends itself particularly well and with particular dangers to the uses of artists.

Leaving aside the definitional subtleties not germane to this study the essential principle of Neo-Platonism in its impingement on the work of Michelangelo is the continuum it establishes between the natural object, the work of art dependent on the natural object, and the divine. The artists of the northern Renaissance could hold to such a continuum by a simpler theology: the doctrine of the creation. All things were created by God, therefore all things equally reveal the grace of God. Consequently, all things deserve and receive the most loving care and are equally radiant with the symbolic light. Michelangelo loved natural forms (particularly the human body) with a comparable passion but his intellect was far too much developed to permit the acceptance of so innocent a conviction. Things could not be accepted in the unqualified innocence of their being, for within the thing is its essence, which it must reveal, and above all things and their essences is the essence of beauty and the ultimate essence of all beauty is God. This account of reality has serious flaws as a Christian theology: it is static and not operational; it is inadequate to the Incarnation, as it puts matter at the bottom of a hierarchy of ideas and the created order becomes a clog on the spirit rather than an instrument of grace; it upsets the balance between the Hellenic and the Hebraic and thus defines Christianity as a system rather than making the system a tool of faith. It has not worked for many people. It worked for Michelangelo.

It worked in its own odd fashion. When he could hold the system with confidence his work is least Christian. As he became increasingly aware that the system was not adequate to experience yet could not be surrendered, his work becomes increasingly revelatory. With other artists in this study the relation between nature and grace is a harmony of increasing complexity and depth of consciousness of the human experience; with Michelangelo nature and grace are in harmony only at the beginning of the work when the principle of harmony was humanistic and not particularly Christian. Increasingly there was, not a harmony, but a bitter tragic tension between nature and grace, which tore him apart and made of his life a personal tragedy hardly to be equaled by other artists except Van Gogh. He believed passionately in both, he could betray neither, he could not deny their integral relation. Yet he could not see them in harmony, only in tension, and within this tension his work developed.

Other artists lived tragic lives without any comparable results. Rembrandt contended with more personal tragedy than Michelangelo and turned even more obsessively to the tragic themes for his subjects, yet there is no comparable struggle with nature in his art. There is a refinement of his sensitivity, a quieting of the action, an increasing radiance of the light, but nature remains the instrument of grace and within the tragedy or Rembrandt's subject and his awareness there is a majestic and compassionate serenity. Titian has no such personal tragedy, except the tragic isolation of great age, but he turned increasingly to the tragic themes with a comparable radiance and majesty. Yet Rembrandt in his Bathsheba and Titian in his Danaë could use art's greatest symbol of sensuality – the naked body of a woman – within a presentation of the economy of grace and therefore make nature at its most intimate an instrument of grace.

In his early work Michelangelo saw the continuum between the natural order and the divine and his idealizations were an instrument for the establishment of the essential beauty within the surface appearance of nature. Since there was no tension but only harmony, the natural object, the body, is the proud bearer of the sense of its own ordering within divinity. It is not arrogance, for Michelangelo was too much a Christian for that, but it is grandeur, majesty, the glorification of the human. The culmination of this statement is the ceiling of the Sistine Chapel.

Michelangelo was involved in the world of his own time and observed it

Fig. 27

with an intimacy rare in an artist. As it became increasingly apparent to him that there was not a simple continuity between nature and grace the struggle became more intense. Less and less could he see nature as a bearer of grace. Theologically this reflects an inadequate grasp of the doctrine of the Incarnation, the sense Rembrandt had so clearly that God acts within the finiteness, the evil, and the very contingencies of human experience. Humanly it is of incomparable significance in its revelation of the spirit of man transfigured by faith within the bondage of doctrine.

Michelangelo loved his material and his work with the passion that a true artist must have. As his life in the world made it increasingly clear that matter could not so simply carry the divine across the distance of the Neo-Platonic hierarchy, the tragic dissociation took place. He could not forsake the natural object, the body, yet he could not see the ultimate beauty so clearly in it. The body, then, is given over to passionate struggle or tragic despair. The divine is the wholly other, distant and unattainable to man whose only response now is not the grandeur of his awareness of his calling, as carrier of the divine, but the despair of imprisonment in matter which keeps him isolated from the holy – the high and lifted up. Out of this awareness came the Medici Chapel and the "Last Judgment".

Fig. 34

The tension of this struggle is nearly unbearable to the sensitive observer and must have been inhumanly intense for Michelangelo, the tension between nature passionately loved and grace passionately longed for. The consequence in his work is a gradual loosening of his tie with the materiality of the earth, the Platonist yearning to be free from the obstruction of matter. The result was finally the Rondanini Pietà, so abstracted from the material as to be as nearly bodiless as sculpture is likely to get, a work which seems to be a repudiation of all he had stood for, yet is the logical completion of all his thought.

Fig. 27

Yet Michelangelo remained an artist working out of a lifetime of passionate concern with the material of his work. He could no more repudiate the body than he could repudiate breathing. Every element of hiss ensibility was informed by his understanding of the body and every element of this statue responds to that sensibility. The statue has always seemed "medieval" because it is so given over to the expression of pure spirituality and simultaneously so "modern," because it is so far abstracted from experience. In truth it is pure Michelangelo and only Michelangelo. He had finally come to the vision that grace is only given, never won, that the union of nature and grace, the divine in the human, is tragedy. The result is silence.

The consequences of this could only be catastrophic for other artists. The work of a great artist can have various consequences. Some close off an epoch simply because they have solved the remaining problems and there is no place left to go within that style. Others establish the problems and generations of artists can nourish themselves on the body of the work. Michelangelo's influence was ruinous, not because he dominated others by the sheer greatness of his work, but because his work developed within a spiritual tension which others did not know or could not bear. The scavengers took his vocabulary and made it into an orthodoxy. The academics took his idealizations and made them into ends. His only worthy successors were the mannerists who could feel his tension but did not know his grace. In a world without God, without grace, they still could not know nature other than as the bearer of ultimate meaning and the ultimate meaning could for them only be the warping of nature to a proud and arid denial of hope.

So far the main themes of the artists selected for a view of the Renaissance have been drama, gesture, and rhythmically ordered space with another important characteristic barely mentioned in connection with Botticelli. One of the main themes in the bill of indictment drawn up by those who would cast the Renaissance out of the Christian communion is sensuality. Just as there is reason and evidence for so much of what is asserted about the Renaissance so there is to this, also. Those who accept and pursue the nature of man as they see it and not as sermons say it ought to be, will see in man a compulsive drive to sensuousness and sensuality. Those who make it a part of the integrity of their personality to pursue to its full conclusion those things they see as inseparable from the nature of man will become aesthetes or sensualists and the Renaissance had an ample supply of both. Yet again it is too simple to say, "They were sensualists, therefore they were non-Christian." As was true of their concern for individuality and for power the Renaissance often paid a fearful price for the knowledge it gained of the nature of the senses. Yet the full vision of man would not have been possible without their work. It cannot be said that the Renaissance resolved the problem it stated or pursued the situation to its furthest conclusions (which was not achieved before Rembrandt's "Jewish Bride" and "Bathsheba") but at least it made the later development possible.

The first thing made possible by the Renaissance was the acceptance of the nude body as in itself a proper object of delight and of study. There are paintings of the body which deliberately exploit the basest of man's drives and there are paintings of the body which glory in the beauty of creation and man's physical creativity in it. Just when a work can be classified as manifesting the innocence of the Garden before the fall and when the corruption of the Garden after the fall is a matter of personal judgment. Examples of each will be found in the Renaissance as well as works which examine the body, including its sensuality, with the coolly analytic vision which was so important a part of the Renaissance achievement.

The most vivid illustration of this is Titian. Titian, too, follows the development so vividly seen in Donatello, Botticelli, and Michelangelo, moving as he does from the humanism and sensuality of the main body of his work to the tragic vision of his late years. His movement within that general pattern is, however, peculiarly his own. His essay in Renaissance humanism as seen in his portraiture is one of the most important of all. His paintings of the nude body are the finest statement of Renaissance sensuousness. Inseparable from the sensuousness of the painting is the significance of the paintings for the development toward modern art, for they are the first paintings of which it can be said they exist for themselves alone, using the subject equally with the material substance to create an object for human delight. Thus the human body is seen outside the judgment of morality and is relevant only to the act of painting and of the apprehension of painting. Such an attitude involved a revolution in human belief.

Titian's art moved, however, deeper into the human situation and the passion paintings of his late years represent another of those distinctive visions of the meaning of the redemptive sacrifice which are so significant a feature of the Renaissance. He brought to these, not ecclesiastical submissiveness in portraying what is told him by others, but the quintessence of personal experience as felt by a mind finely drawn through decades of the most arduous discipline. If the price which had to be paid for these paintings was, in lesser men, the abuse of man's individuality, the price then is part of the human tragedy. The game in this case is well worth the candle.

Lending, however, a particular poignancy to this achievement is the fact that Titian, unlike Michelangelo, did not turn away from that great instrument of Renaissance art, the nude body. Alongside his passion paintings there are nudes drawn from mythological subjects which transfigure the human body as nothing else in art. Titian's early nudes are solid, earthy, rhythmically articulated, sensual. His Danaë is vital and alive but is a vision beyond materiality, a vision out of light. In his old age Michelangelo could see only tragedy. Titian saw tragedy as fully as any man but he saw too the glory of creation, the body transfigured to accompany his vision of humanity redeemed.

Fig. 29

Fig. 30

Fig. 32

VIII

THE

RENAISSANCE

AS PARADIGM

The Renaissance has not only its singular charm which has been exercised over the imagination of men for centuries but a singular usefulness in this investigation because its variety and intensity give it the quality of a paradigm. The older world entered into it both transformed and as a survival. The modern world grew out of it. It is therefore possible for modern man to see humanity not just as a foreign race thinking in terms of foreign problems but his own ancestors working on the world he still inhabits. There are, therefore, other artists and other problems of the Renaissance whose consideration might contribute further understanding to the questions raised here. If, in the initial examination of the phenomenon of the Renaissance it was best to look at the art works first and then see how the proposed categories impinged on them, it might now be of use to follow through the categories somewhat more systematically and see their reference to the Renaissance. This procedure might serve to clarify, not only the Renaissance but the categories themselves.

There is a problem involved in the interpretation of the category identified as "the arts of creation," and a problem of singular felicity. Briefly put, the problem revolves around the fact that delight in the nature of creation and in the act of making the art work is diffused so generally through man's work that it is difficult to the point of impossibility to determine when the source of this delight can be claimed as specifically Christian. In fact it is questionable whether it would be worth the effort, for delight too closely examined ceases to be delight and becomes something else and the least the artist can ask of the observer is that he share the experience with something of the same unquestioning naïveté which characterized the making of the work. It is best then to recognize that delight in creation is a dimension of man's experience and a demonstration that the Garden is not simply a part of man's mythical history wholly soiled by his sin but a possibility of his present experience. Since delight is an aspect of the Garden experience it is in many ways pre-Christian, a part of common humanity and one of those happy places where the Christian can share his life and work with his fellows.

On the other hand, to the Christian, the fact of sinfulness in man's experience is a living reality and the experience of man's sinfulness is a fact of history and the present common life. Creation is seen less as a Garden to delight in than a thing to lust after, to dominate, to possess by force. The innocent vision is a gift granted to children and to the artist almost alone among men. But to the artist who cannot find his spiritual or intellectual home in innocence within the universal rape of nature, delight in creation comes not always of itself but only through grace, and he cannot present that delight except in gratitude to the Christ who opened his eyes and purified his soul to the reception of those things his eyes saw.

In general, Italians, particularly the Italians of the Renaissance, were too objectively rational to give way to that innocence which is the reference of the category of the arts of creation. There is, however, one man, Giovanni Bellini, who can be said to have won through to an innocence that makes him perhaps the greatest master in this category. "Won through" is the proper term since there is no lack in his work of the full development of Renaissance science. Yet for all the rational skill evident in the construction of his paintings there is a radiance of light and color suffusing his work. This radiance is perhaps most clearly seen in all its existential

richness and theological significance in Bellini's masterpiece, "Saint Francis   Fig. 6
in Ecstasy." In most of his other works the radiance is a dimension of the
setting of the painting. In this painting it is both the subject and the reality
of the painting and its source is made explicit in the figure of St. Francis
in ecstasy before his vision of the glory of God in creation. Every object is
seen with perfect clarity, in the integrity of its own being and the place in
the whole, and radiant with the light that can proceed only from the throne
of grace.

The only artist whose work contains a radiance comparable to Bellini's
is the Fleming, Jan van Eyck. Again, the radiance which enriches his vision
of things is, in the most of his works, a part of the setting. In one, however,
"The Adoration of the Holy Lamb," the glory of creation is not quite so   Fig. 5
directly the subject, which is clearly specified by the title, but certainly it is
an inseparable dimension of the subject as well as the major element of the
formal language. The whole of creation is under the judgment of God
but the whole of creation proceeds from the hand of God and nothing is too
small or too great to be radiant with the glory of God. It would be the
part of arrogance for the Christian to claim credit for this type of respect
for either the small or the great things in creation. There is hardly, in
Western art, anything to excel and barely to equal the attention a Japanese
or a Chinese artist of certain styles gives to a blade of grass. The element
that distinguishes the Christian work is comprehensiveness. All things
proceed from the creative hand of God. Therefore, all things reveal the
glory of God and neither the small nor the great are exempt.

It is a truism, often contradicted but not always successfully so, that
modern rationality took its rise in the Renaissance. Whatever the truth
of the general interpretation, no characteristic is more fundamental to the
life of the Renaissance spirit than its search to understand and to control.
This makes the second category, "the art of man in the image of God,"
particularly relevant. The Renaissance represents a major stage in the
fulfillment of the completeness of man's nature in its attempt to find the
names of things and their proper relation to each other. It is difficult to
isolate any single example of this as more worthy of recognition than others
for the rational control of the stylistic language and the search for a rational
structure in the observed world is a part of the essential posture and act of
the Renaissance artist from the beginning to the end. This attitude finds
dramatic illustration in Uccello's passionate search for the meaning of
perspective space, in Alberti's coolly rational account of the mathematical

structure of the arts, the relentless anatomical researches of many Renaissance artists. Perhaps the greatest example of the scientific attitude in Renaissance art and life is Leonardo da Vinci. It would not be true to say that Leonardo's is the most realistic of all styles for the nineteenth century excelled him in that. But it might be closer to the truth to say that he is the clearest manifestation of the Renaissance work in the area of the arts of the image. Nineteenth-century realism is, in various ways including both Courbet and the impressionists, a linking of art with the pure optical act. Leonardo's work is optical but it is also intellectual, a probing not only into the things he sees but the things he knows and the organizing principle of so many of his paintings is not description but the evocation of the informing principle of the events which are the object of the painter's own act.

Fig. 13   Thus, the "Last Supper," celebrated as one of the most popular religious paintings, is less religious than it is psychological. "The discovery of the world and of man," famed as a description of a main stream of Renaissance thought, is brought together in this work. Leonardo's essays in perspective construction are well known, the orderly control of space by the rational intellect and its use as an expressive instrument of the artist. His researches into anatomy, into the variety of human gesture and appearance, into the description of the surface and the organizing principle of objects are equally well-known. He does not, however, pursue these in isolation (as Uccello did perspective), except in his notebooks and drawings. In his paintings, and particularly in this one, his researches cohere into an integrated search into the reality of human action. The event is described, not as a kind of journalistic realism, but as a significant dramatic action whereby in the totality of external act and appearance the inner nature and meaning of the relation is uncovered. Thus the "Last Supper" is a single-minded analysis of the complexity of human act and relation. The central event is stated, "One of you shall betray me." To this central event the various persons react in their own personal ways, in the fullness of their personal reality. There is nothing distinctively Christian about the central act. It could be the act of any leader of any human enterprise when he is aware of his imminent betrayal. The significance of the act lies not in its Christian reference but in its human drama and its function as a tool for the dissection of the human personality. This painting and the stylistic attitude it betrays is a major example of the autonomous intellect at work.

This analysis moves the discussion of categories quite close to the next, the "arts of the fall." Insofar as Leonardo was concerned with the discovery of the nature of objective reality there is no more cause to sit in judgment on his work than there is for sitting in comparable judgment on the comparable work of a scientist searching out the nature and the structure of things simply because he does not have an overtly pious purpose in his work, or even, for that matter, because he is a violent atheist. Insofar as Leonardo, and others like him, emphasized the autonomy of the intellect, however, they begin to assert, not man in the image of God but man usurping the functions of God. In point of fact this is rarely a major attitude in Renaissance art, even though it is present in the personal attitudes of Leonardo and other Renaissance artists. Generally the Renaissance artist is so concerned with the objectivity of his painting and the reality toward which his painting is directed that he is less concerned with asserting his own autonomy. He may not always have considered himself a servant of God but he did consider himself a servant of what he could see, of what he could know and discover in the world about him, and what he could make in his work of art. It remained for the romantics to see the artist as God.

The ability of the artist to protect himself against this temptation by the objectivity of his interests was not shared by all elements of Renaissance society. Notably many of the humanists, who lost touch with the objectivity of the world around them in their passionate search to revive the classic, could not shield themselves against this temptation. The tradition of the arrogant scholar got either its start or major encouragement from the scholars of the Renaissance. They, however, were not able to lead the artists after them. Another characteristic Renaissance man, the prince, the tyrant, or the princely personality was more successful. These men were among the sources of commissions for artists and a substantial amount of Renaissance portraiture is given over to the visual statement of these personalities in all their arrogant autonomy. For example, there is Titian's portrait of "Pietro Aretino," Verrocchio's "Colleoni," Piero's "Sigismondo Malatesta," Donatello's "Gattamelata." It is still difficult, however, to classify these as "the arts of the fall" for the artist is not responsible for the character of his sitter. All these manifest the character of the sitter and so they are important essays, not only in Renaissance art, but in Renaissance political philosophy. But they are essays more nearly in the scientific spirit. These men were part of the phenomenon of the world and deserved to be recorded, manifested as such, and it is a splendid presentation they receive.

Portraits are more relevant to this argument when the work of art does not simply present and analyze the spirit of the sitter but manifests that spirit in

Fig. 21
Fig. 23

its own forms and rhythms. Obviously this is not easy to demonstrate and probably the demonstration would be impossible without some use made of subject matter to serve as clue to the artist's intention. There is, for example, the Malatesta Temple. There is something singularly characteristic in the arrogance of a lustful and infatuated Renaissance tyrant converting a Christian chapel into a memorial of his passion and there is something equally interesting about the artists who lent themselves to the enterprise. Even so it might have remained no more than another commission had not the form of the building and its ornament manifested so tense and autonomous an expression that its harmony with the tyrant's purpose is painfully evident. It is an exquisite work. It is also a seductive work in which things are opened up in the imagination of men which might better be left closed.

It is tempting to include the physical riot of so many Titians, the seductive Venuses, the passionate Bacchanals. But is this temptation simply the reaction of the Puritan mind against the honest fleshiness of the Mediterranean? Too many factors of personal psychology are involved to make an answer easy. Titian can be defended. His Venuses and Bacchanals have, for all their fleshiness, a dimension of joy in texture, movement, earth, air and sky, color, bodies, which make them a celebration closer to the idea of an Arcadian classicism than to the idea of the flesh as sinful and the fall as basically sexual. It remained for Goya in the arrogant sexuality of his two Majas (and the "Clothed Maja" is more sensual than the "Nude Maja") to state sexuality without qualification as a part and a privilege of autonomous personality. It would be a mistake to try to baptize Titian's painting of this type or to construct a Christianity which could conform to so materialistic an ideal. This style is without question profoundly materialistic. That it is, however, materialism and not altogether a fallen sensuality would appear to be demonstrated by the transfiguration this syle undergoes. Just as his pageant of Christianity (so much a part, too, of his Venetian materialism) is transmuted into one of the most powerful statements of suffering incarnation, so his celebration of the flesh and the beauty of the body is transmuted into the visions of the glory of the body in the Venuses of his old age, the allegories of earthly beauty receiving its glory from the divine. Not until Rembrandt's "Bathsheba" and "The Jewish Bride" is there the equal of these in finding within the harmony of the Christian faith a comparable statement of the character and quality of the flesh of the body.

The standard interpretation of Veronese would make his work relevant to the analysis at this point, as that work appears to be concerned chiefly with the indulgence of fleshly appetites, although in wonderfully effective and persuasive tones. From this point of view, the Inquisition which took Veronese to task for his "Feast in the House of Levi" may have been wholly wrong in their claim to dominate the work of the artist and they may have shown the usual official inability to grasp the formal language of the painting, but their instinct was right in mistrusting the painting which asserts an ideal quite contrary to their own.

In contrast to this, Professor Phillip Fehl has recently offered a reinterpretation of Veronese's style, which finds Venetian sensuousness and materialism a setting for a very sensitive and delicate statement of the central significance of the historic acts of the faith. The analysis is quite persuasive and entirely relevant to the course of this argument.

It is an unpleasant task, and not particularly profitable to try to select artists who manifest the fall in this fashion. It smacks too much of sitting in judgment. More useful and ultimately more significant is the examination of those artists who are aware of the abyss of man's sinfulness, the tragedy which his sin involves. This is not always simple to do in the Renaissance for its peculiar mission was to discover and affirm, to glorify and exalt, not to give voice to tragedy and despair. But there were great men in the Renaissance, men whose work penetrated far beyond affirmation at the facile level which characterizes the imitative figures of the Renaissance, and beyond or deeper than the optimistic affirmation which, for all its grandeur is still one-sided. Perhaps the greatest of these were Donatello, Michelangelo, and Titian.

Donatello, whose work contains some of the major statements of Renaissance affirmation, produced in his "Magdalene" one of the most Fig. 38 intense expressions of tragedy to be found in the range of Christian art. It fits well with the Renaissance glorification of the nude, for the subject is inseparable from the interpretation. Mary Magdalene is the prototype of the sinners of the flesh. All the eloquence of Donatello's great stylistic powers is given over to the presentation of the dissolution of the flesh as symbol and allegory of repentance. There is in the work an extraordinary power of tension and intensity of expression that make of it an eloquent testimony to the Christian insight into the nature and consequences of the fall. Similar expressionism is to be found both before and after this work but it is doubtful if such expressive power were conceivable except against the background of the awareness of the nature and the appearance of the flesh and on the foundation of all the technical skill of the Renaissance artists in the presentation of the human body. The fall here is not a theological principle but a fact of alienation and the overcoming of that alienation involves the most terrible consequence in mind and body.

One of the most oppressive statements of the frustration which follows man's inability to extricate himself from the intolerable dilemmas which follow the fall is to be found in Michelangelo's Medici Chapel. Far more than most artists, Michelangelo was sensitive to the life of his own times and involved in the spiritual history of his own culture. It is with the greatest despair that he contemplated the end of Italian liberty, the destruction of the humanist ideal which he himself stated so grandly in his "David" and his early "Pietà." In the Medici Chapel, however, the figures, in all the power of Michelangelo's conception of the human form, twist in on themselves, are locked within tight compositional outlines. This is the world of matter, the world of earth, and only frustration and despair is the lot of man on earth. The figures of Medici dukes, however, risen from the tomb, sit inertly, lifelessly, paralyzed. The architecture itself imprisons its own elements within tight enclosures and enhances the general despair of the chapel design.

This could take its place as an eloquent statement of unqualified despair and frustration were it not for the note which looks beyond the despair and links the work to Christianity. The program would appear to be basically involved in the Neo-Platonism of the time (although this interpretation is still moot) but it is significant that, while even Mary sits with the curious paralysis of all the other figures in the chapel, only the Christ child moves with complete freedom in an eloquent upward spiral. The program is incomplete, so there is no way of saying what the over-all effect would have been had Michelangelo been able to finish the work. Apparently there was to be a painting of the Resurrection in the upper portions of the chapel and drawings exist showing a triumphant Christ soaring out of the tomb. But the work as it survives shows only the deadening despair and frustration which seem to be man's lot on earth.

The most explicit counterweight to Titian's Venetian materialism is his "Flagellation." This work, dark and gloomy, torn by the flickering torches, imprisoning the tortured Christ, is reminiscent of Rouault and his "Miserere," "Man is a wolf to man." The central figure cuts back and forth, canceling out its movement and action in a way reminiscent of Michelangelo's Medici Chapel figures. Around it cut the violent, mindless figures of the torturers revealing the violence of man's lust for pain.

The major works which set forth the Renaissance apprehension of the nature and significance of redemption have been discussed in the previous chapter. Donatello's great pulpit series cover the passion in all its dimensions, from the pain of injustice to the torment of the sacrifice, the agonized triumph of the Resurrection, the soaring glory of the Ascension. Michelangelo's "Pietà" is one of the great works of the tragic spirit of man but it is redeemed from pure tragedy by the arching compassion and suffering of the mother, here treated not as the Queen of Heaven nor as the Mother of God but as embodied compassion, which points beyond the sacrifice to its ultimate meaning. Titian's "Pietà" accomplishes something of the same end. The passionate figure of Mary Magdalene can speak only of human despair but the great majesty of Mary rescues the work from pure end to the glory of its ultimate significance. And Piero's "Resurrection" is pure triumph.

IX

TYPES OF CHRISTIAN
STYLES

There is nothing inherent in the character of the Renaissance which should give it so prominent a place in this discussion, anything that could give it a normative status in the Christian understanding of the arts. It deserves to be rescued from the indifferent position to which it has fallen from its once high estate. The variety of its manifestations make it singularly useful in the outlining of the issues of concern here. It must not be exalted, however, at the expense of other expressions of the Christian faith of equal validity. All human expressions of the faith are partial, for that is the nature of man. Thus, no one period or one style can be taken as representative of the true faith and the most necessary articles of equipment are flexibility, openness, catholicity.

The picture therefore, would lack any reference to completeness if the Christian categories were defined altogether by reference to one stylistic period. Since, however, this is not a history of Christian art, but an outline of the approach to the criticism of Christian art, it may not be necessary to go into as much detail in discussing the other periods except to indicate certain typical approaches and attitudes toward the faith as they appear at other times.

The distinctive concern of the Renaissance was rationality, understanding and control of the artist's means toward the most organized statement of his typical interests. This rationality is not the exclusive possession of the Renaissance artist for no art exists without the rational control of the artist's means toward his chosen end. It is a matter of degree and flavor, not any uniqueness of possession. Even in affirmation, in celebration, or in despair the Renaissance artist remains more self-conscious in his rationality than most artists. While this distinctive rationality was a heritage of the later styles through most of the nineteenth century, justifying the assertion of some historians that the Renaissance as a period did not end until the nineteenth century, it is not so central a preoccupation to most of the later artists. It remains, then, to define something of the distinctive contributions made by other historical epochs to the development of the Christian consciousness.

If it is possible to move away from the Gothic as the normative statement of the Christian faith, it is not necessary to stay away from the Gothic as an essential expression of this faith. Yet it is necessary to be more specific than is usually the case with the proponents of the Gothic style as uniquely Christian. The medieval period lasted for centuries and included not one stylistic attitude but a number. They were closely related, to be sure, but not to be handled under the same description as though they equally represent the Age of Faith. It is perhaps not too much to say that the history of the Gothic period as Christian expression remains to be written, despite the large extent of the existing literature. How is it possible, for example, to unravel the strains of motives which went into the building of the great cathedrals? How is it possible to determine when the motives of the builders were devotional, theological, or humanly sinful as manifested in civic pride and personal ostentation? How is it possible, for another example, to determine the Christian nature of an event when a great window is endowed out of arrogance, prideful display, or as a part of political maneuvering? Yet there it stands glowing in such harmony and serenity as pass human understanding. These questions can be directed at the major Gothic monuments, those which make up the concentration of

157

monuments referred to under the rubric, the "Age of Faith." What, then, of the complex of motives and styles which make up all the provincial expressions outside the main lines of creativity?

In a history of Christian art, these questions must be answered. Otherwise the full dimension of Christian life in those times is lost. It does a violence to the humanity of these people if it is thought they were moved by any less complexity of motives than the people of any time or place. Yet this kind of detailed investigation would, perhaps, be out of order here where the concern is rather to establish the form of the essential categories. Therefore, the remarks will be directed at the major concern of the Gothic style, the defining concern as seen in the major French monuments. That remarkable phenomenon known as the late Gothic style will be treated briefly a little later and in a different context.

If the violence of the Romanesque period and the singular character of the late Gothic style are for the moment laid aside, then the central Gothic experience stands out with a clarity which deserves all the attention it has ever received. It was important to the Christian doctrine of man that the Renaissance should discover and state man's rationality in the way it did. But rationality has a way of obtruding itself at times between man and the apprehension of much which is central to his experience. There is nowhere in any art of any time anything quite like the serenity of the Gothic sculpture of the first half of the thirteenth century. This is not to say that serenity is not a concern of other artists. Much oriental art is given over to the search for the full statement and being of serenity, the contemplative Buddhas, the great Chinese landscapes. It is a compliment to the integrity of these works that they are not to be confused with the Christian contemplation of the Gothic period. Theirs is an absorptive contemplation, a feeling of the soul for the essence of the natural order. In Oriental contemplation as seen in their painting there is no definition of the individual but rather the overcoming of the individual in the unity of things.

The essence of the contemplative serenity of the Gothic is individuality. It is also true that the essence of that serenity is the lack of personality, else there would have been no work for the Renaissance. The problem of combining personality and individuality with serenity has never really been solved, although Piero came about as close as any artist to that achievement. Personality is realized in the visual arts only by drama or dramatic relation and drama obtrudes itself on serenity. The problem of combining serenity with individuality was fully resolved in the high Gothic sculpture.

The great portals of the Gothic cathedrals center on a figure of Christ, Fig. 26 calm, majestic, serene, Lord of all he surveys, in infinite charity and compassion. Ranged on either side are the subordinate figures, saints, apostles, martyrs, confessors. Each has his own characteristic form, described with accuracy and sensitivity within the limits of the necessary stylization. There is not the distinctiveness of facial gesture that is necessary to reveal the individual personality within the distinctiveness of individual form. Thus the harmony of the group is not weakened by action or fully realized dramatic relation. The faces are, rather, calm, expressionless, of a serenity corresponding with the great figure of Christ in the center. This was the visual statement of the peace of God. It is not quite the peace and serenity of Piero. His was an achievement of the intellect, overcoming passion and drama, attaining to the balance of forces which look back on sin and suffering overcome, a broken world defeated. Gothic serenity is more direct and naïve and is built, not on an awareness of sin and brokenness healed, but sin destroyed and the primal unity restored as though the sin had never been.

Gothic style develops toward movement and intensified dramatic relation, thus breaking loose from the architecture and dissolving the serenity and the harmony which was the brief achievement of the high Gothic style. After the singular achievement of its late period the possibilities of the Gothic style were exhausted and the problem stated for the Renaissance. Then a new world and a new style began.

The Gothic style is primarily a style of affirmation, the serenity which comes from unity restored and brokenness banished. The Baroque style is also a style of affirmation yet in quite a different way and with its own complications. In some respects Baroque is a worldly style, more worldly than its predecessor with the worldly reputation, the Renaissance. As the high Gothic could state the faith with simplicity and naïveté, so the Renaissance could explore rationality with simplicity and naïveté. Naïveté was no longer quite so possible in the Baroque period and it is so often a style of self-conscious sophistication. Yet it was a style which lent itself with singular felicity and flexibility to Christian purposes of various kinds, Catholic and Protestant, mystical and dramatic, active and contemplative.

For Christian purposes the greatest of these artists were Rubens and Rembrandt (deferring El Greco for the moment as presenting certain very special problems). These were men antithetical in personality, in worldly position, in the type of their faith. Yet in many stylistic features they belong under the same general heading. Some of these are technical matters of no particular interest to this analysis but some are highly relevant.

For the Protestant mind the proper understanding of Rubens presents the greatest difficulty, for his work is the antithesis of some of the ascetic ideals so central to the concerns of Protestantism. It is the quality which moves even so sophisticated a spectator as Paul Tillich to say of a Rubens' Madonna, "It is wonderful to look at, but nobody would think that this is the Mother of God in the Catholic symbolism of this relationship." (*Christianity and the Existentialists*, ed. Michalson, p. 142). (Cf. chapter III, p. 38).

Such a comment misconstrues the natural relationship between subject and painting, a relation which needs to be dealt with in various ways throughout this analysis. Rubens provides a graphic illustration of one aspect of this problem, for he, more flagrantly than most, ignores archaeological accuracy and draws his figures from a particular social setting of his own day. Rubens seems incapable of realizing on his canvas the poor, the tragic. His people are physically powerful, luxuriously dressed, set forth in color of unparalleled richness and composition of unequaled dynamism. The fitness of this for the presentation of the idea of Incarnation, filled as it is with the sense of the humble, the ordinary, the commonplace life among poor peasants and villagers in Palestine is a question which comes perhaps naturally to the mind.

The question is not, in fact, improper. If it is assumed that subject matter is a thing of consequence in a painting, then an artist is responsible for the interpretation he makes of the subject matter, the manner in which he presents it. Yet the examination of this subject and what it reflects of the character of his faith must not start from the assumption that the artist is basically an illustrator trying to set down in visual form what things might have looked like when they happened. It must be remembered that subject matter is, after all, part of the artist's material and therefore can be manipulated for his purpose in making the work of art. Under this interpretation it might be seen that Rubens contributed a note to Christian art which is found nowhere else, certainly not with such clarity and energy.

Rubens is, above all others, the painter of exultation. Christianity comes in humility, in the meekness of the Incarnation, entering not as a conqueror in triumph but as a babe in a manger. Yet Christianity is the final revelation of all the glory, majesty, and power of God, and it is this glory, majesty, and power which Rubens exalts. With a single-mindedness which runs through all this work he celebrates this glory and realizes it in the forms of his paintings. More truly than with most artists, Rubens pursued this vision through all the great variety and vitality of his production. To Rubens, the world and all in it manifests God's grandeur and glory. The incredible abundance of his overpowering bodies is not sensuality but an exulting in the power and glory of creation.

If Rubens is thus obsessed by the material he works with, no less important is the sense of order which pervades and controls the grandeur which he feels so deeply. Perhaps the most important of all Rubens' instruments is movement, movement downward to the black abyss of hell, movement outward in the glory of the earth, movement upward to the transfiguration of creation which is the ultimate glory of God. This movement, pervading all his work, is the instrument of order which controls and directs his exultation. The importance of this cannot be exaggerated. Rubens was one of the finest intelligences to perform the act of painting. Exultation in its simple directness is not foreign to Christian art. In the hands of Rubens it becomes finally an exultation in the glory of the order of creation.

The intent of Rubens is not, therefore, the search for understanding, the penetration of the order of existence, or the setting forth of the redemptive act. It is the glorification of the majesty, the creative power, the ordered glory of the almighty God.

Rubens should not necessarily be taken as representative of the Baroque period or the Baroque style. It was too varied a period and too flexible a style for that. The existence of alternative approaches to art will be perfectly evident from the discussion of Rembrandt and El Greco to follow. Even the main stream of the Baroque style, which Rubens does represent, could be used for the most arrogant display of ostentation or power, or, particularly in its later stages, the most frivolous kinds of lasciviousness. But a major element in this main stream of the Baroque style, in all the arts (see, for example, the German Baroque churches), was this same overwhelming health, this sense of a profound and meaningful order, an affirmation of the glory of God and his creation.

Rembrandt presents a somewhat different problem of interpretation, particularly in a Protestant community. Although he has played a very small part in the public life and art of the Protestant communities, he is accepted by Protestant intellectuals as the Protestant artist without comparison and quite often considered the very type and model of the Christian artist. It does not simplify the problem for this study that this judgment is very largely accurate. It errs only in the way which all such judgments necessarily err: a part cannot be taken for the whole and Rembrandt's art cannot represent more than a part of the total sense of the meaning of the Christian faith. But interpreting his art according to the Christian faith is a little too easy for the purposes of a study, which has for its purpose the elucidation of categories which can give some sense to the proper approach of the Christian to all art.

Rembrandt, nevertheless, must play a central role in this investigation. More than any other individual artist, he comes to the events of the Christian faith in their biblical record with no preconceptions, responding to them by no inherited scheme but in the fullness of his awareness of the meaning of life in the light of Christ and through his own profound sense of meaningful form. Thus the aesthetic so basic to this study finds a particularly vivid development in Rembrandt. As much as an artist can (no artist can wholly escape his heritage), Rembrandt responded to the reality of life directly with the materials and the forms of his art.

Of all artists, Rembrandt is the most deeply moral, in the sense of his obsessed preoccupation with man's moral situation poised between time and the eternal. This dilemma, this paradox of condition, is the principal source for the concerns of Rembrandt's maturity and old age. It determines the choice of subject, it informs the treatment of the subject in the painting.

In his choice of subject, Rembrandt is profoundly human, with a deep sense of the common life of his time. Leaving aside the bombastic Baroque of his early years, his subjects, biblical or non-biblical, are drawn from the life of man on earth in man's essential humanness. There is no concern for power, rank, status, any of the means whereby man attempts to avoid or add to his native humanness. It is Rembrandt's concern to dig back into the substance of man's existence, not paint his persona or his paraphernalia.

The most direct expression of this choice is obviously the portrait and the self-portrait which make up so important a part of Rembrandt's work. Yet the portrait as a subject for his art is not an exception and, in fact, can be fully understood only in the context of the whole body of work and the moral vision represented by the other types of subject chosen.

The point of these other subjects is not the statistics of choice (although such a statistical study is revealing) but the points of orientation. Rembrandt's chosen subjects are the nodal points of the moral life, the relations which determine the moral life: man isolated before God; man in his institutionalized relations such as the family, or the structured associations of his work; man caught inextricably in a moral dilemma on which his being might turn; and finally, the core and key to his work, man involved in the work of Christ and responding to it. In each case the subject is revelatory. The posture of a man in his relation, the agonized awareness of the dilemma, the vision of Christ, all uncover the humanness of man as Rembrandt sees it.

Thus his choice of subjects from the Bible tends to come around to such stories as Susannah and the elders or Bathsheba. Susannah was faced with the choice of losing her virtue or her reputation, Bathsheba with losing her virtue or disobeying her king. There is a peculiar poignancy about these two subjects and a human depth which gives them unusual significance, even in Rembrandt's work. They show forth the paradox of human choice in the way which Rembrandt finds so revealing. But they also show this choice in a context of wider significance and stand therefore among the major documents in the attempt (all too seldom pursued) to find a genuine Christian attitude toward the flesh and the desires of the flesh. Rembrandt is no Manichean. Susannah and Bathsheba are not abstractions or puppets. They are women with the full physical reality and desirability which can characterize women. They are not idealizations of women as the Renaissance artists saw women. They have the sense of actuality which lends a singular poignancy to their moral dilemma. Artists painting the female nude are nearly always preoccupied with their sensuous or sensual appeal and the figures then become morally two-dimensional, lacking either psychological or spiritual depth and reality. Rembrandt stands almost alone among artists in his awareness of the human reality of these persons without in any sense diminishing their physical appeal. They are thus three-dimensional characters in his moral drama, their essential humanity enhanced rather than weakened by the fact that it is not simply the drama of sensuality which is his concentration but a particular manifestation of the universal entrapment of human beings.

The theme of sensuality in the human experience is important both to Rembrandt's development and to this argument and it must be resumed in a moment. The concern here, however, is with the various subjects, the choice of which reveal so clearly the major preoccupations of Rembrandt's work. The moral dilemma is often manifested in the subjects that concerned him, for he chose the stories of Lucrece, and Joseph and Potiphar's wife. There were, however, others of like nature. His imagination worked a number of times on the stories of David and Saul, Peter's denial, the prodigal son, Abraham and Isaac, Hagar.

Apart from the great works dealing with the ministry and the sacrifice of

Fig. 31

Christ, perhaps the most revealing of his subjects are those dealing with the moment of revelation, the uncovering of the divine within the humility of reality. In those subjects already identified as concerned with the moral dilemma, Rembrandt resolves that dilemma in his last versions by treating them, not simply as drama, but as revelation. The early version of the prodigal son is a characteristic Baroque drama. The last version is the embodiment of mercy and forgiveness. The denial of Peter is cut by a light out of darkness which rends not only the darkness but the soul of man. The supper at Emmaus is perhaps the most explicit reference to the kind of revelation which was so much a part of Rembrandt's vision. One of the greatest is his small "Philemon and Baucis." It was not possible for Rembrandt to attempt directly the representation of God the Father as so many artists before him had done. He was not an orthodox Calvinist but he was too orthodox for that. Under the guise of the classical myth he could show the Trinity in terms of Zeus, Hermes, and the light which proceeded from them toward the aged couple bowed in adoration in their poverty and humility. Under the guise of a classical myth he has here created one of the most deeply Christian of all his works and one which can stand most usefully as a key to his intentions. His art is profoundly an art of the Incarnation. The world has been created by God and is good because it proceeds from the hand of God and is irradiated by the presence of God. In this, he does not differ in principle from many another artist, such as his predecessors in Flanders of the fifteenth century. His concern is rather with the entry of the divine into history, the intersection of the timeless with time. History in the larger public sense of the word plays little part in his work with a few significant exceptions ("The Conspiracy of Justus Civilis," perhaps the "Polish Rider") but history in the sense of the involvement of man with time, the sense of the passing and the changing, subject to free choice and action, is a dimension of his work which is fundamental to its proper understanding. In this, too, he does not differ fundamentally from other artists since the sense of the passing and the changing, even the sense of free choice, appears as early as Donatello and Leonardo and is a common element in Baroque art. What is unique to Rembrandt is the intersection of the act and purpose of God with the drama and relation of man.

Thus neither time nor the timeless are the exclusive preoccupations of Rembrandt but the structure and quality of their relation. The shift in his own style reveals this perhaps as clearly as anything could. In his early work he chooses many of these same subjects and treats them solely as dramatic

Fig. 20

acts. They are all movement and dramatic intensity, external, even super-ficial. In his late work, when he returns to the same subject, the movement is either potential or completed, although present implicitly. But such movement is held under powerful control, trembling beneath the surface but never escaping. Primarily there is a great stillness, a peace out of power, a suspension of the event under the vision of God. The picture has become presentational.

The presentation is not that of Piero who transcended time into a vision of the peace of God. This is the vision of the transfiguration of pain and power into the compassion of God.

In his last works this principle is the key to the understanding of them all. In the rest of his career it is the key, in that his style, in its working out, moves toward this vision. Thus the theme of sensuality is one of the most important in his account of the human condition. As a man he was deeply involved with the women of his life. As an artist, he dealt many times with the human body and for the same reasons that other artists have felt attracted to the body as a subject, its unparalleled variety and depth of artistic significance. These are caught with a vividness of realism which should content a follower of Courbet, yet as often as not they are in action or in context. He sees the body as a part of its meaningful environment, but this context is always the ordinary human context of daily life. Thus the sensuality he presents in the bodies of women is a natural attribute and not a romantic addition to them. Even the classical myth of Danaë is presented exuberantly, not with the clean edged polish of the Renaissance style, but in a Dutch bed with plump pillows and a sagging mattress. Yet the body glows with unparalleled richness.

The "Danaë" represents an early exuberance of attitude toward the attractiveness of the flesh and is untouched by the sense of the moral dilemma which is so fundamental to the later work. Bathsheba, modeled by his beloved Hendrickje, has an even grander sensuality. It is one of the greatest images of the feminine and the female in all art. Yet the letter in her hand presents her involvement; the indescribable loneliness of the fine head isolated against the infinite depth of Rembrandt's space communicates in the language of painting the tragedy which has grown out of her beauty.

This too is not fully comprehensible except in terms of "The Jewish Bride." This is perhaps the only work of art which sets forth a truly defensible image of the Christian concept of the relation of man and wife in the flesh. With infinite tenderness the man takes possession of the body

Fig. 33

165

of his wife, not just symbolically but actually in laying his hand on her breast. With equal gentleness she receives his gesture. The posture of the figures is quiet, noble, presentational. The composition encircles them, draws them together, the colors of the clothes of one are found as accents and highlights in the clothes of the other, joining them in form as well as gesture. They incline toward each other, yet look off into space, pensive, and lonely. They have joined as one flesh, yet they are divided by their unassailable individuality. As nearly as it is possible to do in a single picture Rembrandt has brought all dimensions of marriage into this one.

Thus it is against the background of this vision of the relation of the flesh in marriage that the great problem pictures must be seen. The human body is created out of the providence of God and is a rightful object of desire, gift and possession in marriage. The dilemma of Lucretia, of Bathsheba, of Susannah was not a dramatic problem useful for the making of a spectacular narrative painting. It went to the root of their moral personality, it was the occasion for their meeting the problem of good and evil and out of this meeting more than the dramatic situation emerges. The reality of a human personality is manifested in the flesh which can be a place of human beauty and glory as well as the opportunity for human shame.

This is one instance only, albeit one which has a uniqueness of treatment, but it shows the structure of Rembrandt's humanism. It is the consciousness of this moral and personal depth as shown in Bathsheba, in Saul, in Peter, that informs all his work, including the portraits. Portraits are difficult to interpret conclusively in these humanistic terms since by definition they lack the dramatic dimension which makes the other paintings accessible to the discursive intellect. But seen as a part of the total context of man's work and thus joined inseparably to the others, it is apparent that Rembrandt's portraits are far more than records of external appearance. They are probings into the reality of the human personality. These portraits are not understandable except as statements of Rembrandt's vision of the moral personality. Man is isolated in an immensity of undefined space. Man is not little, he is not a cipher, he has the fullness of his personality and his individual body. But this humanity is seen in a majestic loneliness, man isolated before the throne of grace and judgment. No institution, no hierarchy, no dogmatic structure can intervene to fix the outline of his relation to God or explain away his responsibility. Although Rembrandt, in the nature of his portrait commissions, explored the various dimensions of human relationships, his people remain isolated and alone.

The discussion of Rembrandt's contribution to the working out of the language of Christian art has stayed close to the choice of subject and the manner of his treatment of that subject. This is as it must be in an artist who was so concerned with his response to the human condition. Yet it should be emphasized that these are not literary essays on the subject but paintings, and Rembrandt's unique handling of the subject is made possible only by an equally unique and personal handling of the artistic means. Rembrandt's concern is with the least palpable quality of humanity and the least material aspects of their relation. These can be achieved only by the use of the least material means at the disposal of the artist, light, space, atmosphere, color. Rembrandt's lines, for example, do not describe edges nor define the clarity of things but they suggest motion and the lines of tension which hold things together. His color is not the precise descriptive color of the Italians but a fluid thing, dissolving masses, fading away to re-emerge elsewhere in the painting, evoking the figures while it penetrates them and joins them to the space which is the context of their spiritual life.

In many important ways Rembrandt would seem to be diametrically opposed to the concerns of El Greco. The one is the great Protestant humanist, the other the great Roman Catholic visionary and mystic. The one is all earthy realism (albeit a realism transfigured), the other all stylized distortions. Yet in their different ways their concern is with the same dimension of the human experience in the context of the Christian faith.

Again, the choice of subject and the treatment of it is a clue to the intentions of the artist. El Greco is never concerned with man's moral dilemma, nor with his dramatic relation in the context of earthly experience. There is a long series of portraits of the greatest importance in the understanding of his work. There is one landscape which is less a true landscape than the mystical vision of the city of Toledo. There are no history paintings except as history is seen in the light of miracle. There is no interest in genre, in ordinary life, in women as women, in children, in any aspect of normal human intercourse or relation. The subjects in his paintings are largely religious subjects. None is from the Old Testament. Most are those important to the Spanish aspect of the Counter Reformation.

El Greco, then, is concerned primarily with subjects which were of no concern to Rembrandt (except for portraiture) and entirely uninterested in those things which make up so important a part of Rembrandt's work. Nor, except in the most general sense, is there any close relation of style. Rembrandt's style is rooted in the closest observation of the actualities of human life and action. It has the taste of earth and the observation of the quality and texture of man's life. El Greco's is dream and vision, fantastic shapes and colors, swirling, zigzagging compositions, steel hard, inhuman people.

Yet their basic concerns are in common, for El Greco sought always the point of intersection of time and the timeless, history and eternity. The direction of his concern was different and in their differences they complement each other. Where Rembrandt sought the intersection of the timeless with time, the impact of the sacred on human life, El Greco sought the intersection of time with the timeless, the transfiguration of human experience into the heavenly vision.

The distinction involved here is not incidental. There have been other attempts in the history of the Christian church to represent the mystical vision or some aspect of the divine reality. This is a constant preoccupation of Byzantine art, for example, and much of medieval art at various times. In these forms, however, the art work embodies the victory of the visionary over the actual. Only the vision is felt, not the actual substance of the earthly event. Other Baroque artists have felt the same concern, particularly in Counter Reformation Italy, yet here the actual conquers the visionary and there is less a realization of the vision than a dramatically effective picture of the person experiencing the mystical event (see for example, Bernini's "Ecstasy of St. Theresa"). Only in El Greco is there the sense of the actual transcended, the transfiguration of history into the eternal, the physical into the divine.

It is true of El Greco as it was of Rembrandt that it would not be possible to interpret his portraiture in these terms if the form of the analysis had not been worked out by means of his more complex paintings. Yet this act having been performed, his portraiture can be seen both as prolegomenon to his mystical paintings and part of the general interpretation of experience most clearly seen in them. His portraits are by no means a small part of his production, nor are they confined to any one time in his career. They are, therefore, of major significance in the understanding of his work.

A close examination of El Greco's portraits reveals an acute eye for distinctive individual forms. They are excellent portraits considered simply as portraits. Yet the memory carries away from them an impression of remarkable unity and even sameness. The origin of this impression is partly social. Spain of his day was compellingly controlled by a social ideal which compressed individuals into a common mold and it is not surprising that this should be reflected in the portraits of the time. Even more compelling is the formal language of these remarkable portraits. There is the quality which appears in all portraits when the artist is not willing to subordinate his own vision altogether to the personality of the sitter. These are not just formal records but paintings by El Greco and they share the common structure of El Greco's art. They have more in common and this is expressed most forcefully in the look of the eyes. Gesture in any painting of this period is of fundamental importance. This is particularly true of El Greco who carries much of the burden of the visionary by means of ecstatic and symbolic gesture. A portrait does not gesture but only looks and El Greco has concentrated into that look all the expressiveness which otherwise is carried by the whole figure.

The use of this direct look is important quite apart from its expressive quality. Almost without exception the portraits look directly out from the canvas to the spectator. Almost without significant exception the sacred paintings have the figures with their attention turned inward or upward rather than outward to the spectator. The exceptions are revealing. They include many portraits of saints, who are usually men of the past whose appearance must be imagined by the artist but who, nonetheless, are involved in historical actuality and are not part of an interpretative vision (although it should be said that many are conceived in the visionary context and not always as portraits of historic persons). There are also many of the visionary paintings with one or more figures withdrawn from the scene and staring at the spectator. These are often explicitly, always implicitly, the links between the world of history in which the spectator stands and the world of the vision in which the sacred event takes place. Often by gesture of the hand they present the scene to the worshiper and the worshiper to the sacred persons.

The only other exception is Christ himself in certain of the paintings, such as the great "Resurrection" painting. All is vision and Christ floats weightless above the tumult of the earthly event. But he stares calmly at the worshiper. Christ is mystical vision and the source of meaning. He is also the key to history.

Fig. 3

In the portraits the quality of this look is itself a major factor in El Greco's art. The look is important in a Rembrandt portrait too but its quality is altogether different. It begins with a dramatic, often vulgar, Baroque abruptness but as his art matured the look turned more and more inward until Rembrandt's portraits become a concrete illustration of the old saying that the eyes are the windows of the soul. They are still, silent, brooding, deep. They seem to uncover the inner nakedness of the essential person and the sensitive spectator turns quieter too, almost shamed at this intrusion into the privacy of another person. At the same time there is a sense of pride and enlargement of the spirit in this identification with the essential being of another person. A student of Rembrandt's art, who is by no means a religious person or particularly sympathetic to religion, said of his "Syndics of the Cloth Guild" – ostensibly a record portrait of some tough Dutch business men – "It made me love my wife more." This was not meant sentimentally. All great art ennobles the spirit and enlarges the sensitivity of those who come to it receptively, but Rembrandt does so with a quality which peculiarly affects the deepest emotions that are involved in the relation of person to person.

Fig. 22

El Greco's eyes function differently. They are not the same, despite having in common the same intensity. At one extreme is the Grand Inquisitor, Cardinal Niño de Guevara, perhaps the most terrible realization in art of the fanatic, great in intelligence, in personality, in character and devotion, all nourishing a single-mindedness inconceivable to others without this interpretation of it. At the other extreme – not very far off – are the few female portraits which come as close as El Greco ever comes to gentleness and tenderness. All share the single quality of intensity. The eyes come out from the canvas like weapons. They bring to mind the description in the Letter to the Hebrews: "...living and active, sharper than any two-edged sword, piercing to the division of soul and spirit, of joints and marrow, and discerning the thoughts and intentions of the heart. And before him no creature is hidden, but all are open and laid bare to the eyes of him with whom we have to do" (Hebrews 4:12-13).

It is perhaps relevant that I once before used this same passage to account for something of the distinctive quality of Rembrandt's art. It cannot be applied in exactly the same way to each man but the fact that it does reveal something of the nature of each man's concern emphasizes again the closeness of his art in the context of the Christian interpretation of things. The passage actually refers to the word of God and has something of a direct relevance to the work of Rembrandt. The word of God, in the sense both of the Bible and of God's rational act among men, is the center of Rembrandt's thought and what his art in its maturity shows is the consequence of this piercing division, the human soul under the conditions of the word.

El Greco approaches the problem a little differently. The Word is embodied, not in the hierarchical institution, but in the common activity of the visionaries in the church. Thus their individuality, while present, is transcended. They become carriers of the vision, of the Word. Their physical form is the form of historic persons. The look of their eyes has no part in earthly experience but is the expression of souls consumed by the Word and thus transmitting the Word to others in the setting of the earth.

El Greco was not an unconscious artist or a victim of either psychic or physical disorders as some would have it. Even so intangible a thing as the look of the eyes is under perfect control. In those portraits which are most like straight portraits for a commercial purpose, the intensity is there but is subdued to earthiness and could be attributed to the peculiar and distinctive quality of the Spanish aristocratic ideal. In others the quality and intensity of the look becomes a measure and a revelation of the state of their souls, including as it does the fanaticism of the Inquisitor, so horrifying to the more liberal mind of the twentieth century, the flesh-consuming intensity of that living death's head, Cardinal Tavera, the more humane but no less intense look of Don Diego de Covarrubias.

This account of his portraiture states the essentials of El Greco's art, although the analysis could not be made without the other paintings. It is in these other, devotional, pictures that El Greco's essential artistic personality shows through. Again, the subjects show his continual pre-occupation with the intersection of the divine and the human, time and the eternal. Yet again, the contrast with Rembrandt is instructive. Rembrandt shows the effect of the divine in history, Christ teaching and healing or calling the children or suffering in the full radiance of his humanity, human beings acting within the moral order which is established in a world determined in form and relation by the fact of Christ, the divine revealing itself in the life of man. El Greco, shows the opening of heaven, the whole realm of the sacred, and men being drawn up from the earth to it. This appears clearly in three of his largest and most famous compositions, "The Burial of Count Orgaz," "The Martyrdom of St. Maurice," and Fig. 25 "The Dream of Philip II" (Adoration of the Name of Jesus). In each case the essential spiritual and compositional movement is upward to the heavens which reveal the source of life or receive the worshiper in his ascent. In each case, the events of history are no less present than in Rembrandt but the spiritual atmosphere is wholly different.

In all his work El Greco shows that eye for the actual which is so central a part of nearly all art yet the actual in the devotional and visionary paintings is lengthened into a symbol and a carrier of that which is beyond the physical and is more real than the earth itself.

X

THE

HOLY

AND THE TRANSCENDENCE OF DRAMA

Thus far this analysis has concerned itself entirely with the west European tradition since the medieval period. It is not unlikely that a certain cultural nationalism is involved here, yet the device might serve well enough to isolate certain varieties, certain types of the response of the Christian in art. There are, however, two types which must be found outside this west European tradition and the analysis could not pretend to any comprehensiveness without them: the art of the catacombs and the Byzantine icon.

The art of the catacombs can be included only by means of a certain charity in the definition of the word art. The works found there vary somewhat in quality but for the most part they do not belong, in depth and flexibility, with that range of art which is so fundamental to the understanding of the history of the human spirit. Yet they do indubitably state something fundamental to the understanding of the Christian consciousness and function uniquely in the life of the early church. This function is found, overlaid by others, as a constant theme in the life of Christian art. In short, the art of the catacombs is made up of visual prayers, the concretion of prayer.

Byzantine art, on the other hand, is one of the highest and most significant of the world's styles, considered strictly as art, yet it, too, is the purest expression of a function of Christian art which remains fundamental to the full interpretation of that art. Byzantine art is the embodiment of the vision of the liturgy. It is the concretion of worship.

Both styles lack a dimension that has been a major factor in the preceding pages. It is historically of the greatest significance that west European art cannot be discussed apart from the structure of the moral order which has been the preoccupation of the preceding pages. The European mind is incorrigibly dramatic and even those artists who move outside or above the dramatic do so only by absorbing and then transcending the dramatic vision which is so fundamental to the western mind. It is of the essence of Piero's art, for example, that the dramatic is vividly present to give the tension of life to the timeless presentation which is his primary concern. The reciprocal relation between this sense of drama and the development of the Christian consciousness of the meaning of things is a question too large for this study and perhaps too large ever to be answered. Yet as the discussion of the Renaissance attempted to show, this sense of the moral drama is fundamental to the understanding of the Christian cosmos and is not to be dismissed simply as culturally limited and therefore "relative."

The desire to establish this sense of the moral drama as fundamental to the activity of the Christian mind cannot and must not lead to the conclusion that those art forms which ignore it are less Christian, just as it has been necessary to reject the conclusion that the wrestle with the moral drama is itself not Christian. If this study aims for one general result it is the attainment of some genuine catholicity of awareness of the significance of man's forming.

Thus it must be accepted that the great enterprise of the Byzantine artist and the catacomb artist is partial, as all man's enterprises are, and, therefore, doomed to the same ultimate death which faces all that man does. But the enterprise itself was devoted with a single-mindness and fanatic intensity to the establishment of an attitude and an act within the faith which could not and cannot conceivably be eliminated or ignored. This is the concretion of man's response to the act and the being of God.

So far this discussion has largely ignored, by intention, that dimension of any work of men which is decisive in making it religious, the sense of the holy – the numinous. Since it is decisive it cannot be ignored permanently except as a rhetorical device, but it is necessary to see it properly and in proper relation to the whole consciousness of the Christian. The rhetorical device of putting second what could defensibly be treated first is made necessary by the present temptation of the Christian intellect. The Christian mind of our time is weighted down with the consciousness of the abuse of the idea of morality which came out of the work of our predecessors. Morality was defined in terms of conduct and the obligation of the Christian defined, therefore, in terms of acts in social context. It is one of the false attacks on contemporary theological thought that it denies this ethical obligation, as the life of many a contemporary theologian can witness. But it is still possible to say that the thrust of much of contemporary Christian thought has veered away from the ethical and therefore the more deeply moral and has concentrated on abstract principles and ideas of which the sense of the holy, in terms of its modern definition, the numinous, is not the least important. It is the purpose of the ordering of this study to restore to a position of primacy the sense of moral structure which is the basic characteristic of the Christian mentality while stating and perhaps demonstrating the inalienable necessity for the sense of the holy as a part of it. This ordering of things would appear to have biblical precedent. The risen Lord pursued the repentant Peter with the repeated question, "Do you love me more than these," thus establishing the centrality of his own person to the faith of the church whose rock he was addressing. Yet the response demanded of Peter, the definition of his relation to the source of meaning, was love, and the command laid on him was "Feed my sheep." The answer to the requirement for his credentials was the transforming power of the gospel in the very suffering bodies of men. And, "Seek ye first the kingdom of God and all these things shall be added unto you."

There is, therefore, in the very words and acts of Jesus, the sense of the inspiriting centrality of his own holy divinity and the sense of the transformation of man's moral sensibility and the ethical acts which proceed from that morality. Without this morality we are as sounding brass and tinkling cymbals. Yet the morality has its source in the power and holiness of God in Christ.

Without the sense of the holy there is always the danger, amounting to a certainty, that the dramatic concerns of western man will degenerate into narrative, moralism, or pietism. This in fact has been the course of Christian art for more than two centuries and is amply demonstrated by the vast bulk of the art of all branches of the Christian church today. There is, therefore, compelling reason to turn in humility to the Byzantine and the catacomb artist. It is unlikely that the consciousness of Western man can nourish itself on either style for any period of time. Once the revelation of the moral order through the dramatic problem has been seen, to turn away from it would be an evasion and a flight approaching the unforgivable. Yet it remains true that perhaps the purest expression of man's worship and devotion is found in these two styles, and the awareness of their meaning may restore to the consciousness of the church something of what it has denied to the impoverishment of its corporate life.

Having once stated the intent of catacomb art there is little more to say about it for it does not bear any analysis of formal structure which is so essential to the proper examination of the other works discussed. In the larger sense this is not fully true for there is never an act of forming which is not relevant to the question of the development of artistic styles, and the very succinctness of the catacomb paintings establishes the type of style which later artists were capable of developing at a much higher and more expressive level. But this kind of expression and communication was, so far as we can tell, altogether removed from the intent of the artists. This is sepulchral art, and contrary to sentimental popular opinion, the catacombs were intended only for cemeteries and small private and brief acts of worship connected with the dead. Thus the art works could not be intended to teach, inspire, present, or any of the innumerable purposes characteristic of artists. They were prayers and only prayers.

Fig. 41

It is important to this argument that these people could conceive of prayers as visual, that to them the three men in the fiery furnace, or Jonah coming out of the belly of the whale, stated on the wall the prayerful hope for the deliverance of the dead from the bonds of death. Thus the artist approached his task with an untrained eye and hand, uninterested in technique or structure, simply stating his hope in prayer and thereby establishing a fundamental type of Christian art. Without style, without "art," the statement has a directness and a simplicity rarely achieved again for rarely again can the making of a work of art be pursued with so single an intention. Yet the work of art as a prayer, as both act and offering, will be an element of fundamental importance in the history of the art of the Christian church. There are many times when Christian artists do not so conceive their work and make it didactic, rhetorical, or something else. But in the background there is the sense that a work of art done in the context of the Christian faith is more than a creation of man in his isolation but is a part of his service to almighty God.

Fig. 42 This attitude carries over into Byzantine art but the focus of the attention of the Byzantine artist is rather different. It was no longer possible to see the faith and the church in such simplicity and directness. The prayer which could be so uttered in the catacomb now became the most elaborate liturgy the church has known, even though the catacomb prayer is present in its essence. The art work was now public and carried with it all the responsibilities a public art so conceived might have. It received, too, a highly developed intellectual structure and purpose for, conceived overall, Byzantine art is a clear statement of Byzantine cosmology. Appropriate to all this they had developed a highly refined technique and formal language.

At the core of Byzantine art the intent was comparable to the art of the catacombs, to make concrete the relation of man to God in the liturgy, to set forth in the material the act of service and praise man makes to God. Thus it never occurred to the Byzantines in their formal art that they were describing the earth or analyzing the moral drama. There is in their art an adulteration (or a human flavor) of ostentation, or power, of all the things which can be a part of man's most essential act of service. But basically they approached the making of a work of art as though they were walking on holy ground. More than almost any other artists of any time they felt the power of the numinous in the sacramental. The space of earth falls away obliterated. Their main intent is to overcome the materiality of the earth, transcend the space and the things which stand between man and God. Thus their figures are flat, weightless, all expression concentrated in those amazing faces and the expressive rhythm of their bodies and the forms in the mosaics. Space is transformed into gold, the most spaceless of all colors, lifting the persons or events up from the earth into the realm of that which lies beyond the earth.

The organization of all this is basically liturgical and Byzantine art realizes, therefore, more clearly than any other kind of Christian art the sense of the primacy of the act of worship. Since it is basically sacramental, conceived as the locus of God's communication with man, it cannot concern itself with the things of the earth as the other styles discussed here might. It, therefore, realizes the numinous more single-mindedly than any other style so far considered. In fact, it might be said that the realization of the numinous is the major purpose of Byzantine art, the mystery of man before the holiness of God. With Rembrandt it was man before the goodness and the judgment of God but the moral plays virtually no role in Byzantine art. It is non-dramatic, even anti-dramatic, for drama is of the earth and this art is of heaven alone.

Such a style is bound to become false for it has too little attention for those aspects of human existence which infect everything man does. The Byzantines, as everyone else, could not escape history and time, yet their art is suspended out of time. It was inevitable that it should on many occasions and finally almost altogether have become rigid, rule bound, inexpressive, and in many ways an obstruction to the spirit of man. Yet no less can be said of many styles and there is no greater fault in the rigidity of Byzantine art when inspiration had departed from it than in the sentimental narrative of pietism which was the end of the western concern for drama. It was inevitable that each of these great styles should develop its own concern to the ultimate and that this ultimate should inalienably have been corrupted by the finiteness and pride of man. Yet the one without the other becomes painfully distorted in the whole context of the work of the church. Out of this conclusion arises a lesson for the work of the artist in the church today.

When a study of this kind turns from the descriptive and analytical to the prescriptive it treads on very dangerous ground. It is rare that any attempt either to predict the forms of future styles or to impose a prescriptive style on the work of the artist is successful. Perhaps the dangers of prescription might be avoided by keeping close to the diagnostic and allowing the prescription to suggest itself by the implications of the diagnosis. In any case, if this analysis is correct, much of the problem of art in the contemporary church can be discerned.

The art used by the contemporary church or made under its influence is, at best, almost always art of the second or third rank. The church does not attract the significantly creative artist nor use his work significantly because nothing in the church informs his sensibility and his work cannot be a meaningful part of the sensibility of the church. It is too easy to attempt to account for this simply by saying that the artist or the art of the church is of lesser rank, for the flaws in the work run deeper than such appellations suggest.

The Christian and the Christian artist live now as heirs of a long tradition but heirs of the collapse of that tradition as well as its greatness. Both the moral and dramatic tradition of the art of the Western church and the liturgical and numinous tradition of the art of the Eastern church fulfilled themselves and fell into the inevitable senility and the contemporary church artist cannot go beyond them because he cannot free himself from them. He feels it an inevitable necessity to be narrative and he feels it an equal necessity to be charismatic. He can pursue neither alone with single-minded passion and he has not learned to weld them into the unity of a new style, hence his work is almost inevitably an artificial combination of disparate elements linked only by conventional stylizations which have lost their original impulse. If the conventional art of the church is hopelessly sentimental, the serious art is almost as much so, in the precise meaning of the word sentimental, the excess of the forms of expression over the motivating emotion.

Thus the church's dissociation of sensibility is characterized by a dissociation of nature and grace. The Western emphasis on nature, the Eastern emphasis on grace never, in the eras of their fruitfulness, lost the sense of the other. The sense of the holy was the passionate concern of the Eastern Christian artist but it was the incarnate holy he sought and many monuments of the Eastern church are profound and meaningful statements of the narratives they recount. The sense of history, the event in time, was the passionate concern of the Western Christian artist but the event is the channel of grace and is transfigured by the holy. Each succumbed to its own characteristic weakness, but in its strength each had its own wholeness.

The contemporary church artist cannot succeed by turning into a manner the stylistic devices of the tradition, even when these are overlaid by the forms of contemporary styles. Perhaps he can succeed, if he can succeed at all, only as he can free himself from the weight of this tradition and seek in the attitudes of the past what he could not find in its devices.

XI

MANNERISM

AND THE TRAGEDY OF CREATIVITY

It is characteristic of the body of evidence so far presented that it deals with the most actively creative times of man's history, the period of great styles as represented by one of the most actively creative of the stylistic periods. Yet the argument must also accept the fact that not all of man's life is lived within periods of cultural creativity and the study of history has been afflicted by too exclusive concentration on just such periods. It is not possible now, or relevant to this argument, to deal with those periods of no cultural activity at all. It is necessary to deal with those periods generally considered to represent cultural decay or sterility. It is illusive, humanly complex, indirect. The preceding chapters present the case in terms of men who knew their own mind, worked for definable goals, created a body of work identifiable in its shape and purpose. This chapter deals with men whose goals were diverse, deliberately concealed even from themselves, quixotic, paradoxical. Their contribution to the Christian understanding of the arts is not of the same order, yet humanly it is revealing beyond much of the more coherent evidence.

The word mannerism has a curious history. As is so often the case with art historical terms it began as a term of opprobrium, applied to those artists of the sixteenth century who, in their own words, worked "in the manner of" certain of the great masters of the immediate past. It must be confessed that those who succeeded in this purpose remain among the duller artists of the times but the professions of this purpose managed to conceal for a long time the inherent worth of the development that was taking place beneath this superficial surface. It is one of the major achievements of criticism in recent years that it has succeeded in discovering and defining much of what took place among those artists who were the creative voice of the period.

Mannerism continues to have its specific reference and clearest development in the period which gave birth to the idea that defines it. The working out of its principles has redirected attention to the same phenomenon as it appears elsewhere and makes of mannerism a perennial event in the working out of the spirit of man.

The presentation of the idea of mannerism here presupposes a certain periodic development in the arts, for the style (or attitude, as mannerists do not always share fully in the common attitudes that make up a style) appears in a curious position between the major periods. A true style, Renaissance, Gothic, Baroque, is a pervasive thing, affecting the form and language of many different works of the period. Mannerism, on the other hand, is the style of an elite, of the sophisticated, as often against society as it is expressive of the overt purposes of that society. Its intricacy makes it less accessible to the untrained majority and it is thus an art for the wealthy, for the socially elite.

These major styles give birth inevitably to a mannerist style unless there is some decisive interruption to it in its final stages. This process of a style "giving birth" to something is not nearly so idealistic as the anthropomorphic terminology might indicate. A major style is born when certain problems in the formal language are stated in such a way that they capture the imagination of the artists who follow. No historian will venture to explain why this problem is imaginatively significant at this point and not earlier, but once the event has taken place the later development is understandable without resorting to elaborate images such as the unfolding spirit of man.

The first statement of the problem may, in terms of absolute value, be as significant and as fine as any later statement, but it does not work out all the implications of the problem nor develop all the technical resources necessary to the working out of the potentialities of the problem. The succeeding generations assume the task of carrying out the common problem in this way and it is to this working out that we have the fascinating successions of artists within a single style, some deliberately branching off from the main stream of a style they fully recognize, others enthusiastically working out the implications and possibilities of the defining problem. Inevitably the time comes when all the technical devices have fully developed and are entirely understood, when all the expressive possibilities have been used up. It is not a matter, as the German idealists would have it, of a personified spirit of the age dictating to men how they should work and express themselves. It is much more a matter of simpler materialism. All the techniques necessary to discuss this particular problem have been worked out and exploited. All that can be immediately said within those techniques and problems has been said. The style, then, is "exhausted" and the time is ripe for a new set of problems if the creativity of man is to go on. If the new style, the new problems, have appeared then the old style can die an unlamented death because no creative person is any longer interested in it. If, however, the new style is not ready at hand or still has not appeared in so challenging a form that it can command the attention and interest of those who are still productive, there is a curious interregnum when there is often a tremendous productivity in art work yet a very restricted range of possibilities for creativity.

Such a time is obviously the favorite of the academic style. There is no longer the arduous duty of discovery and invention which makes the earlier period the despair of the pedant and the conservative. All has been learned and reduced to rules. The techniques that took the full devotion of the earlier men are now codified, set forth in exercise books, taught by rote. This is the time of the jackals feeding off the blood and flesh of their fallen betters. Such art is sometimes correct, mildly interesting, often pretentious and of no consequence to this argument.

There are those, however, who hold in command the techniques and have in themselves true creativity and yet have found no way into a new world where creativity has the joyous expressiveness of the new style. These are the old men, whatever their years, the men who are no longer intoxicated or deluded by the dreams of their youth, the men who know that discovery

is not their fate but who know also that their skill is as great as their predecessors and their minds clearer.

The effect of this realization varies widely. There is no enthusiasm in a
mannerist style, no joy. It is often a dead world, airless, congested, frozen
into immobility, or tearing itself apart in a frenzy of movement. It can be
sardonic, with the skeptical cynicism of the man who has no more illusions
about the world. It can be frantic with the desolation of the man who has
no more hope for the world. It usually lacks almost all those qualities
featured in the previous pages. It has no joy, no peace, no serenity, no
dignity except occasionally the frozen dignity of the outraged but withdrawn aristocrat, no delight, no force.

It is an unpopular style. Universally, the mannerist periods are rejected
and held in little esteem in favor of their predecessors. The fifteenth century
or the high Renaissance (the first quarter of the sixteenth century) is far
more popular than the later three-fourths of the sixteenth century. Early
or high Gothic is universally admired at the expense of the Gothic of the
fourteenth and fifteenth centuries. Hellenistic art is universally criticized
unfavorably when compared with the fifth century and many histories of
Greece actually or effectively stop with Alexander the Great.

Popular taste is not wholly wrong. This later period is dominated in bulk
by the dullness of the academics and even the creative mannerists are often
perverse and succeed in being merely bizarre rather than significant. The
earlier hits a higher level of quality and even those works which cannot
sustain that level of quality often make up in charm what they lack in
depth. There is no charm in mannerism, no concession to popular taste.
It is not remarkable that it should not be a popular style, yet this should not
conceal the poignant, deeply meaningful, human expression that gives
to the period its amazing human relevance.

Those who do not know the field professionally, yet wish to follow the
argument, deserve an example of the rise of a mannerist style and the best
one is the most obvious, the mannerism of the sixteenth century.

Any attempt to define verbally so complex a thing as the essential
problem of an artistic style is doomed to distort the reality it discusses.
If that difficulty is realized, however, the attempt can be made meaningfully.
The defining problem of the Renaissance might be described as the objectively understood dramatic relation and action within a rationally
constructed space. The problem of the formal language of the Renaissance
was so stated by Giotto (it is relevant to the problem of value that no later

Renaissance artist excels Giotto in value and few are his equal). The later development is by no means a single-minded working out of this problem. Some are reactionary, going back to the older style, through conviction or incompetence. Some are trimmers, using the externals of the newer style to be fashionable while basically adhering to the old. Others go madly off in different directions because of their different interests. Nevertheless, the working out of this problem is the central concern of the Renaissance artists and it can be traced almost as though it were a separate living thing through its individual users (the German idealists were not complete ignoramuses). Some artists strongly emphasize one side of the problem, others another: Piero was primarily interested in space, Donatello in dramatic action and relation. The same style can be used to express the deepest piety or the wildest sensuality. Through all these various manifestations the integrating problems run, tying together diverse individuals into a common whole.

That grand moment common to all styles, its classic period, arrives in this development with the high Renaissance. Again there is nothing particularly mysterious about this culmination. The techniques adequate to any problem have been developed and learned but have not become dulled by repetition. The problems have been solved yet still have the clarity of their full resolution without the boredom of long familiarity or the disillusionment that comes with the realization that this, again, is not the end of man's pilgrimage but only another premature heaven. Thus the classic moment is the moment of balance, harmony, serenity, majesty, dignity. After that, mannerism.

Mannerism appears in many different places and in different individuals. Michelangelo was a high Renaissance artist in his early period. In his middle period, he was the greatest of the mannerists and his late work anticipates the Baroque. Andrea del Sarto was the soulless technician of Browning's poem so long as he worked with the language of the high Renaissance. Spiritually he was a mannerist and his greatness is found in his mannerist works. Others, Pontormo, Il Rosso, for example, are pure mannerists. It is in these men that the phenomenon of mannerism appears in its purest form or at least its clearest form. Here pure must include all the curiously impure contradictions that characterize this style.

It is no more a service to mannerism than to any other style to reduce it to a few general observations. It is even less accurate than it might be with other styles, for the defining characteristic of mannerism is the individualism, pained and isolated, with which it pursues its enterprise. It would be a particular disservice to mannerism to attempt to reduce it to any conventional religious category for it is not of the nature of mannerism to be conventional. Rather the mannerist takes over the conventional subject matter of the period out of which he has come and uses it for very personal expressiveness. It is rarely in the specific subject that he finds the means for his expressive act but rather in the style itself. This, obviously, is one of the sources for the unpopularity of mannerism as a style for the popular audience depends heavily on subject matter for its appreciation and cannot understand a work of art that depends primarily on style with the subject simply an element in that style.

Fig. 36   Thus, Rosso's "Crucifixion" and Pontormo's even more curious "Deposition" must, to the orthodox and stylistically untrained Christian eye, appear perverse in the extreme. There is in this style nothing that enables the unsophisticated believer to lay comforting hold on the work. Space, which the Renaissance sought so avidly, is here all powerful by virtue of its explicit denial. This is not the spaceless world of the manuscript illuminations but a work from which all space has been pressed, leaving only the dregs of its former greatness. Gesture was always the most effective instrument of the Renaissance artist, developing character and drama simultaneously. Here the gestures are either unmotivated and thus move in the same purposelessness as the lifeless space, or they are exaggerated, going beyond the rationality of the action into a world where the rational is no longer in force. The color, which was a major instrument of the Renaissance painter to establish the great order, serenity, and harmony of his work, is clashing, painful, antagonistic.

All this is a deliberate affront to all that went before. The serenity and order of the classic style is denied, sometimes ridiculed, sometimes caricatured. There is no finding of the relevance in the subject or in some orderly interpretation of the subject. It is only as a cry of the human spirit that such works can be understood.

Such language might be acceptable to some mannerists but it is likely that many would take a sardonic view of so emotional a terminology as applied to their works. Mannerism generally works only at the extremes, with the wildest expressions of emotions or with the severest suppression of them. Yet honesty compels the use of the term. For mannerism is the cry of the fully educated, fully civilized man who finds that neither education nor civilization suffices to change the essentials of man's experience. It is here that much of the deepest human experience of mannerism is to be found. In the creative periods man is sustained by the excitement of discovery, by the intensity of the work he is called on to do, by the manifest order he can bring into being. In the mannerist interludes man has absorbed all the technical and intellectual lessons built up through the years past and he finds that they too do not suffice.

Mannerism, therefore, is the great style of disillusion. It is negative but being negative it is preparation. Man cannot sustain himself. Having tried all he can, he sees only his work in ruins and the world he made, when he was as God, has only created its own destruction. It is not the work of mannerism to be creative or positive. The work of mannerism is to strip man to his nakedness, to rescue him from culture, to see him only as a man.

Thus a premature value judgment has often led the critics to pass over part of his own humanity. In the nakedness of man's isolation, the mannerist often makes discoveries that are vital to man's comprehension of the meaning of his own enterprise. It is probably true that, by and large, men will continue to prefer the order and serenity or vitality of the creative periods, but to use this as an excuse for the neglect of the disagreeable styles is to impoverish the imagination.

It is not all disagreeable. The "mannerist" period of the Gothic and the Greek styles produced images of an infinite tenderness and gentleness, the lonely loveliness of young girls. It is all part of the same fabric. Mannerism is the means whereby man can reflect on his own isolation and the collapse of his own pretensions. It is preparatory to the reception of God alone as God.

XII

CHRISTIANITY

AND THE ART OF THE TWENTIETH CENTURY

So far as the essential points of the argument are concerned, the evidence is now in. This is not to say that everything has been said that could be said, only that enough has been said to test the argument. The evidence should not be closed off, however, without a close examination of the singular problem presented by the art of our own day. There is an obvious relevance to the making of a special examination of the art that happens by chronological accident to be closest to the observer. This is what we live with and if the categories and operating principles are to have any usefulness they must function in the art of our own times.

There is, however, a special problem created by the art of the twentieth century; special, that is, for the Christian critic. The art of the late nineteenth century and early twentieth century is, perhaps, the most important body of western art created outside the influence of the church and often is in open rebellion against all the church stands for. The categories do not permit the rejection of art that does not use a Christian subject matter. Yet it is not fair to attempt to baptize these men against their will. Rather, it is required that their work be taken seriously in all the integrity of their purpose and achievement. Thus the serious Christian critic must be able to determine his attitude toward this very important body of art.

There are certain answers that must be rejected as unfair to the material or improper in method. Among these must be included Paul Tillich's much publicized statement that Picasso's "Guernica" is the greatest Protestant work of the twentieth century. The theological implications of that statement need to be explored at great length in ways inappropriate to this study. Suffice it to say that "Protestant" is here identified with the act of protest against the powers of the earth. This casts a pretty wide net, for all times and all places have had those who are able to make this protest. Thus the identification is another of the attempts to baptize prematurely something that belongs elsewhere.

It is too easy, also, to claim the modern artist as a theologically significant analyst of the plight of contemporary man. This is to overlook the fact that art is essentially constructive, not destructive or analytical. The artist is concerned with making an object which had not been there before. He might be, as Picasso certainly was in the "Guernica," deeply concerned about tragedy and destruction. It is only, however, as he succeeds in incorporating this into the work of art as constructive that it becomes truly a work of art. In a study of this kind it is only the principle of construction that determines the character and relevance of the work.

This is not to say that the work of the contemporary artist is irrelevant to the study of the discontinuities of modern life. As a human being the artist can manifest the brokenness, the discontinuity of life as well as the next man; but when he does so he is functioning as man and only peripherally as an artist. He becomes a cultural symptom rather than an artist. An artist's work is interesting as art precisely to the degree it succeeds in speaking the ordered and integral language of art. We might learn more about the brokenness of the world by looking at the work of this or that artist but we see that brokenness through the temperament of a maker, a sensitive and ordered vision, which sees brokenness only in terms of its own integration. Art is one of the essential elements of hope in the chaotic life of man. It exists only as order. The artist who excuses his work because of the chaos of his times is using the times as a cloak to conceal his incompetence. Only as he achieves unity of vision, coherence of execution, order of effect can he deserve the name of artist.

This is particularly true of the criticism of cubism, the style which has endured more interpretative rhetoric of this kind than any other. Unless they are pulling the public's leg (a likely possibility) even the verbal statements of the principal cubist artists are as theoretically confused as are all those writers who have spoken of cubism as expressing the brokenness of modern society. There is great seriousness to their concern with the blending of space and time but there are few better examples of the boredom of irrelevance than the claim of the critics of cubism that the artists analyzed the object into its appearance from various points of view and then presented these appearances simultaneously. There is one critic, at least, who doubts seriously if either artist or critic has ever experienced a cubist painting in these terms. Occasionally a critic will note that the object virtually disappears in a cubist painting and this seems a little odd if, in point of claim, more of the object is included in the painting than is ordinarily the case. But this rarely encourages the critics to reject the received dogma about the significance of the cubist style.

Fig. 19   In point of fact, in point of the actual experience of the painting, cubism is the most profoundly constructive of all the twentieth-century styles. Further, or in other terms, it is the most profoundly ordered of the twentieth-century styles (with the possible exception of constructivism which might be described as a purified cubism).

Thus the brokenness of the world is an irrelevant concept for cubism. The breaking up of the object is intensely important in the history of the twentieth-century mind but, in terms of the theological relevance of cubism, this is a liberation, not a breaking. With Cézanne, and the cubists following his lead, man was liberated from the tyranny of the object. Man was free now to use the object in pure poetry, not subserve his creativity to the dehumanized fact. Cubism is not a combination of different aspects of an object. It is a pure construction that makes allusion to recognizable objects for a structural purpose only. A work of pure abstraction or, more accurately put, of non-objective art, is a thing in its own right, independent of all other things. This is quite legitimate and must be touched on in its place, but it is not cubism. Cubism alludes to the object, partly for technical reasons, partly for human reasons. Technically, the allusion to objects detaches parts of the painting from the ground, and therefore, helps establish the particular space construction that is one of the primary concerns of the cubist artist.

Humanly, the purpose is more relevant to the Christian critic. The allusion to objects asserts man's control over the object, its subservience to human purpose. Cubism is often witty and playful, particularly in its later stages, often rather somberly intellectual. In either case it liberates or celebrates the liberation of man from the object.

Cubism is not, because of this, Manichean or dualistic. It is against the nature of art to be Manichean, for art is by its nature irrevocably united to the goodness of matter. Cubism is not even Manichean in its handling of the subject for, whatever specific attitude the artist might take and however distant he may make the object portrayed, he always treats it with respect. It is a fit part of the order of his art work, the object new made to set forth the consciousness of man of the deeply controlled, sensuously delightful order felt by the artist.

The Christian church can claim no part of this achievement. No other work of mind has been more creative of the essential posture of the twentieth-century intellect, and the church or the faith has been wholly detached from it. This has a homiletic purpose for the church. It is a shame and a call to humility in the church that the spirit of man was liberated from subservience to the least creative aspect of physical things by those working in complete indifference to the work and purpose of the church. Worse, the church was indoctrinating and continues to indoctrinate its members in this coarse and insensitive subservience to the most superficial and sentimentalized appearance of things, sacrificing to those outside the church the task of creating the visual and intellectual structure in which contemporary man can find completion.

There is no way to baptize this achievement. It was done without the church and the faith and it was a good work. There rests on the church the burden of guilt for whatever perversions this liberated spirit might achieve. It is not of the nature of man to endure his freedom with grace and charity, and liberation is always liberation into the possibility of new offenses. The work of the twentieth-century mind, proceeding in part from this liberation from the object, is no exception and nowhere has the church as an institution provided guidance or the means of control or direction. Even in its awareness of its own guilt it cannot fail to acknowledge the greatness of the order that proceeds from cubism.

Cubism is not the whole of twentieth-century art and it is not, in fact, of greater value than some other styles. It has been one of the most decisive of the modern styles and the modern mind is inseparable from the accomplishment of cubism. There are other manifestations of this liberated creativity, however, and they deserve at least a brief statement.

The general character of the achievement of cubism applies in much the same way to the other styles, although each is modified by its own particular concerns. One, constructivism, goes further than cubism in liberating art from the object outside itself since constructivism eliminates the object entirely and makes of the painting an object in its own right. The various forms and degrees of expressionism and surrealism still place a great deal of emphasis on the known world outside the work of art since objects as known from that world are both purpose and instrument of their work. It would not be possible to approach these styles, however, unless it were clearly understood that the greater use they make of recognizable objects in no way indicates a greater subservience to those objects in the nineteenth-century sense. The attention of the artist is directed toward the outside world, either in the sense that he seeks to express some characteristic of it or some aspect of his reaction to it. It is safe to say, however, that the main stream of twentieth-century art has sought to bring these things into the painting as a painting.

The twentieth century has an incorrigible urge to journalism and whenever its art pays too close attention to the object it tends to journalistic superficiality. (There are exceptions to this generalization; e.g., Andrew Wyeth.) As a rule the twentieth-century artists lack the ability to generalize about the object in the way that makes a realist painting of the Renaissance so humanly meaningful. Those artists who pay too close attention to the object tend to date badly as their parochialism shows itself. Those artists who nourish themselves on natural appearances without being journalistically parochial are generally deemed eccentrics from the main line of the development. Of this type, John Marin and Morris Graves might be noted. The value of their work might be as high or higher than many others but they are judged to be somewhat apart from that main stream of the century's art, which has sought to explore the art work in itself and for itself more or less alone. This would reflect itself in this argument. The work of such men has great value yet it can be handled in terms already developed for this study. It is the so-called main stream of the twentieth-century style, represented in good part by cubism, that presents the unique achievement and the unique relevance of twentieth-century art.

The primary concern of cubism is with structure, held under tight intellectual control. In its later stages there is an element of delight that was to be a foretaste of comparable developments later on, but at the beginning this enterprise took the fullest and most concentrated attention of the mind of the artist, and what emerged was a profoundly organized structure. Yet this concern with structure is somewhat different from the earlier artists with similar concerns. Theirs was a concern with the objective structure of the world as it is. The modern concern is more nearly with the structure of the painting as an object created by the mind and the hand of man. It should be obvious that the distinction here is one of emphasis. Too much has already been said of art as constructive. It is true that the center of gravity has shifted to the art work itself.

Interestingly enough, much of this statement would apply equally well to the less intellectual, more subjective, and emotional styles of the century. Expressionism is, by definition, an art that violates natural appearances for the sake of a stronger emotional expression. In its more hysterical forms the structure becomes loose and empty but in its profoundest exponents, Van Gogh, for example, or Munch, the picture leads its own structural life. Fig. 40 The difference lies not so much in the general category applicable to them as it does in the organizing principle. In cubism the organizing principle is a kind of gravity, a force of tension and relation that holds the parts together. In expressionism it is force, movement, action, but the result is an ordered painting to be lived in its own right, quite within the structural principle of twentieth-century painting.

Surrealism follows a slightly different road to something of the same end. Of necessity it reproduces some aspects of the visible world with greater accuracy than the other twentieth-century styles, yet it does so in a manner quite in harmony with this general interpretation of the century's art. The objects are torn loose from their natural context and used to construct a new world wholly under the control of the will and the imagination of the artist. It purports, as a style, to reach beyond the real to the reality that lies in another world. Since there are certain obvious limits on the ability of the artist as a human being to see this kind of reality, the work is a construction of his imagination and his will, a thing to impose on the imagination of the spectator.

Thus the achievement of the twentieth century is constructive, the creating of a type of object and a type of making that had not existed before. This was a liberation of man from a kind of oppression of his imagination and represents clearly man as himself the creator. Perhaps the purest form of this creator-activity is constructivism which reproduces most nearly the type of creativity which might have appeared had God been less concerned with freedom and more with order. Constructivism is the ultimate expression in modern art of harmonious serenity above the muck of the human struggle. Few artists have been able to sustain constructivism both creatively and purely but when it is achieved it is the cleanest note of the twentieth-century work.

This liberation of creativity had consequences beyond this kind of making. Man was liberated into creativity. Ever since the Garden, man has taken his liberation as an opportunity for self-assertion and the free creativity of the twentieth century has been no exception. Thus the theory of much of twentieth-century art has led many artists to the most unrestrained assertion of their godlike creativity which has, perhaps, ever come from an artist. It has, in fact, given rise to a whole aesthetic of free creativity, the understanding of the art work as wholly subservient to the creative activity of the artist. Having overcome the tyranny of the object the artist now makes of the painting an object which can demand of him no more homage than any other object deserves. It becomes a record of his physical action, the field within which his action takes place. The isolated artist is supreme in his godlike creativity. The style emerging from this aesthetic is often referred to as abstract expressionism but is more aptly known as "action painting."

The Christian must not only admit but assert that this aesthetic is wholly false. No man is an island unto himself, either as man or as maker. The attempt to make himself wholly isolated and wholly in command of his own destiny and reality can only lead to destruction, as it has done with a few of these artists.

The obvious conclusion is a false one. In terms of the categories set up it would appear that the art produced from such a theory could only be classed under the heading of the arts of the fall, a manifestation of the incorrigible evil at the heart of man. An honest look at the paintings themselves should suffice to show that this is not at all the case.

It is a characteristic of a period such as this that a variety of stylistic themes should be working themselves out. The basic problems of the twentieth-century style have been worked out and the inevitable result is a proliferation of academic art. The wildest explorations of the modern artist have been reduced to rules and are taught in academies all over the country. At a more serious level is the considerable quantity of manneristic art. This phenomenon made the previous chapter essential to the argument, since otherwise the term in this very important context would have been virtually meaningless. Nevertheless, much of contemporary painting is mannerism, with all the characteristics of complex spatial structures, clangorous colors, sophisticated compositions, emotional intensity. There is present in such paintings all the pathos, all the sardonic awareness of evil and suffering, all the detachment, which characterize a truly manneristic style.

At the same time the works produced by some of the painters with the   Fig. 37
most extreme statement of demonic individuality are, in fact, works of singular loveliness, works that bring into art, at an entirely different level, the quality of delight that is found only in the innocent eye. The difference of level comes in the nature and object of the delight. The delight seen in the earlier style is inseparable from the delight in the physical world. The delight of the contemporary artist is delight in the art work alone. Curiously enough, even in the works of the most verbally extreme of these men, a genuine objectivity enters into the painting. It is no longer the Renaissance objectivity of the seen world but an objectivity that respects the private life of the painting and all the elements in it. Colors, shapes, lines, masses, movement, tension, all the component elements which at all times have been the work of the artist, work out their own destiny and establish their own relational life. This obviously false anthropomorphic language might serve to elucidate the characteristic life of a contemporary painting. There is a great similarity in many of them simply because the modern style has become academic but there is, too, that body of works which tends to resemble each other because the elements have their reality and their life which the artist controls but respects so what we have is not the similarity of dullness but the similarity of a creative style.

The creativity is in the delight, in the life of the thing. Contemporary art has become a matter of following out this life of the forms, the integrity of their vital relationship. They fall, therefore, under the category of the arts of creation, not in the perverted sense of the verbal statements that claim man to be a god, but in the purest sense of man delighting in the nature of things and bringing into being their effective relations.

It is obviously too broad a claim to say this description belongs accurately to all works of modern art. It is too richly varied a period for that. Not only are there different styles, but this same style lends itself to somber, tragic motifs as well, reminiscent of tragedy and evil in the world outside the forms of the art work. Yet it is not simply a perverse desire to swim against the critical stream that impels the appellation "delight," for the larger portion of contemporary art. So much of it has an innocence of delight that makes it all the more unfortunate that prejudices do not make it more generally available. Mannerism is deliberately anti-popular. It is sophisticated, it depends on a knowledge of past forms that no one but the specialist can have, it is consciously strained and painful. The mannerists in contemporary painting are no exception. But so much of contemporary painting is composed so largely of innocent delight that it could be available to anyone who is willing to look with innocence of eye rather than with an eye corrupted by subservience to the object. Freedom is hard bought and dearly held and most are afraid of it. But the rewards of liberation are great.

There are more things about this style relevant to the thought of the Christian. Not the least important of these is the difficulty of man effecting either his own salvation of his own damnation, by his own intent, and unaided power. It is promised to man that his salvation shall come to him as an addition to his proper work and service. If it becomes his professed aim and entire purpose it is a life he loses rather than gains. Similarly, the intent to achieve what the Christian must condemn as the damnation of isolated individualism fails of its own weight with those who seek it through their work. It is the nature of art to be constructive. It is also the nature of art to be something outside the person, a thing which can appear in integrity only if the essential integrity of its relations and qualities of existence are scrupulously observed. A man might be a liar, a cheat, and a corrupter of persons but if he tries to be so in his art, he does not achieve a corrupting object but a bad work of art. It is the nature of the art work that it require integrity and order, otherwise there is no art work. Whatever the claims of the artist, the work survives.

EPILOGUE

ART IS THE MORALITY

OF THE IMAGINATIVE LIFE

The argument is closed in the presentation of its typical elements. The problem of identifying the work of Christian art has, at least, been located. This location can be determined by its two co-ordinates, its two dimensions. The art work finds its life between nature and grace and the great creations of Christian art are to be found at the intersection.

The artist lives within the natural order and his celebration of it makes the art of creation. He explores and analyzes it and makes the art of the image of God. He sees and mourns its brokenness and makes the art of the fall. He lives within its healing and makes the art of redemption.

Seen in its other dimension art can be wholly within this world, wholly concerned with the natural vitalities where religion is irrelevant. When the imagination takes on the quality of awe the work becomes implicitly religious. If the sense of awe is conscious, if the sense of the holy is fully present, then the work is explicitly religious. Where the essential spirit of Christianity is present the work is implicitly Christian. When the work is consciously incarnational it is explicitly Christian and the one dimension has met the other.

Distinctions of value are irrelevant to these concepts. They differ in relevance and power, not necessarily in aesthetic value. Nor can one supersede another or usurp its place. All the works of men are partial and in every case a primary concern of this study has been to present art as the place of the working out of man's deepest concerns. All these things are essential to the wholeness of the human enterprise. Yet even when this is said it is necessary to go further and say that this enterprise and the place of the artist in it cannot be seen except in terms of the point where the essential dimensions intersect. This is the point of definition by which the wholeness is seen as whole, the point where art's hope and quality as consciously incarnational and redemptive is determined. Out of this grows the sense of the holy, the intersection of nature and grace which is the essence of Christian art. So the argument must push a step beyond the demonstrable in order to suggest the essence.

Christian art, generally speaking, has been concerned with all the basic Christian doctrines. Christian aesthetics, however, finds its center of gravity in the doctrine of the Incarnation.

The parallelism must be retained. In his way, the Christian artist has been concerned, sometimes obsessively concerned, with the doctrine of re-demption, with suffering, with the drama of relation, with all those things that make the fabric of Christian experience. Even these concerns must be seen against the background of stillness that is the nature of the thing seen rather than the thing acted out in time. The definition of what an artist is essentially lies in the sense of the Incarnation, that the material substance of the earth was deemed worthy not only to proceed from the creative hand of God but to be radiant with the Godhead himself.

All art is incorrigibly materialistic. Its very being is found in the substance of the material from which it is made. Its meaning is to be found in the nature of that making, the manner in which the physical material is given shape, the posture that shape takes in the wholeness of the human experience. Philosophical idealism in any form is not possible to the artist, a fact which Plato knew perfectly well. For the artist there can be no higher reality than the material nor meanings that are superior to their expression in the physical substance. An idealistic philosophical system that finds darkness in material, art as an obstruction to the spirit of man, can find no truth in the arts or no more than a dim and distorted reflection of truth. Thus it is essential to aesthetics that the artist be free to find his meaning and his expression in his material.

Few artists are philosophically inclined and most go about their work in complete indifference to such a controversy. Their work and its meaning are a part of the material and that is the nature of things. Furthermore, few if any artists can afford to be indifferent to the radiance of the material, the sense that the material is the meaning of his life. An artist who hates his material or is indifferent to it becomes a contradiction in terms, for such an attitude makes art impossible. He lives fruitfully in his material or he is no artist.

Thus the Incarnation is a reality in a limited sense even to those who never heard of it. It behooves the Christian to be respectful to the very fact of art which, by existing, testifies to the glory of the created earth.

The Christian artist, however, goes further. Physical material is not only the habitation of his work, it was judged worthy to contain his Lord. It is thus radiant with the glory of creation and the new creation that proceeds from the Incarnation. If the theological justification of art in general proceeds from the Incarnation, the radiance of Christian art in particular grows out of this more acute sense of the glory of that which was given in the grace of God. One measure against which the Christian artist must be measured is his sense of the glory and the radiance of things.

Does this indicate that Christian art must be "realistic"? The answer to the question is not obvious. It can be, but this has been asserted of every style. It can be asserted that the norm from which the Christian artist departs only at his peril is the sense of the radiance and the integrity of things seen. To deny the goodness of the earth is to deny the goodness of creation, to be Manichean.

The injection of this principle complicates the argument so far advanced. Many of the styles discussed specifically assert the goodness of the earth. Others are obsessed by the agony of the human experience and the material becomes the instrument for their expression of this pain. Nature is twisted and distorted out of its serenity and dignity to give to the work the sense of its impact with the tragedy of human experience.

The first answer to this dilemma is a very practical one. A work of art is limited as any human act is limited. There are many other aspects to Christianity than the affirmation of the goodness of the earth and it is required of some in the exercise of their responsibility that they grapple with the vitalities of tragedy and contend with the abyss of contradictions that cuts across human relations. There is no insuperable problem here. The great tragic artists in any form react to existence and make their world out of a powerful conviction of what things are. They respond to the despair, the meaninglessness, the cruelty, the ugliness of the earth, out of a profound sense of what life and the earth are in their essence and the rhythms of their work; the principle of coherence within it reflects this sense of life. The great expressionistic artists, the great tragedians, are always affirmative in their strength, even though – particularly though – their affirmation has nothing to do with the mindless optimism of an effete society. The affirmation that characterizes the great tragic artists is something quite different from the curious Manicheism of Ivan Albright, or the casual brutalities of much Roman work, or the fecund vitalities of South Indian sculpture or the brute masses of Soviet, Nazi, or American commercial architecture. The denial of the health of creation does not come from the tragic artists but from those who sentimentalize nature or drama, those who prettify the natural order, those who work by rote rather than by conviction.

By its nature the work of art is rooted in things. It is itself a physical material, a combination of physical materials, each with its own particular character. Its life is found in the relations it sets up among the physical qualities of its component elements. All art that is true art is a communion with the nature of physical things and for the Christian this is, by definition, a probing into the reality of God's creation. Thus, to the Christian, no art is a matter of indifference since all true art is man's response to created reality. The most significant art for him is that art which responds under the light of grace, but all art has relevance for his life and thought.

Thus it must be reaffirmed that all good art belongs to Christ as all the goodness of creation does. At the same time it must be reaffirmed that some art is relevant to the life and thought of the Christian in a very special way. It is hard then to say that any art is "Christian" in the sense that persons are Christian but there is some art that grows out of a life under grace, that reflects the thought and the labor of a Christian working out his responsibilities in the material that is the substance of what he does.

Thus it is very common to the arts that the artist should glory in the fact of creation, delight in the earth, and in its natural vitalities. But the style that reveals most to the Christian is the style that grows out of the dialogue of nature and grace. Naturalism can teach much about the earth, but it is holy naturalism that speaks to the need and the condition of the Christian.

There are many great artists who have explored the structure of the created order and the structure of the art work that can manifest the power of man to extend and comprehend that creation. The great and singular experience of the art of the recent past has been the most rigorous exploration ever undertaken of the nature of the created object as made by the artist rather than produced by the exercise of external laws and appearances. There is a special relevance for the Christian in the work of those men who affirm, not the isolated creativity of the godlike artist, but those who fulfill the purpose of man under God.

The sense of the void, of the abyss, of man's alienation from man and the fruitful order of existence, of cruelty and despair are a part and a vital part of man's work on earth. Any Christian who isolates himself from these experiences because the answer given or implied is other than his own, impoverishes not only his faith but his understanding. Yet there will be in him a special concern for those who see tragedy not as the end of man but as a rent in the wholeness of creation, the consequence of sin and the seed bed of hope.

The final category belongs to Christians alone, for redemption is an act of God that is not generally apprehended except under the grace of God. This is the transfiguration of earth, the search for the grace beyond hope. This is the holiness of Christ penetrating the material and bringing into being the new earth.

Thus what we may call "Christian art" is not sheep separated from goats but a dimension of the general human experience. Man does not sit in judgment on the honest work of his fellow and the Christian is not in a privileged elite or a ghetto isolated from the general human work. His work is a part of the whole, the salt or the leaven. It is only as he understands that quality which gives to certain works of art a special relevance that he can in any way speak of "Christian art." This quality is to be found, not in the choice of subject, nor even in morality but in its rootedness in man's general work transfigured by the numinous.

The relation of art to morality is a complex one, and is not relevant at the moment to the subject at hand. Yet the thesis so far developed would not be complete without this assertion: art is the morality of the imaginative life.

Morality in personal life is built up of choices. It is rare that choice is simple except in abstract principle but in that principle man chooses between right and wrong. He can choose either and build a life out of his choices or pursue his life to its destruction by the error of his choice. The morality of art is different. Art grows out of the fecundity of the imaginative life, out of the disorder of impressions, ideas, passions, hopes, fears, and all else that make up the work of the mind. It is the art work that enables man to bring order out of this chaos and find meaning in the meaningless. Yet to do so man must bring to his work a rigorous integrity that can only be called morality. If he does not do so he does not create an evil work of art but no work of art at all. The integrity of the creative act is an indispensable ingredient in the making of an art work. Only in obedience can the artist create. Only in subservience to the nature of his material and his operation and in the honesty of his own character can he make a work of art at all. This has nothing to do with the morality of his personal life. He might be any kind of immoral man and artists probably run as high an average of immorality as any other profession. But in the practice of his profession he is a moral man or he is nothing.

Already there is established a principle that should give humility to the Christian who would sit in judgment and separate the sheep from the goats. There are few other places in human experience, with the exception of science and mathematics, where the rigorous morality of personal and professional integrity is so clearly manifest. Yet within this general human creativity there is still that part which is particularly relevant to the life and the work of the Christian. When the morality of art is transformed by the numinous, by the holy awe, then the work is religious. When religious art stands under the grace of God in the love of Christ, then in a distinctive sense the work is Christian. In pursuing the categories that can guide the search through the ambiguities and complexities of the things man has made, it is necessary to see that the general work of men is fully present in the search that, for Christians, is the search for the orders of God's creation. When this search is touched with the sense of eternal mystery, when the tension of the work is transformed by the awareness of the awe of the holy, the power, and the glory of God, then man can be led out of himself to an awareness of the ultimate meaning of his world.

This quality is not entirely inaccessible to the reasoning mind. Part of the integrity of the work of modern intellect is the integrity with which men have pursued the meaning of the human experience and isolated those factors which compel the conclusion that the work of the artist had in its purpose and in the reality of its being the quality which marks it as touched by grace. Ultimately, however, the numinous is received by those who would receive it and thus goes beyond the reach of rational categories. It is part of the humanness of man that he should maintain his rationality and the rational control of his understanding as long as he can. Yet humility lies beyond the control of the conscious mind and the transfigured earth is a world to live in, not to chart from the outside. *The Christian artist is the artist who has gone into that world and has created in it, not just a thing, but a pointing to the Way.*

BIBLIOGRAPHY

BIBLIOGRAPHY

Assembling a bibliography for a work of this kind has singular difficulties. While I have intended that it observe the essential scholarly canons, it is not a work of the conventional scholarly type, built up on the foundation of identifiable contributions from many definable sources. It is an argument based primarily on my own direct experience of art and religion. Yet to reason about either art or religion is not a skill a man is born with and such ability in this regard as may be manifested in this book is owed to many men and books. A bibliography which acknowledged all my sources would, therefore, include everything I have read and studied on the subject of art and religion which would be a pointless enterprise. Yet it would not be honorable to dismiss all my obligations with a general acknowledgment nor would it be useful to those who may wish to pursue the argument further.

In compiling this bibliography I have kept in mind these two purposes.

First, I wish to acknowledge obligation wherever I feel a work has some special relevance to the argument as I have pursued it or where the debt is immediate and conscious rather than general. Second, I recognize that I am writing for two audiences, those interested in art and those interested in religion. Many in either group may be quite unfamiliar with the literature in the other and a selective bibliography can serve as an introduction to further study. This is the reason for the inclusion of references which specialists in either field might take for granted as known to all beginning students in their discipline.

GENERAL

There are three principal areas where general acknowledgments are required: theory and practice of art criticism, religious thought, and the interrelation between religion and culture in general and art in particular.

I. THEORY AND PRACTICE OF ART CRITICISM

Currently dominant in art scholarship is a concern for iconography, connoisseurship, and symbolism – the identification of origins, attribution and the tracing of both relations and sources in the context of the work. While acknowledging the inescapable importance of that work, my own concerns have been with the history of style, the definition of the structure of the style, and the manner in which it communicates the attitude which gave rise to it (this is something of a false separation since it is clear that neither line of investigation can be carried on alone but it does indicate a center of gravity in interest). My sources are to be found, then, in the work of Heinrich Wölfflin, *Principles of Art History*, trans. M. D. Hottinger, (New York: Dover Publication, n.d.), Alois Riegl, *Spätrömische Kunstindustrie*, (Vienna: Österr. Staatsdruckerei, 1927), and Guido Kaschnitz von Weinberg, whose work I have known in articles published in various scholarly journals in Germany but which has now been summarized in handy form in the three volumes, *Römische Kunst*, in the admirable series of scholarly paperbacks "rowohlts deutsche enzyklopädie" (Reinbeck bei Hamburg, Rowohlt Taschenbuch Verlag GmbH, 1961).

I owe much to a very different type of book, Theodore Meyer Greene, *The Arts and the Art of Criticism* (Princeton: Princeton University Press,

1940). This book is less well-known than it deserves, partly because of a painfully scholastic organization and terminology, for which the author acknowledges responsibility, but also because it dares to say simply and directly things which are usually buried under manneristic scholarly terminology.

There are many critics whose work I have admired and therefore been influenced by, too many to mention here. Some will appear in references in the separate chapters. I should like to mention particularly the work of Lionello Venturi and for the sake of the interested layman his elementary survey *Painters and Painting* (New York: Charles Scribner's Sons, 1948), and Nicolaus Pevsner, *An Outline of European Architecture* (Harmondsworth: Penguin Books, 1957), a classic in architectural history and criticism and a model of exposition of the relation between man's purpose and the style of his art. I have made much use of such critics as Patrick Heron, Clement Greenberg, Roger Fry, Bernard Berenson and many others.

Without passing judgment on the philosophical quality of the work of various aestheticians I can safely say that few of them have been of any use to me in my work. The single exception is Harold Osborne whose two books *Theory of Beauty* (New York: Philosophical Library, 1953), and *Aesthetics and Criticism* (New York: Philosophical Library, 1955) represent distinctive contributions to the discussion.

In a special class for my purposes is a book which deserves to be listed under all these categories, Jacques Maritain, *Creative Intuition in Art and Poetry* (New York: Pantheon Books, 1953). I have no personal need for the Thomistic system or terminology but it is presumptuous to prescribe another man's style. I have not re-read the book for years, certainly not since beginning this manuscript, but there is hardly a page of my work which is not influenced by that extraordinary book.

Of almost equal importance to the development of my work is the writing of Herbert Read. The debt here is perhaps less localized to one book but the ones I have used most extensively are *Icon and Idea* (Cambridge: Harvard University Press, 1955) and *Education through Art* (London: Pantheon Books, 1949). There are areas of his psychology of art which I can neither use nor judge since I have no competence to speak of that subject but my thinking on this subject has been deeply marked by his passionate and repeated insistence that art is a genuine way of knowing, not only not subservient to anything else but even primary in man's experience.

Henri Focillon's *The Life of Forms in Art* (New York: Wittenborn,

Schultz, 1948) is a small and splendid book which I return to with profit and pleasure.

Other specific works of criticism appear in connection with separate chapters below. By their example, many belong in such a sketch of books influencing my work in criticism.

2. RELIGIOUS THOUGHT

There is no possibility of making adequate acknowledgments under this category nor of providing adequate guidance to those not already familiar with the literature. I am a theological layman without any formal training. The reading I have done in the process of my self-guided training is not so exceptional to be of more than passing interest to those who already know the field nor has there been anything about it to make it normative for those who come new to the study. Other books might serve the purposes of another person equally well. In work of this kind it has become increasingly clear to me that the necessary thing is to do the kind of study that enables one to think theologically in terms of one's own discipline, thus making it possible for that discipline to speak to theology. It is not a matter of learning theological categories that can be superimposed on the material of the discipline but of using theology to learn more about the kinds of reality to which theology and the discipline are equally directed.

In my own theological reading, the most important single instrument has been the quarterly journal, *Theology Today*, which manages to talk about a wide range of centrally important theological issues without technical terminology and is therefore peculiarly well suited to the needs of the concerned theological layman. I owe too much too diffusely to too many writers and too many conversations to extend the list further in terms of theological study specifically. A good, practical current bibliography is published by the Division of Higher Education of the General Board of Education of the Methodist Church under the title, *The Re-Examination of Faith in the Scholarly Community: A Bibliography*, ed. Richard N. Bender.

The only indispensable part of my own theological training (and I am inclined to make this a general principle) is the close and continuous study of the Bible.

3. RELATION BETWEEN RELIGION AND CULTURE

The most generally useful instrument in this area is another journal,

The Christian Scholar. In the decade of its existence, this journal has almost singlehandedly created an informed community of concern. It also provides much bibliographical material on the general topic as well as in specific areas of the problem. More bibliographical references can be found in the Bibliography published by the Methodist Board of Education and mentioned above.

Some of the best thinking and writing in this area has been done in connection with the specific problem of the relation of Christianity to higher education. Again, it is ungracious to single out a few writings when I owe so much to so many but I will mention those that have been the most important to me. This includes the three classic writings in the field, not yet superseded, Sir Walter Moberly, *The Crisis in the University* (London: SCM Press, 1949); Arnold Nash, *The University and the Modern World* (New York: Macmillan Company, 1944); and John Coleman, *The Task of the Christian in the University* (New York: Association Press, 1947). To this should be added George Williams, *The Theological Idea of the University* (New York: National Council of Churches of Christ, Commission on Higher Education, 1958).

Although, in the text of this book, I take exception to some of his formulations concerning the arts, I still happily acknowledge the debt all of us in this general area owe to the work of Paul Tillich. I owe a great personal debt, also, to the writings of Reinhold Niebuhr, whose *Nature and Destiny of Man* (New York: Charles Scribner's Sons, 1946) was the first serious theological work I read. Professor Niebuhr's concerns are more with society and politics, less with the specifically cultural problems, but what his work first revealed to me was the relevance of Christian faith to the vast world outside personal devotions.

Since I am a historian, it is perhaps natural that much of the writing that has affected my own development has been in the field of history. Again it is cavalier to select when the debt is so general but I have been particularly influenced by Brooks Otis, "Mythos and Logos," *The Christian Scholar* (September, 1955), 219-31, and "History and Christianity," *Faculty Papers*, The National Council of the Protestant Episcopal Church, n.d.; and Burr Brundage, "The Crisis in Modern Historiography," *The Christian Scholar* (September, 1954), 385-95.

There is a specific function for the doctrine of the Incarnation in the text that would perhaps make bibliographical references appropriate to a later place. Two documents, however, have been so basic to my thinking about the relation between Christianity and the material world that I feel con-. strained to mention them here: Joseph Sittler, Jr., "A Theology for Earth," *The Christian Scholar*, XXXVII (September, 1954), 367-74, and Denis Baly, *The Geography of the Bible* (New York: Harper & Brothers, 1957). A worthy third is Nathan A. Scott, Jr., "The Meaning of the Incarnation for Modern Literature," *Christianity and Crisis*, XVIII (December 8, 1958), 173-75.

If a sense of the sacredness of the earth is one essential ingredient in any body of thought that wishes to call itself Christian, the complement is the Christian doctrine of work which is man's way of ordering himself in the body of creation. In this connection I would refer particularly to *Work and Vocation*, ed. John Oliver Nelson (New York: Harper & Brothers, 1954) with particular emphasis on the essays by Robert Calhoun, and Alan Richardson, *The Biblical Doctrine of Work* (London: SCM Press, 1952).

As the problem of religion and culture narrows toward the arts, it is necessary to say that there is a far larger and more useful body of writing in the field of literature than in any of the other arts. An excellent bibliography can be found in *The Christian Scholar*, March, 1958. A few of the more recent books are noted in the Methodist Bibliography already listed. In my own work I have been influenced by Preston Roberts, "A Christian Theory of Dramatic Tragedy," *The Journal of Religion*, XXXI, No. 1 (January, 1951) and by Nathan Scott, whose writings are too numerous to list in a limited bibliography. I shall mention only "The Collaboration of Vision in the Poetic Act," *Cross Currents*, VII (Spring, 1957), 137-53. Also I should like to call special attention to Denis de Rougemont, "Religion and the Mission of the Artist" in *Spiritual Problems in Contemporary Literature*, ed. Stanley Hopper (New York: Harper & Brothers, 1952), and Amos Wilder, *Modern Poetry and the Christian Tradition* (New York: Charles Scribner's Sons, 1952).

I also owe a special debt to Miss Dorothy Sayers. *The Mind of the Maker* (New York: Living Age Books of Meridian Books, 1954) is useful but has less effect on my work than her introduction and notes to Dante, *The Divine Comedy* (Harmondsworth: Penguin Books, 1949, 1956, and 1962). It would not offend Miss Sayers at all to raise the question whether the debt is properly to her or to Dante but her readings have been very relevant to my work. Again, her interpretation of Dante owes much to Charles Williams to whose work she directed me: *The Figure of Beatrice* (London: Faber and Faber, Ltd., 1943) and *The Descent of the Dove* (New York: Living Age Books of Meridian Books, 1956). The "way of affirmation" as expounded by Dante and by Williams is fundamental to my whole case.

There is no comparable body of literature dealing with the problems of the visual arts. Of course, the larger part of scholarly studies in the history and criticism of any art necessarily deals with the problem of religion and art for that is the nature of the material. I owe a very great deal to this body of scholarship and I shall note several of the particularly relevant works in the parts of the bibliography dealing with particular historical periods. Of works dealing with the visual arts from a point of view like that of the large body of literature dealing with the literary arts there is very little. The article by Denis de Rougemont noted above might better have been listed here since it is almost equally relevant. Cyril Richardson's "Some Reflections on Liturgical Art," *Union Seminary Quarterly Review*, Vol. 3, No. 3 (March, 1953) is useful. Nicholas Berdyaev, *The Meaning of the Creative Act*, trans. Donald A. Lowrie (New York: Harper & Brothers, 1955) is generally very useful although it might better come under the general heading of studies in aesthetics just as Maritain's *Creative Intuition in Art and Poetry*, with its many very sensitive critical comments, might well have been listed at this point. Etienne Gilson, *Painting and Reality* (New York: Pantheon Books, 1957) is another excellent book in Thomistic categories.

Several of my own publications might be mentioned. *Form and Reality: Art as Communication* (Nashville: Methodist Student Movement, 1957) is an earlier statement of the case developed more fully in this book. "Protestant Art and the Natural Order," *motive*, Vol. 17, No. 2 (November, 1956), "On the Possibility of a Christian Criticism of the Arts," *The Christian Scholar*, XL, No. 4 (December, 1957), and "The Sensibility of the Church and the Sensibility of the Artist," *Christian Faith and Contemporary Art*, ed. Finley Eversole (Nashville: Abingdon Press, 1962) all deal with the same general problem but from other points of view. Both that issue of *The Christian Scholar* and the Eversole volume contain a number of essays of interest and relevance.

A number of publications, many Roman Catholic, have published significant bodies of reproductions of contemporary work for the churches done by contemporary artists. Largely these are picture books with little more than a descriptive text. The liturgical revival in the Roman Catholic church is producing a considerable body of literature with relevance to the arts. Most of this either appears or is noted in that interesting journal, *Liturgical Arts*. Ernest Koenker, *The Liturgical Renaissance in the Roman Catholic Church* (Chicago: The University of Chicago Press, 1954) deals only incidentally with the problem of art but is extensively concerned with the source of art in the life of the church. In general it is true to say that some of the most important and most useful and relevant writings on the subject of art and the church are precisely those which do not deal with art as such but with ritual and worship. There is a growing literature on the subject. The books which have been of most use to me are Dom Gregory Dix, *The Shape of the Liturgy* (2nd ed.; London: Dacre Press, 1945), and Evelyn Underhill, *Worship* (New York: Harper Torchbooks, Harper & Brothers, 1957). One of the most important books of this general type is Rudolph Otto, *The Idea of the Holy* (London: Oxford University Press, 1923). It is Professor Otto who isolated and defined the principle which he designated by the coined word "numinous" which is so central to thinking of this kind.

Special mention must be made again of an article which hardly mentions art at all, Joseph Sittler, Jr., "A Theology for Earth," *The Christian Scholar*, XXXVII (September, 1954), 367-74. Despite the fact that his concern is not with the arts but generally with the attitude of the Christian faith toward the material of the earth, there are few things I have read in recent years which so directly refer to the essentials of the problem of the arts. It heartened me greatly, as a statement of a responsible professional theologian, pursuing conclusions which increasingly seemed to me inevitable in the nature of the arts. The fullest statement of these principles in respect to the arts is Rudolph Schwarz, *The Church Incarnate*, trans. Cynthia Harris (Chicago: Henry Regnery Company, 1958).

Further reference needs to be made to works which are particularly relevant to the material covered in specific chapters. Again, the principle of selection is to choose those works which have been of particular use to me or which might serve the purposes of the non-professional reader wishing to pursue one or another problem. In the chapters dealing with the evidence from historical periods the most important documents are in every case the works of art themselves and nothing is said which does not grow out of my reflection on those works. At the same time my debt to the seeing and reflection of specialists in each field is larger than I can properly acknowledge. As every honest student knows it is impossible to distinguish between his own insights and those which were generated from the inspiration of another's work. I acknowledge those I consciously remember and give my gratitude to all those whose work I have used without remembering.

BIBLIOGRAPHY BY CHAPTER

PROLOGUE

MacLeish, Archibald. *J. B.* Boston: Houghton Mifflin Company, 1956.

CHAPTER TWO

Goldwater, Robert (ed.). *Artists on Art.* New York: Pantheon Books, 1945.

Kegley, Charles W. "Paul Tillich on Philosophy of Art," *Journal of Aesthetics and Art Criticism,* XIX (Winter, 1960), 173-84.

Langer, Susanne K. *Feeling and Form.* New York: Charles Scribner's Sons, 1953.

—. *Philosophy in a New Key.* New York: Penguin Books, Inc., 1942.

—. *Problems of Art.* New York: Charles Scribner's Sons, 1957.

Tillich, Paul. "Art and Ultimate Reality," *Cross Currents,* X (Winter, 1960), 1-14.

—. "Existential Aspects of Modern Art," *Christianity and the Existentialists,* ed. Carl Michalson. New York: Charles Scribner's Sons, 1956.

—. *The Protestant Era.* Chicago: The University of Chicago Press, 1948.

—. "Protestantism and the Contemporary Style in the Visual Arts," *The Christian Scholar,* XL, No. 4 (December, 1957), 307-11.

—. *Systematic Theology*. Chicago: The University of Chicago Press, 1951.

—. *Theology of Culture*. New York: Oxford University Press, 1959.

Wheelwright, Philip. *The Burning Fountain*. Bloomington: Indiana University Press, 1954.

CHAPTERS FOUR-SIX

(Many of the books which have been important to me in these chapters have been listed earlier under the general topic of criticism. The following works, however, deserve special acknowledgment here.)

Arnheim, Rudolph. *Art and Visual Perception*. Berkeley and Los Angeles: University of California Press, 1954.

Friedlander, Max J. *Landscape Portrait Still Life*. Oxford: Bruno Cassirer, n.d.

—. *On Art and Connoisseurship*. Boston: Beacon Press, 1960.

Gombrich, E. H. *Art and Illusion*. ("Bollingen Series," XXXV, No. 5.) New York: Pantheon Books, 1960.

Stokes, Adrian. *The Quattro Cento*. London: Faber and Faber, Ltd., 1932.

CHAPTERS SEVEN-EIGHT

Benesch, Otto. *The Art of the Renaissance in Northern Europe*. Cambridge: Harvard University Press, 1947.

Blunt, Anthony. *Artistic Theory in Italy*. Oxford: Oxford University Press, 1940.

Fehl, Philip. "Veronese and the Inquisition," *Gazette des Beaux-Arts*, 6e Periode, Tome LVIII, 103e Annee (December, 1961), 325-54.

Scott, Geoffrey. *The Architecture of Humanism*. Garden City, N.Y.: Anchor Books, Doubleday & Company, 1954.

Wittkower, Rudolph. *Architectural Principles in the Age of Humanism*. London: Alic Tiranti, Ltd., 1952.

CHAPTER NINE

Rosenberg, Jakob. *Rembrandt*. Cambridge: Harvard University Press, 1948.

Simson, Otto von. *The Gothic Cathedral*. ("Bollingen Series," XLVIII.) New York: Pantheon Books, 1956.

Visser't Hooft, Willem A. *Rembrandt and the Bible*. Philadelphia: Westminster Press, 1957.

CHAPTER TEN

Demus, Otto. "The Methods of the Byzantine Artist," *The Mint, Number Two*, ed. Geoffrey Grigson. London: Routledge and Kegan Paul, Ltd., 1948.

Lowrie, Walter. *Art in the Early Church*. New York: Pantheon Books, 1947.

Simson, Otto von. *The Sacred Fortress*. Chicago: The University of Chicago Press, 1948.

CHAPTER ELEVEN

Friedlander, Walter. *Mannerism and Anti-Mannerism in Italian Painting*. New York: Columbia University Press, 1957.

Pevsner, Nikolaus. "The Architecture of Mannerism," *The Mint*, ed. Geoffrey Grigson, London: Routledge and Sons, Ltd., 1946.

INDEX

INDEX

79-80; and revelation, 89-90; and the Renaissance, 126-27; and Neo-Platonism, 142, 144; in Christian aesthetics, 196-97
Indian art, 198
Inspiration, 92-93